IMAGES
of America

NORFOLK COUNTY

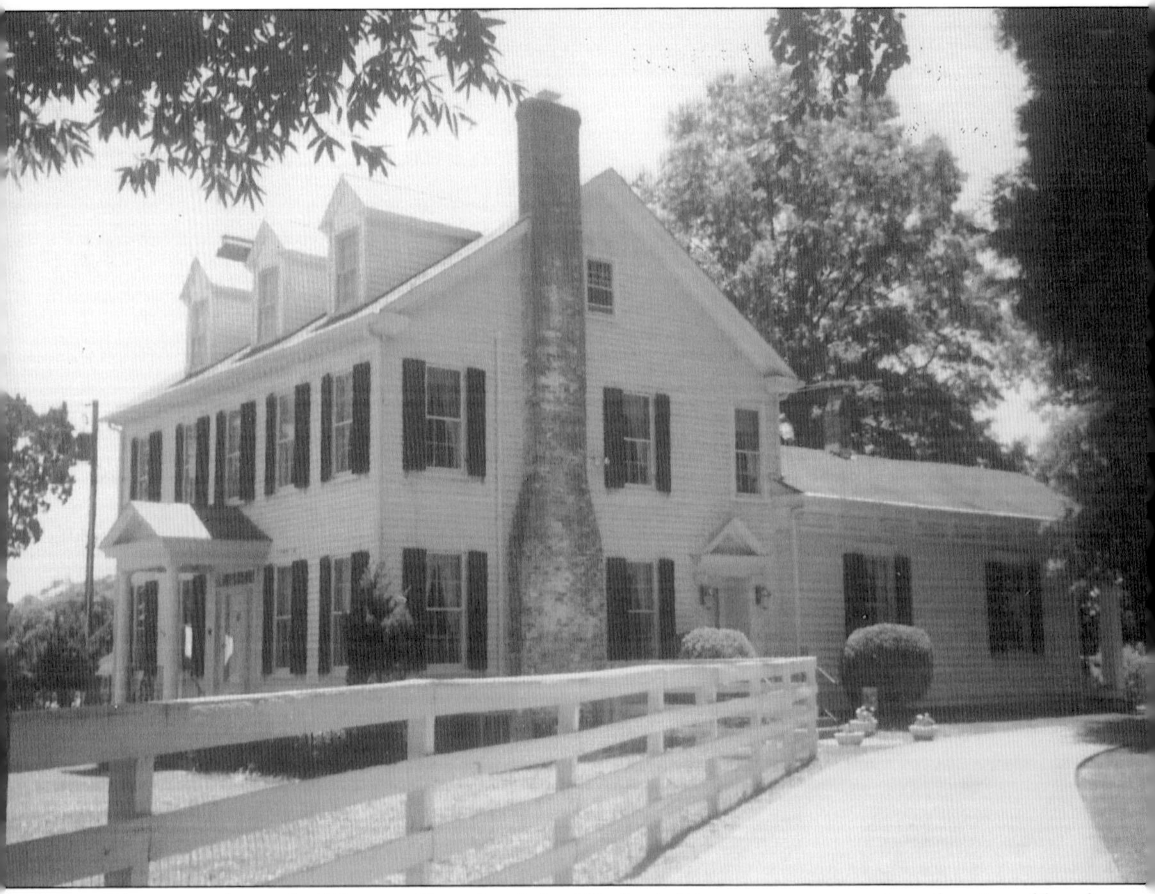

This area, along the Western Branch of the Elizabeth River, was at one time the site of local ferry operations. During the War of 1812, Brigadier General John Hodges built this home and named it "Wildwood." Hodges later sold the place to a Mr. Coffman, who turned the 100 acres into a farm. The Great Depression came, and the bank was forced to foreclose on the property. It was then rented to a Mr. Taylor, who turned it into a gambling house. Mr. John Kirchmier Sr. purchased the property in 1939, and it has been said that, during the renovation process, he found money in the fireplace. In 1963, Dr. and Mrs. Dodson bought the property from Mr. Kirchmier, Mrs. Dodson's father. Several additions throughout the years have changed the style of the home from its original Greek revival to a Georgian style. (Raymond L. Harper, photographer.)

IMAGES
of America

NORFOLK COUNTY

Raymond L. Harper

ARCADIA
PUBLISHING

ISBN 978-0-7385-0650-0

Published by Arcadia Publishing
Charleston, South Carolina

Printed in the United States of America

Library of Congress Catalog Card Number: 00-107108

For all general information contact Arcadia Publishing at:
Telephone 843-853-2070
Fax 843-853-0044
E-Mail sales@arcadiapublishing.com
For customer service and orders:
Toll-Free 1-888-313-2665

Visit us on the Internet at www.arcadiapublishing.com

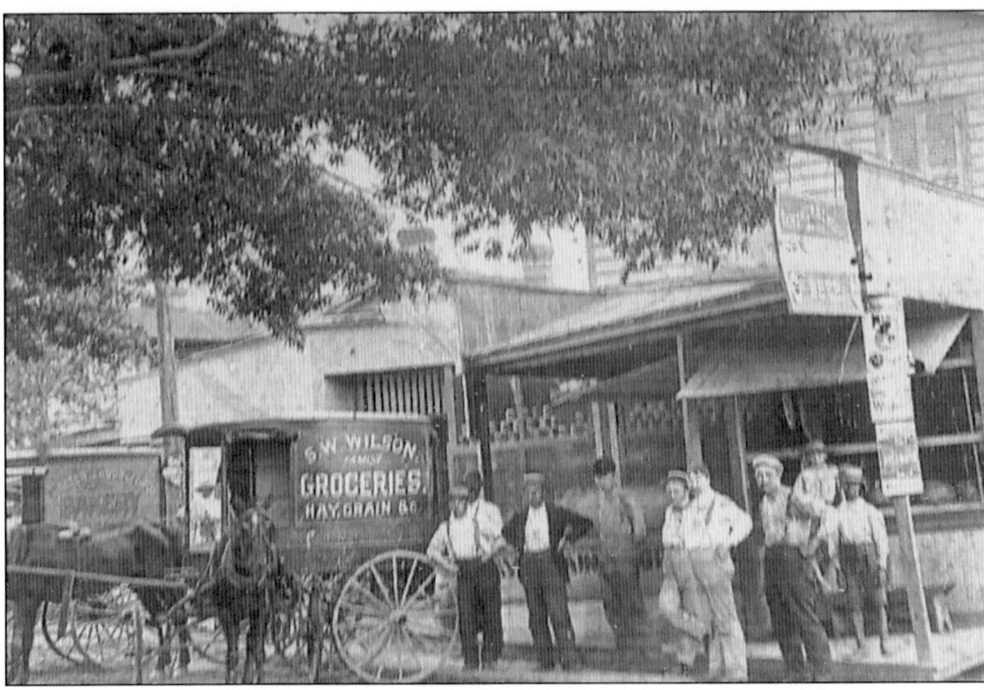

An early business on Liberty Street in the village of South Norfolk was S.W. Wilson family Groceries, Hay, Grain & feed. The first store was established in the front of a two-story house, and the capital stock in the business then amounted to $50. This picture, which was taken in 1888, shows Mr. Wilson's delivery wagon and that of Walter S. Rudd and Bro. Bakery.

Contents

Acknowledgments

I would like to express my sincere appreciation to the many individuals and institutions who contributed their services, knowledge, and photographs used in Norfolk County. I am especially grateful to Ruth Akright; Bill Baker, City of Portsmouth Central Library; Francene King Barber, Richmond County Museum; Ed and Bobbie Beard; William and Janet Benton; Jack Dabney; the Darden family; Hardy Forbes; Harry D. and Betty Fuller; Edward and Nancy Gray; Charles Hackworth, Hackworth Reprographics, Inc.; Lil Hart, Clerk of the Circuit Court of the City of Chesapeake; Williard N. Hill; Vernell Holloman; Mary Consolvo Jackson; Dr. Raymond Jones, vice president, Public radio services, WHRO; Wilmer "Snooky" Jones of the former Norfolk County Police Department; Robert Kinney Sargeant Memorial Room, Kirn Library, City of Norfolk; Myrtle Lambert; Mildred Miles; Doris Curling Morse; Norma Morrison; Frank Portlock; Lillian Pritchard; Stuart Smith, retired sergeant, City of Chesapeake Police Department; D.R. Smithson; Phillip N. Trahadias, Atlantis Photo Processing, Inc.; and Kathleen Wilson.

I dedicate this book to my wife of more than 51 years, Mrs. Emma Rock Harper, to our two daughters, Shari and Karen, our son-in-law, John Rudis, and our three grandchildren, Alexa Raye, Colby John, and Collin Steven Rudis.

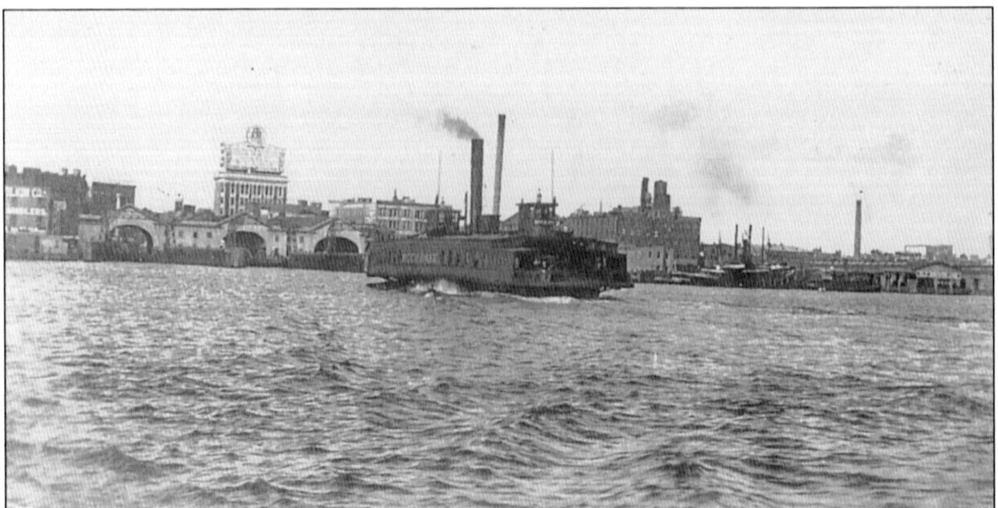

As early as 1636, Norfolk County had a ferry system. By 1637, there were three established ferries in Lower Norfolk County. They were supported by a levy of 6 pounds of tobacco. In August 1702, the General Assembly enacted legislation requiring the ferries to be kept at designated places. At that time the fare from "Norfolk Towne" to "Sawyer's Point" in Portsmouth was six pence for a man and one shilling for a man and horse. This c. 1920 picture is of the *Rockaway*, one of the ferries that operated between Norfolk, Portsmouth, and Berkley.

INTRODUCTION

Norfolk County was formed in April 1691, when Lower Norfolk County was divided into the counties of Norfolk and Princess Anne. The town of Norfolk was the county seat until 1789, when the courthouse was moved to Powder Point (later named Washington and still later, Berkley). After 12 years it was moved again, this time to Portsmouth, where it remained until 1963, when the City of South Norfolk merged with Norfolk County to form the new city of Chesapeake.

The year 1776 brought the American Revolution, and Norfolk County was to bear its share of destruction from the war. When the colonists saw that there was going to be a struggle with England, they began enlisting "Minute Men." Each county furnished an equal percentage of their male population. In November 1775, Lord Dunmore, the Royal Governor, invaded Princess Anne County. This act aroused the spirit of revolt, and Dunmore quickly returned to the protection of his gunboats at Norfolk. Colonel Woodford, who was in command of the county forces, realized the importance of holding Suffolk on account of stores and provisions there. He sent 215 men under the command of Lieutenant Colonel Charles Scott and Major Marshall to fortify the town. Dunmore left his stronghold in Norfolk and entrenched himself at Great Bridge, about 10 miles from Norfolk. This position was well chosen, for the bridge crossed a creek from the Southern Branch of the Elizabeth River, where it divided a small stretch of high ground in the midst of a huge marsh, and the only approach to the stronghold was a narrow causeway on either side. Woodford and his forces came and threw up earthworks on the edge of the swamp. It was there that the battle of Great Bridge took place on December 9, 1775. British Captain Fordyce led the attack but was killed. After that his troops could not be rallied and soon retreated to Norfolk. The fighting lasted less than half an hour. The only injury to the Americans was a slight wound in the hand of one of the soldiers.

Dunmore retired to his gunboats in Norfolk. About 4 p.m. on New Years Day, 1776, his boats fired on Norfolk and a party of British sailors set fire to the wharves and burned the town. It was during this cannonade that a cannonball was lodged into the wall of the old Saint Paul Church on what was to become Church Street (now Saint Paul Boulevard).

In 1779, British General Matthews landed in Portsmouth and made it his headquarters. He captured a large number of vessels that were anchored at Gosport and forced the evacuation of Fort Nelson, which was built on the site of the future U.S. Naval Hospital. The next year, Benedict Arnold held the town and was given orders to destroy as much property as possible. Norfolk County was the last stronghold of Lord Cornwallis before his defeat at Yorktown in 1781.

After the war, Norfolk County rallied and, by the beginning of the nineteenth century, had reached a condition of prosperity again. Norfolk was rebuilt, and with its large harbor, the import and export trade brought great wealth.

It was in 1801 that the Gosport Navy Yard was started and work began on the Dismal Swamp Canal. George Washington was an original stockholder and director in the company owning the largest portion of the swamp. The swamp contains a dense growth of juniper trees and vines that are so thick in places that very little sun can penetrate. The juniper wood produces a dark brown color to the water, and some believe that it has medicinal qualities. During the early years, timber from the swamp was very valuable and reproduced rapidly. Lake Drummond, a beautiful body of water, can be found in the swamp.

In the early part of the nineteenth century, the British began to interfere with American commerce, thus bringing on the War of 1812. In June 1813, the British attacked fortifications that had been put in place at Craney Island, about 5 miles from Portsmouth. The firing was so heavy that the British could not effect a landing and rowed back to their anchorage in Lynnhaven Bay. Norfolk County was left in peace for the remaining two years of the war.

In 1812, the Dismal Swamp Canal was completed and opened to traffic. A large dry dock at the Navy Yard was also begun, and plans for the U.S. Naval Hospital were implemented. The first railroad, the Portsmouth and Roanoke, was completed in 1850. In 1858, Portsmouth became a city, and in 1859, the Norfolk and Petersburg Railroad came into existence.

At the start of the Civil War, the Federals held the Navy Yard, but when they had to evacuate, they burned and sunk all the vessels there and threw the ammunition and small arms overboard. The Confederates went in and repaired the damage as best they could. They raised several of the boats, one of them being the *Merrimac*, which was rechristened the *Virginia*. The famous battle between the *Monitor* and the *Merrimac* was the most notable event within the bounds of Norfolk County. According to an eyewitness account, the *Monitor* was the first to retire. What was the fate of the *Virginia*? She was run ashore, dismantled, and burned by her crew to prevent capture later in the war.

After four years of war, the people of Norfolk County began to rebuild. Great wealth was realized through the success of crops, timber, and the oyster, fish, and game industries.

There are two canals, the Dismal Swamp and the Albemarle and Chesapeake. These connect the waters of the Chesapeake Bay with bays and sounds in North Carolina. In addition to the ferry and railway systems, Norfolk County had a very extensive trolley system that ran to all the suburban settlements. There were also lines reaching out to Princess Anne County, Norfolk, and Portsmouth.

In 1872, Norfolk was squeezed between Smith's Creek on the north and Newton's Creek to the east. On July 1, 1887, the City of Norfolk started a series of annexations that eventually led Norfolk County to merge with the City of South Norfolk. In late 1961, officials of South Norfolk and Norfolk County began talking of a merger to prevent further annexation of land from Norfolk County. The merger became effective January 1, 1963, and the voters gave the new city the name of Chesapeake.

While this book contains images from 1835 to the 1990s, those photographs taken by Harry C. Mann date from 1907 to 1923. During those years, Mann produced many pictures of subjects that included the Jamestown Exposition, early schools as they were built, and various other scenes throughout the area. Later Mann opened a studio at 286 Main Street in Norfolk, Virginia.

Norfolk County at one time consisted of most of the land that is now the Cities of Norfolk, Portsmouth, and Chesapeake. It was famous for its many farms, especially the dairy farms. Remember if you can, when milk was delivered by horse and wagon. You could hear the clink of glass bottles around 4 a.m. each morning. Fresh milk was delivered to your porch daily, and in winter, the cream would rise above the top of the bottle.

By nature, the early settlers were very religious, and the old churches have a special place in the history of the county. Many began in log cabins. There are many old cemeteries in the former county and they provide us with very reliable historical information. Trips to Lake Drummond and the Dismal Swamp were of great interest, and don't forget the Elizabeth River with its ferryboats and tall sailing ships.

Norfolk County was so large that it is almost impossible to include information and images from every part of the former county. When so much material is available, it is very difficult to decide what to include. Probably much worthwhile information has been left out. If this is the case, I offer my apology and hope the reader will accept this work cheerfully as it is presented.

One

Scenes of the Elizabeth

The Elizabeth River was named for Princess Elizabeth Stuart, daughter of King James I of England. There are three branches: Eastern, Southern, and Western. In the early years, the waterway was noted for its fish and oysters. When Robert E. Lee visited the area, he usually carried a barrel of oysters home with him. He described them as "finely flavored and as plump as eggs." Soon after the Civil War, the waterfront became filled with industries dealing in lumber, creosote, fertilizer, guano, and oil. While they provided employment for the local citizens, they also polluted the river. Today, much of the property along the Elizabeth is vacant and there is a movement to clean the river and restore the waterfront.

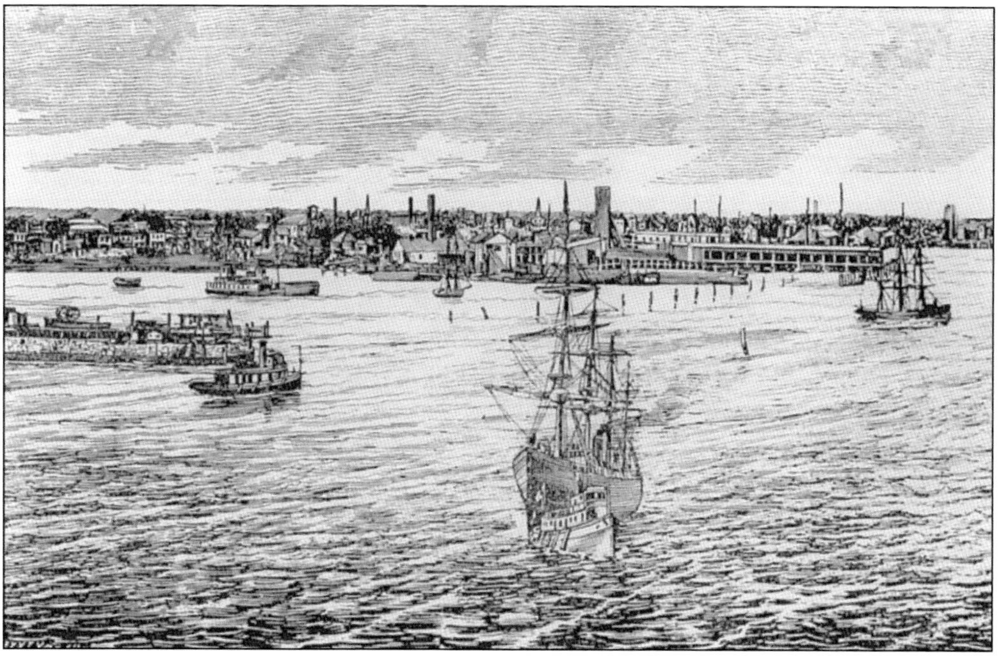

This image titled "Berkley" shows the Elizabeth River as seen by an artist in 1885. It shows several tugboats, the ferry, rowboats, and tall-masted sailboats. The village of Berkley is in the background. A closer look reveals several church steeples.

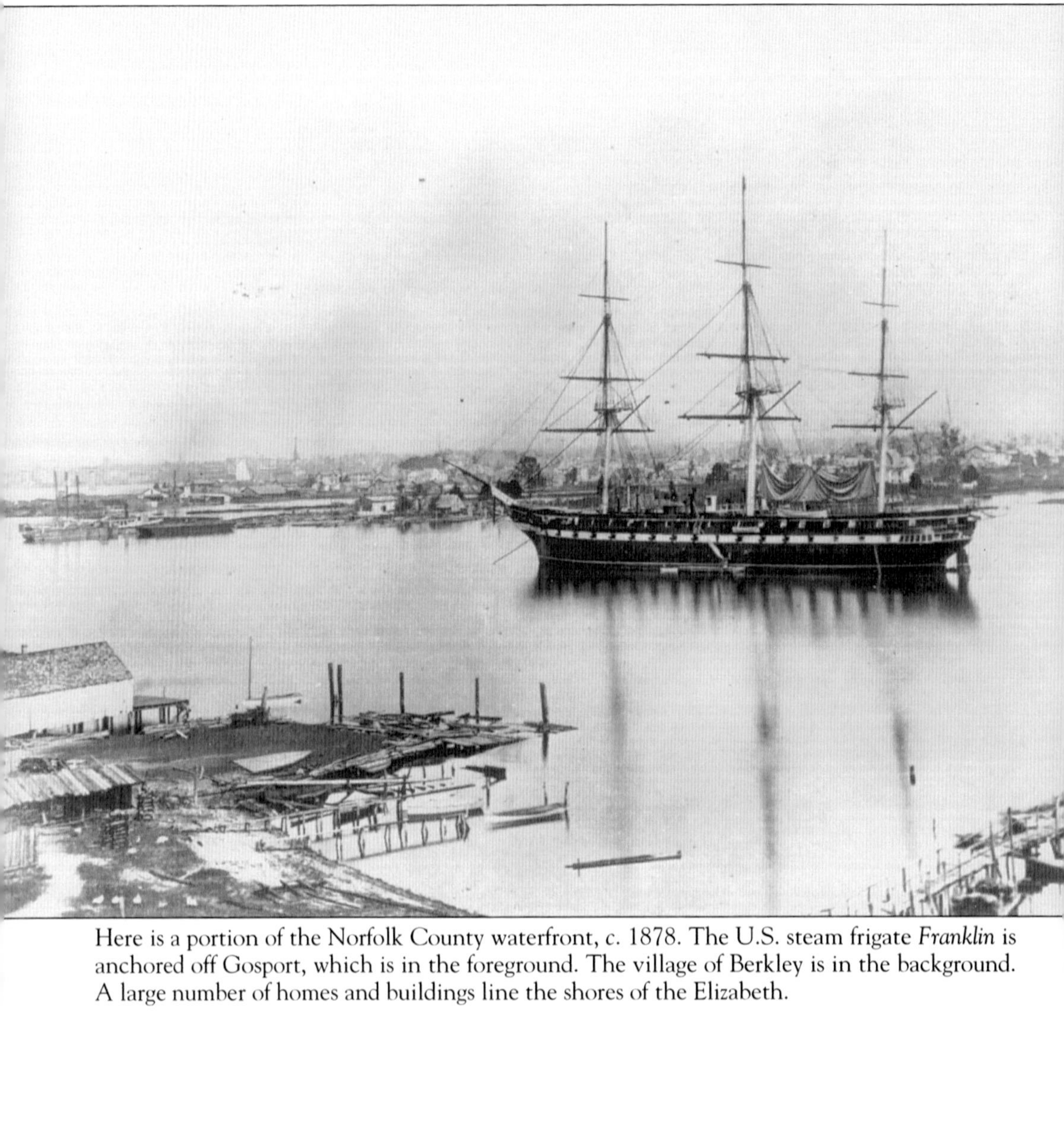

Here is a portion of the Norfolk County waterfront, *c.* 1878. The U.S. steam frigate *Franklin* is anchored off Gosport, which is in the foreground. The village of Berkley is in the background. A large number of homes and buildings line the shores of the Elizabeth.

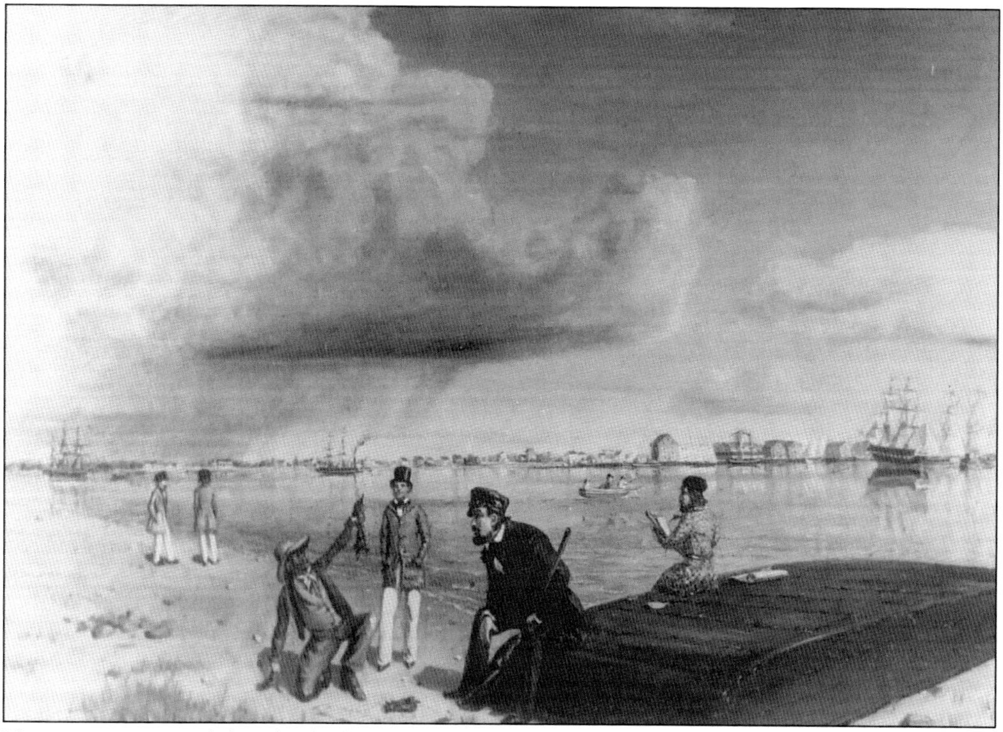

Here is an image of the Elizabeth River in 1835. There are two men sitting on the bottom of the overturned flat-bottom boat. One appears to be sketching a scene to the left of the picture. Another is holding what looks like a double-barrel shotgun, while the man in front of him is holding a duck in the hand of his outreached arm.

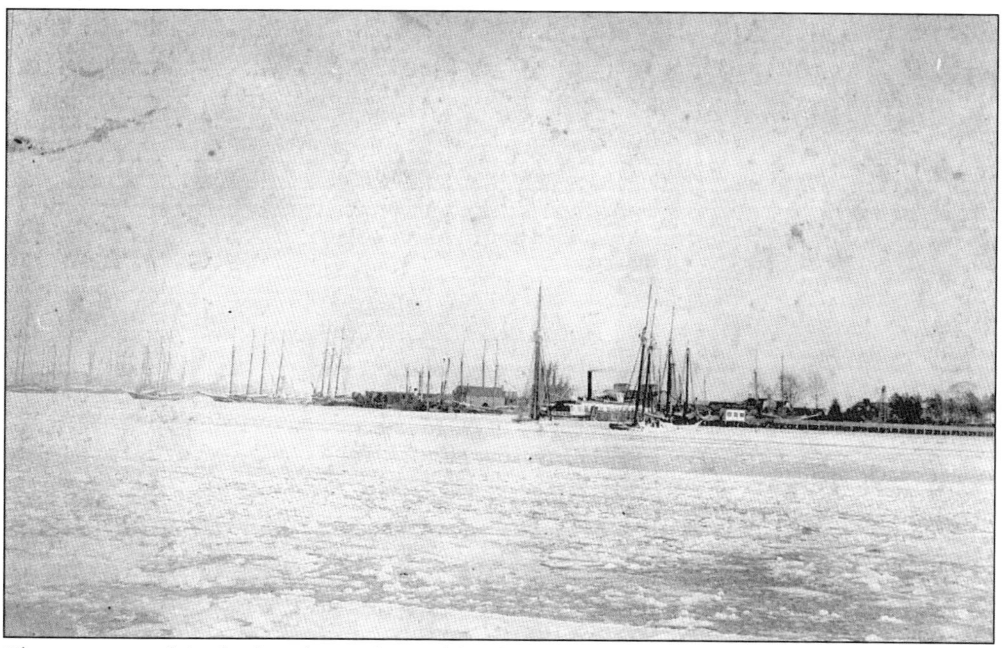

This icy view of the harbor shows the Berkley ferry in the distant background. Taking a closer look at the ferry, one can see smoke coming out of its stack, *c.* 1890s.

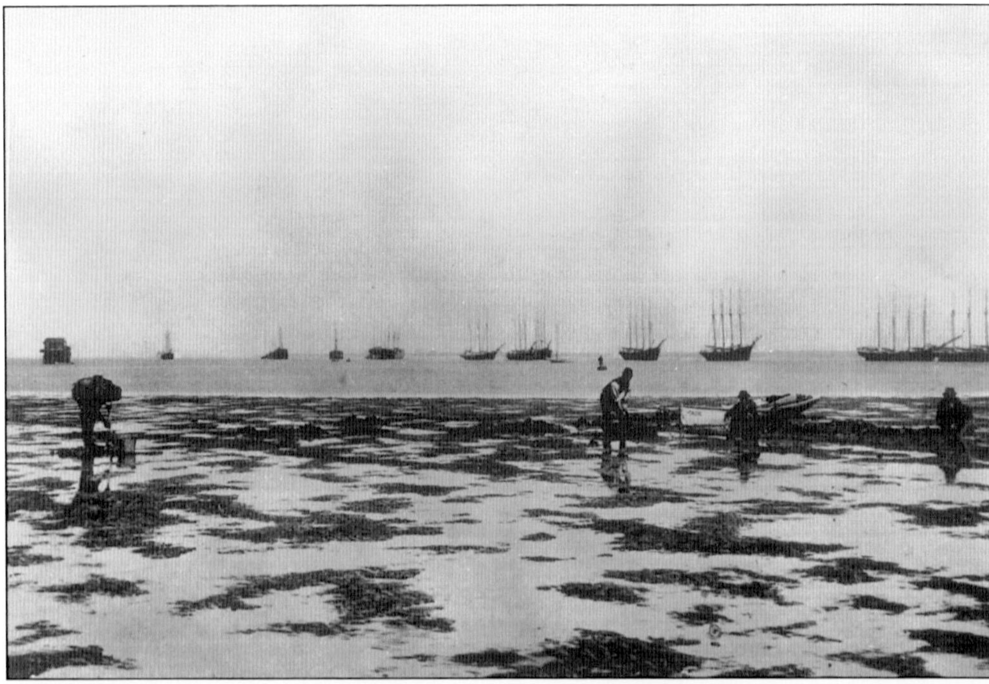

In this 1895 photograph is Craney Island, which is approximately 5 miles from Portsmouth. The group of men seen here may be digging for clams. As can be seen, there are quite a few ships in the background.

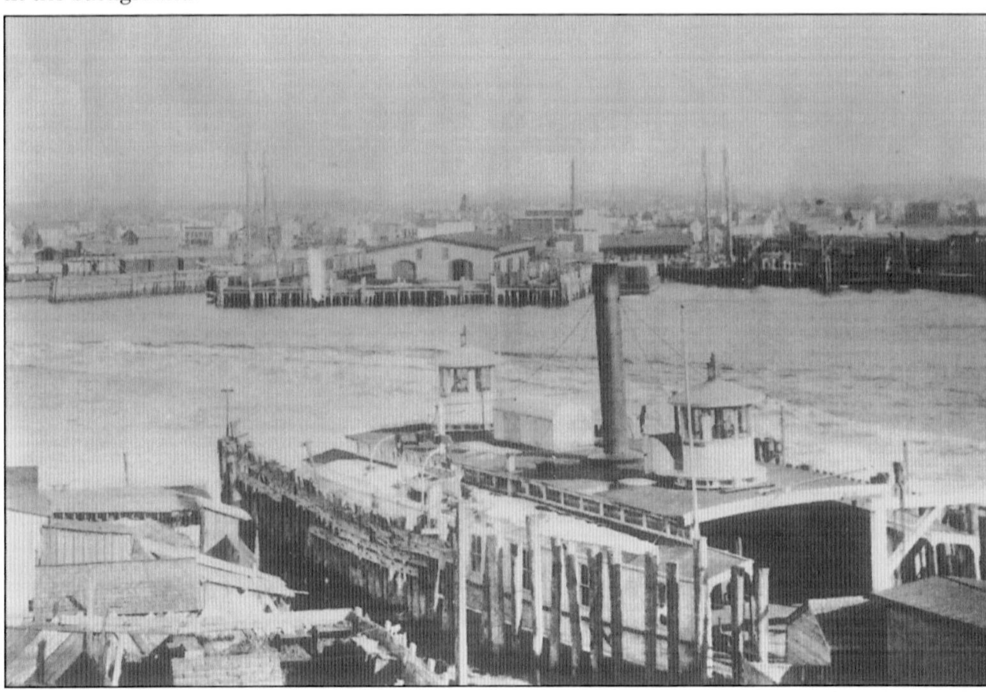

This 1895 picture of the ferry was taken at the Norfolk and Southern Terminals, and the Berkley waterfront can be seen. At that time, the population of Berkley had grown and the village had been incorporated as a town.

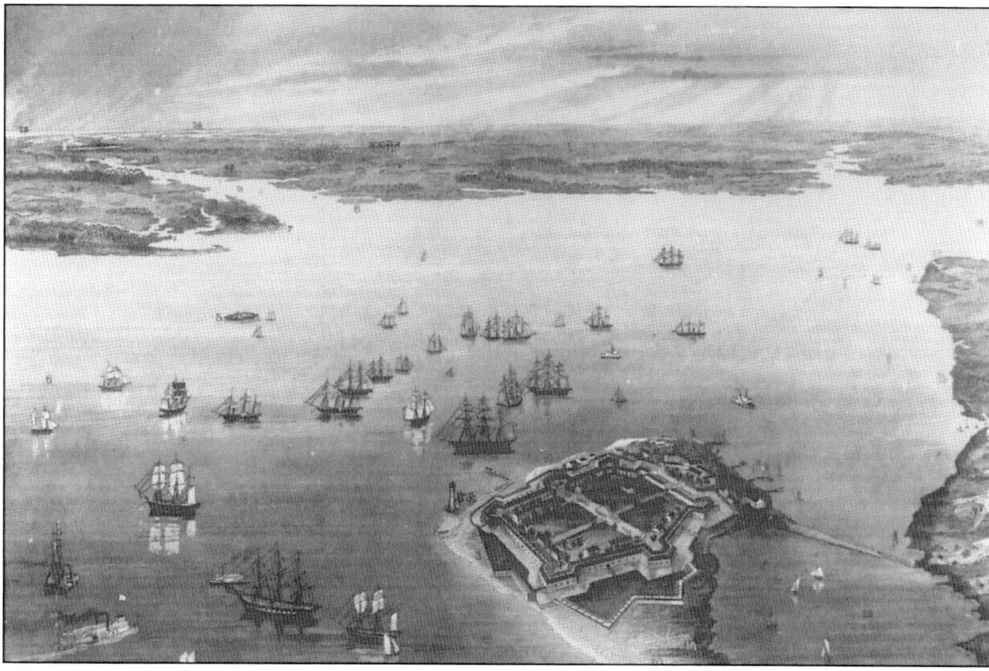

This 1862 image highlights many of the places that border or connect with the Elizabeth River. Among them are Old Point Comfort, Fortress Monroe, Sewall's Point, Craney Island, Dismal Swamp, Norfolk, Portsmouth, Newport News, Hampton, James River, Cape Hatteras (North Carolina), and others.

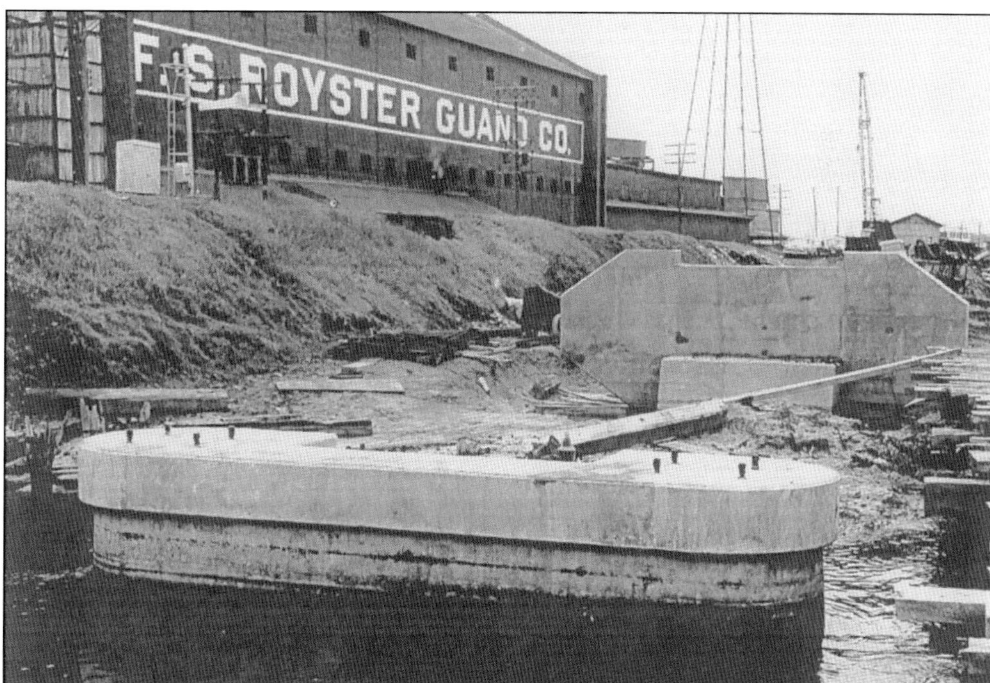

The F.S. Royster Guano Company occupied a large portion of the Southern Branch near the Jordan Bridge. This photograph was taken on February 5, 1957.

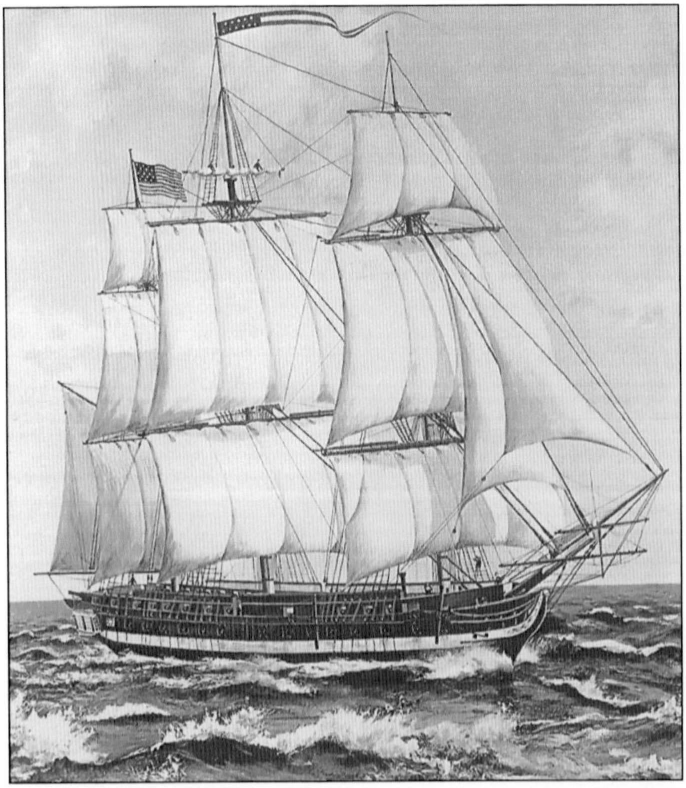

This image, which is used by some organizations to represent the City of Chesapeake, is of the U.S. frigate *Chesapeake*. It was built at the Gosport Shipyard in Portsmouth, Virginia, in 1799. The Gosport Shipyard later became the Norfolk Naval Shipyard.

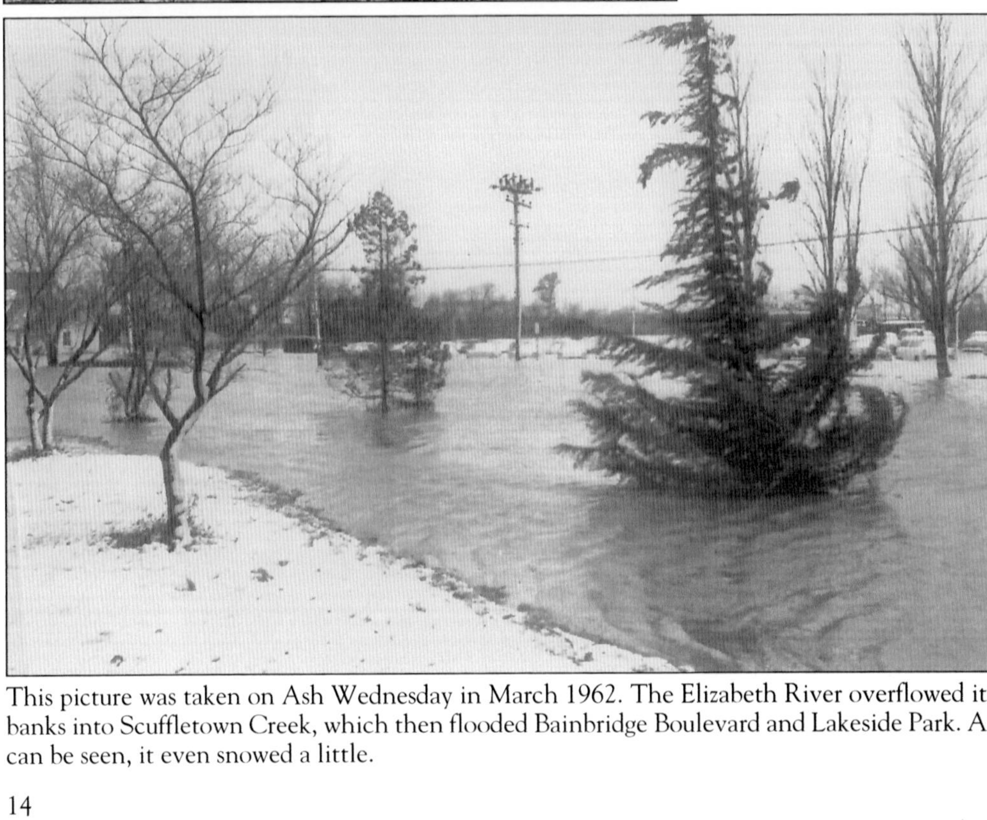

This picture was taken on Ash Wednesday in March 1962. The Elizabeth River overflowed its banks into Scuffletown Creek, which then flooded Bainbridge Boulevard and Lakeside Park. As can be seen, it even snowed a little.

Let us gather at the river. This photograph was taken along the shores of the Elizabeth River in 1909, and everyone in attendance is dressed in their finest. What is the occasion? We can only guess, but maybe there was a fleet of ships arriving or a baptism.

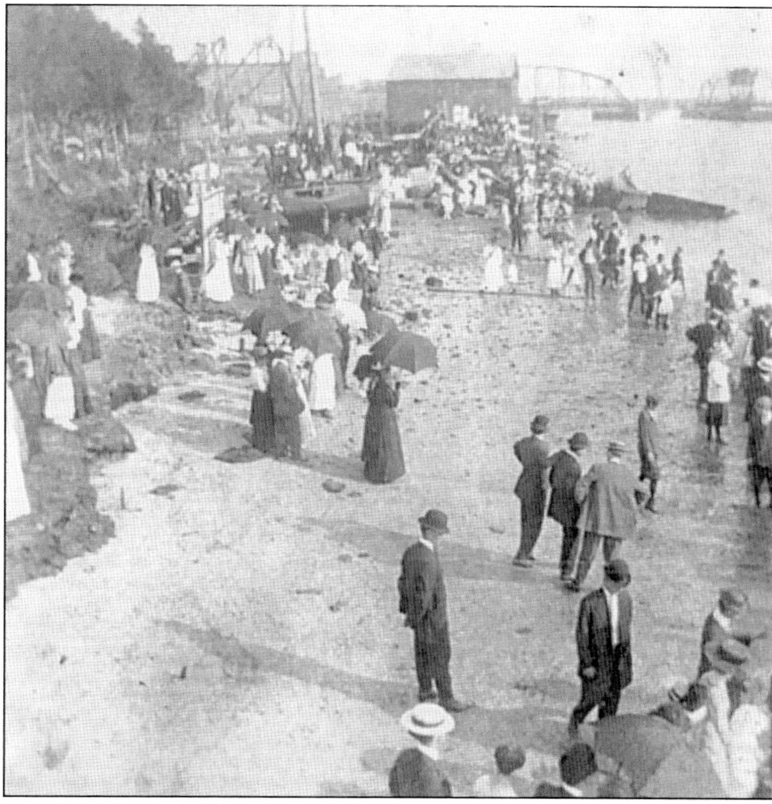

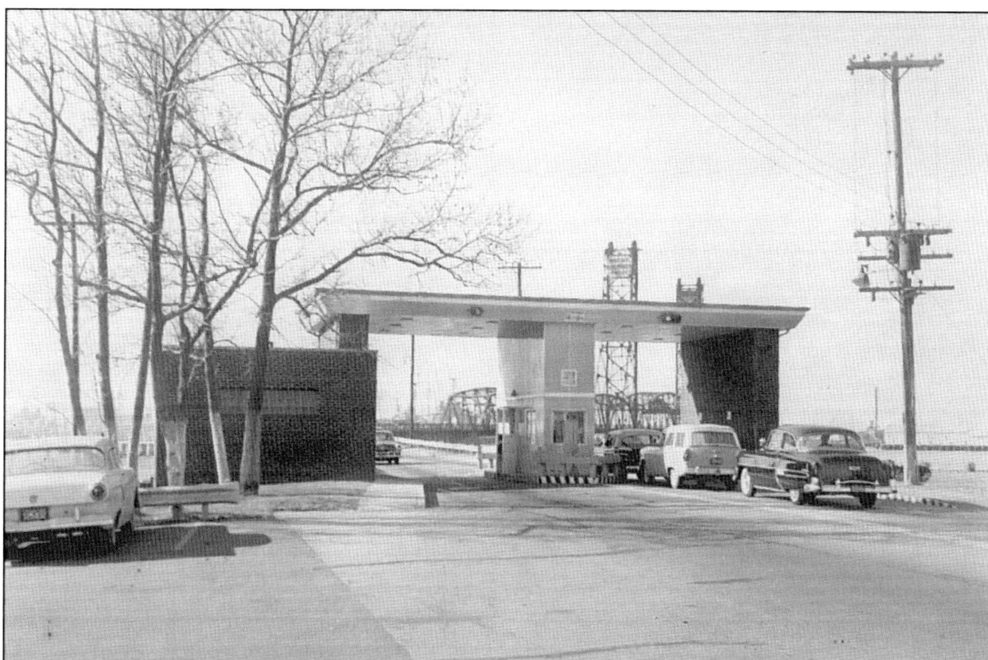

This photograph shows the new tollhouse at the Jordan Bridge. The bridge connects South Norfolk to Portsmouth, Virginia.

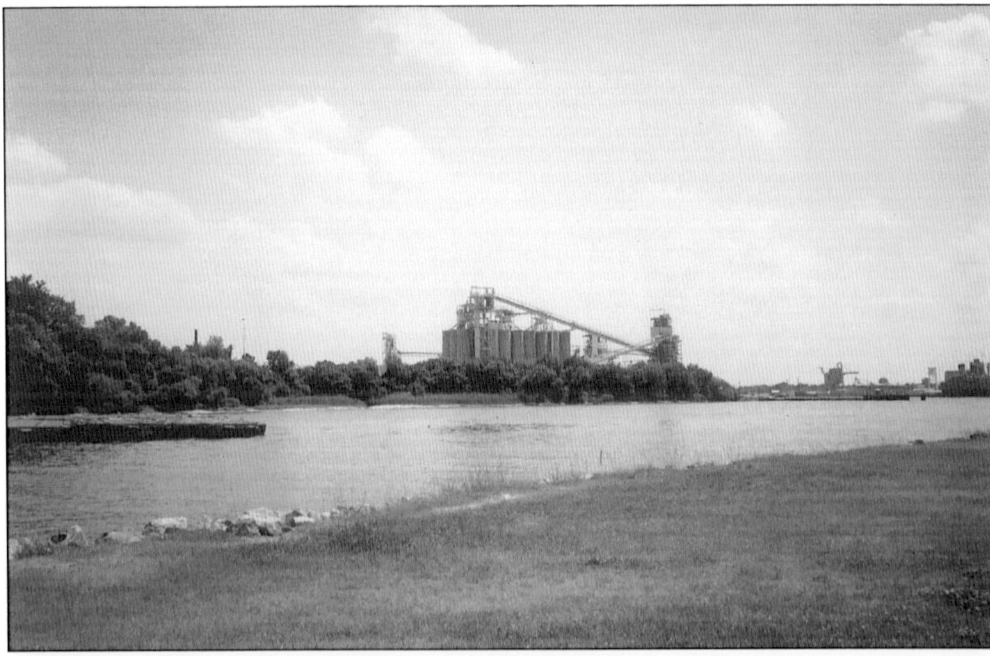

Looking along the Southern Branch of the Elizabeth River, one can see a portion of the Cargill Plant.

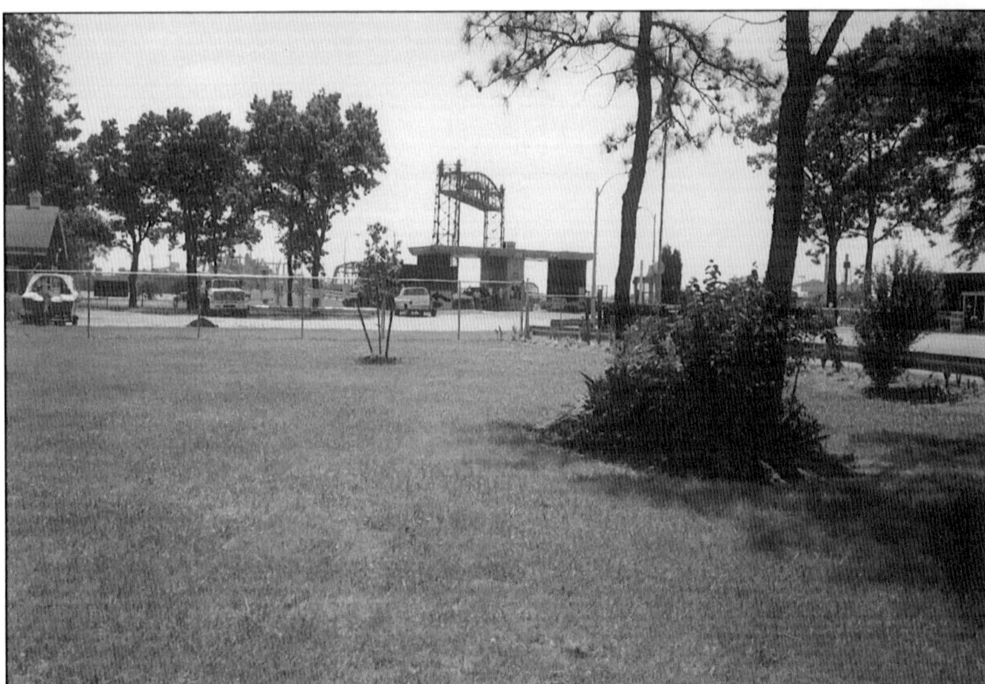

This picture shows the Jordan Bridge stuck in the open position. It was out of service for one and a half years.

Two

Annexed Areas

In 1872, Norfolk was squeezed between Smith's Creek on the north and Newton's Creek to the east. On July 1, 1887, Norfolk started a series of annexations that eventually led Norfolk County to merge with the City of South Norfolk to keep from losing all of its land. Between 1887 and 1955, the City of Norfolk annexed 23 areas from Norfolk County. The images in this chapter were taken from some of those annexed areas.

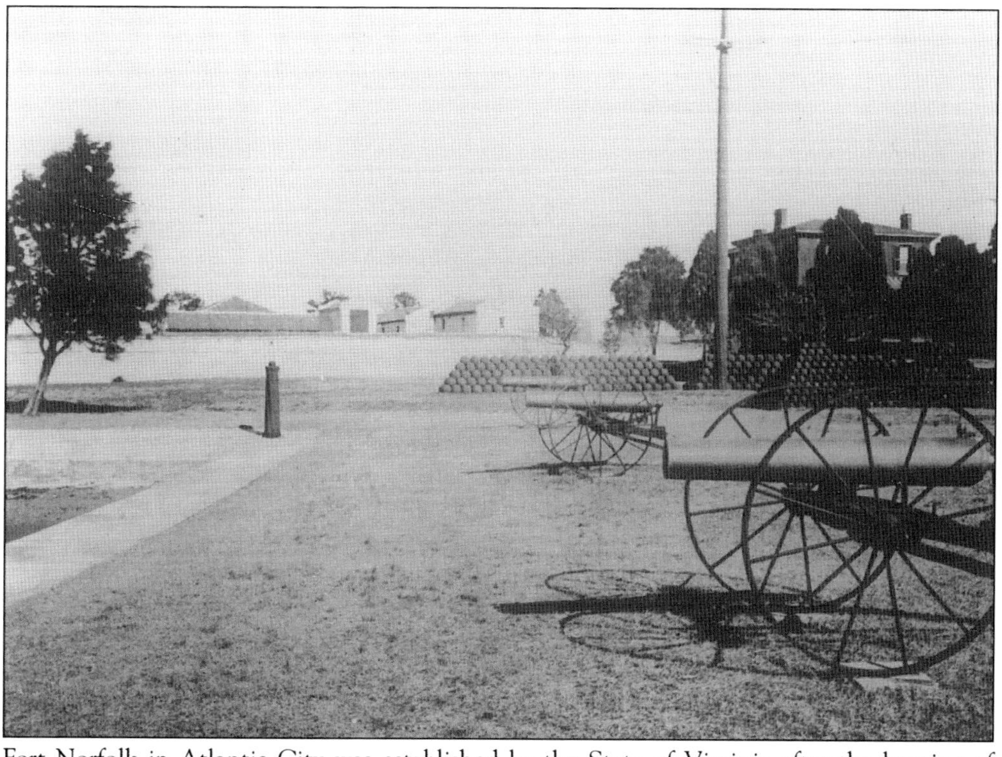

Fort Norfolk in Atlantic City was established by the State of Virginia after the burning of Norfolk in January 1776. It is opposite the site where Fort Nelson, another Revolutionary fort, was built. Fort Nelson has since disappeared and the Portsmouth Naval Hospital now occupies that site. Fort Norfolk served as a Civil War prison and, in 1923, became the headquarters of the Army Corps of Engineers. In 1895, there were a few cannon and cannonballs on display.

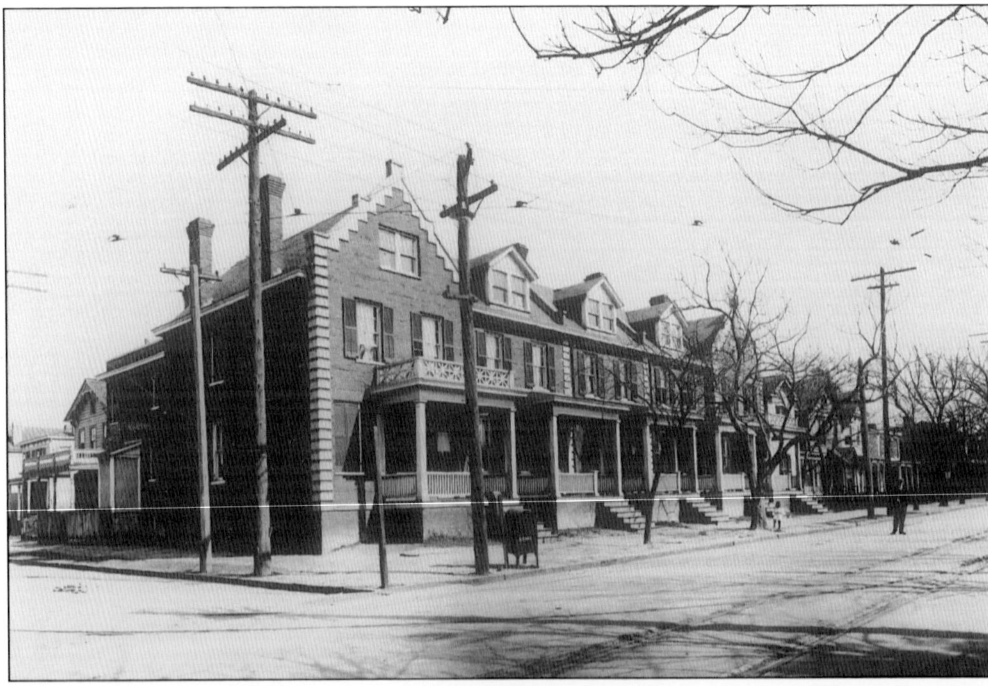

This c. 1915 photograph shows a row of houses facing Brambleton Avenue. The trolley tracks can be seen in the middle of the street. In the right center is a man who is probably waiting to board the next streetcar when it arrives. (Harry C. Mann, photographer.)

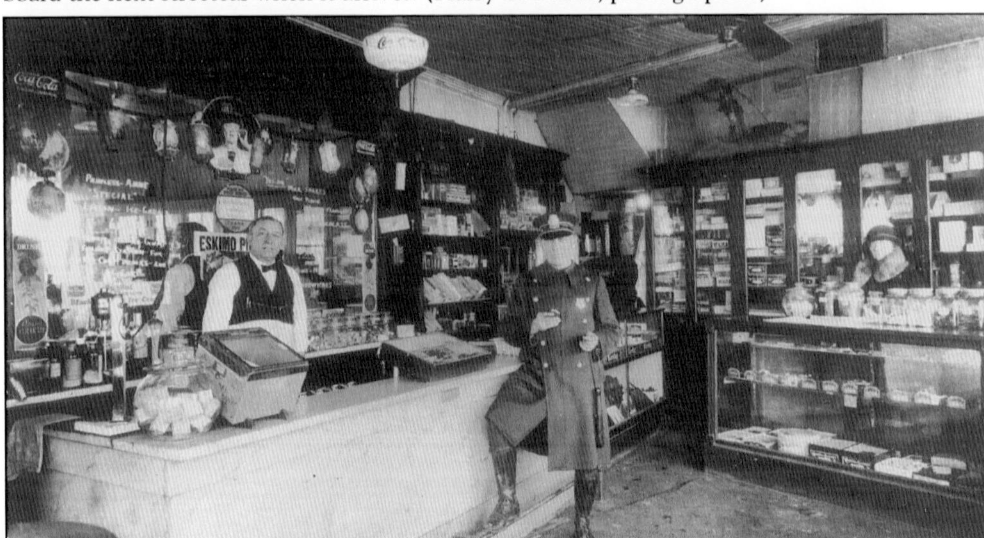

This early photograph was taken inside the Park Avenue Confectionery store on Park Avenue in Brambleton. The police officer, probably walking his beat, has stopped to take a break and visit with the owner. The mirror behind the counter was used to advertise many items and specials that were for sale. One sign is used to promote the "Princess Anne Special," which appears to be lemon ice cream. Other signs include advertisements for the following: Orange Crush, Coca-Cola, milk shakes, chocolates, Eskimo Pies, cigars, and other forms of tobacco. The names of the people in this c. 1920 picture are unknown.

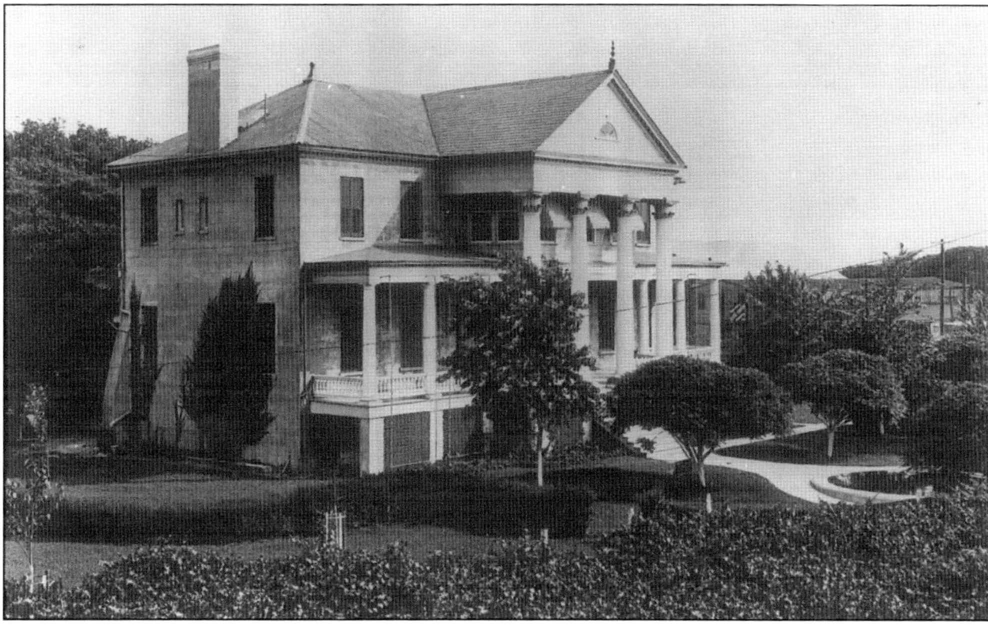

This August 1906 image shows the first marine hospital in the United States. In 1780, the Virginia General Assembly approved a tax for the construction of a marine hospital. The governor appointed a commission to erect the hospital in the town of Washington in Norfolk County, Virginia. The hospital was established by the Commonwealth of Virginia in 1787. (Harry C. Mann, photographer.)

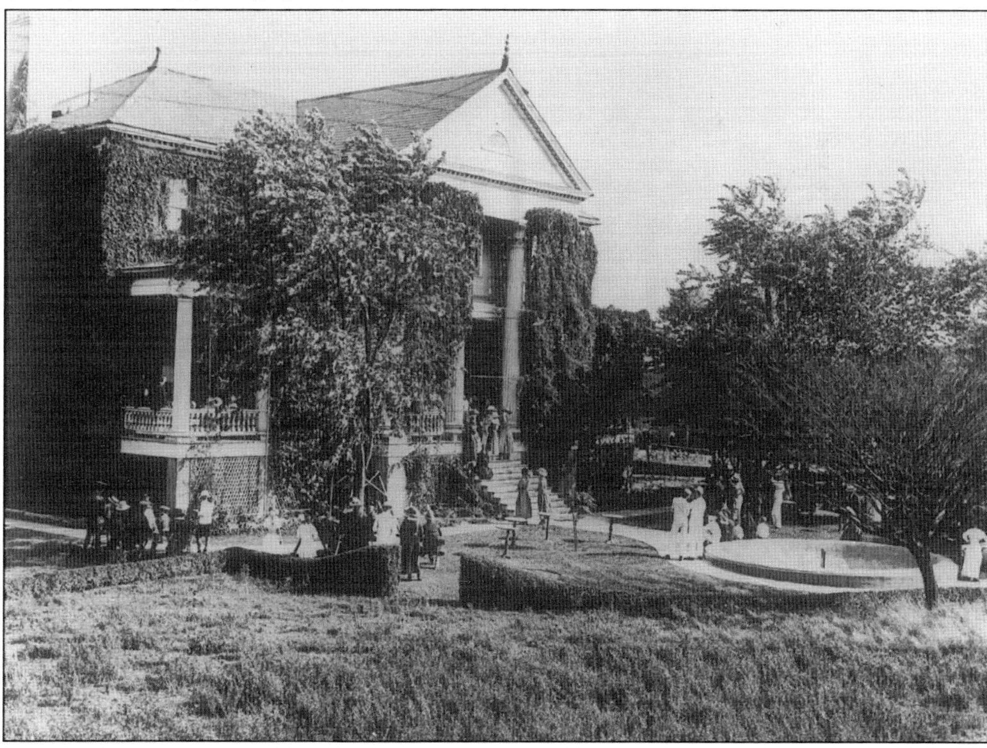

Harry C. Mann took this photograph of the marine hospital at a later date than the one above.

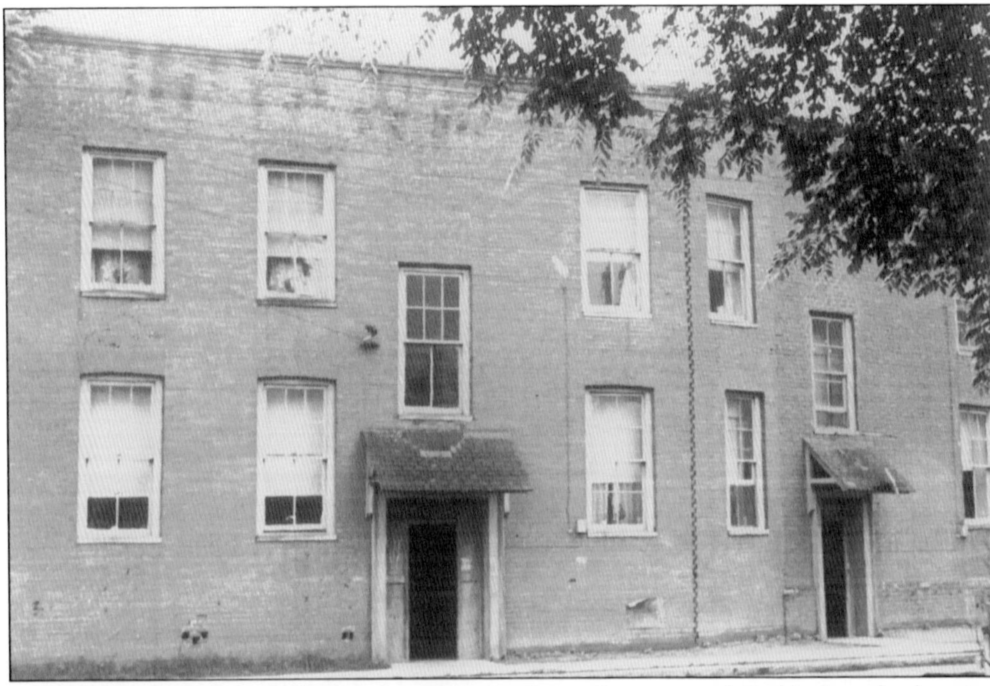

In 1789, the Virginia Legislature chose Powder Point (later named Berkley) as the location for the Norfolk County courthouse. The courthouse was built at the corner of what became Walnut and Pine Streets. In 1791, a lot was purchased from Edmund Allmand for 25 English pounds. According to court records, the first court session at Powder Point was held at the home of a Mrs. Shafer. This picture, which was taken in June 1948, shows the old courthouse when it served as an apartment building.

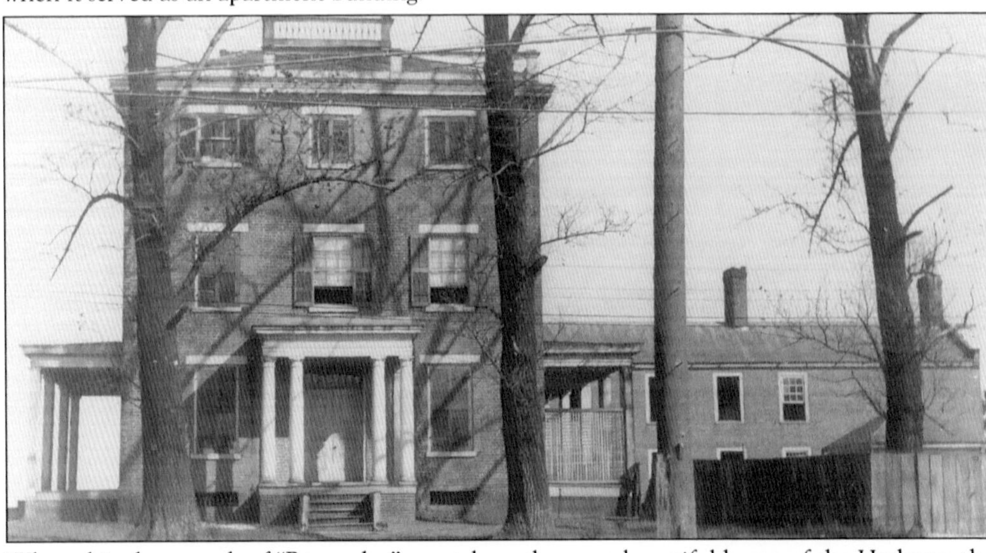

When this photograph of "Riveredge" was taken, the once beautiful home of the Herberts, the Hardys, and possibly others appeared to be approaching the winter of its existence. Some of the windows in the right addition are missing. During this author's youth, the Revolutionary home sat vacant in a field at the foot of South Main Street in Berkley. Eventually it was demolished, and an important part of local history was lost forever.

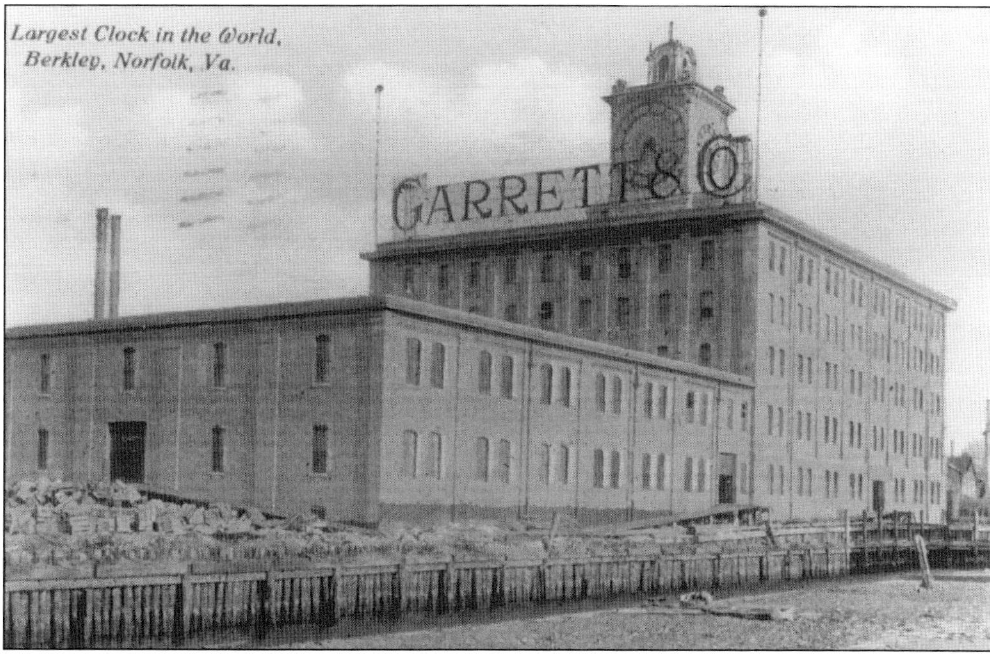

Garrett & Company Winery was established in 1835 in Saint Louis, Missouri. In 1903, Paul Garrett opened this local branch at the foot of Chestnut Street in Berkley. Virginia Dare, a popular wine of the day, was manufactured at the Berkley plant. The four-sided clock on top of the building was publicized as being the largest clock in the world. Garrett operated the winery until Prohibition forced him to close in 1916. Many felt that the era of Prohibition was responsible for the Great Depression, which followed some years later. The Imperial Tobacco Company later used the winery building. (Harry C. Mann, photographer.)

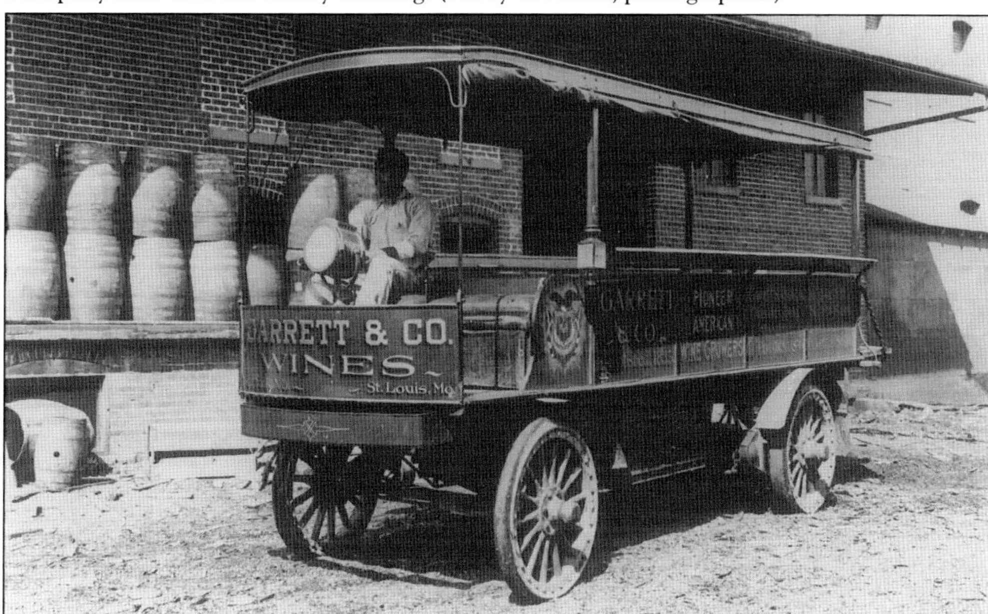

The man seated in one of Garrett & Company's wagons appears to be holding something between his legs. Could it be a searchlight? (Harry C. Mann, photographer.)

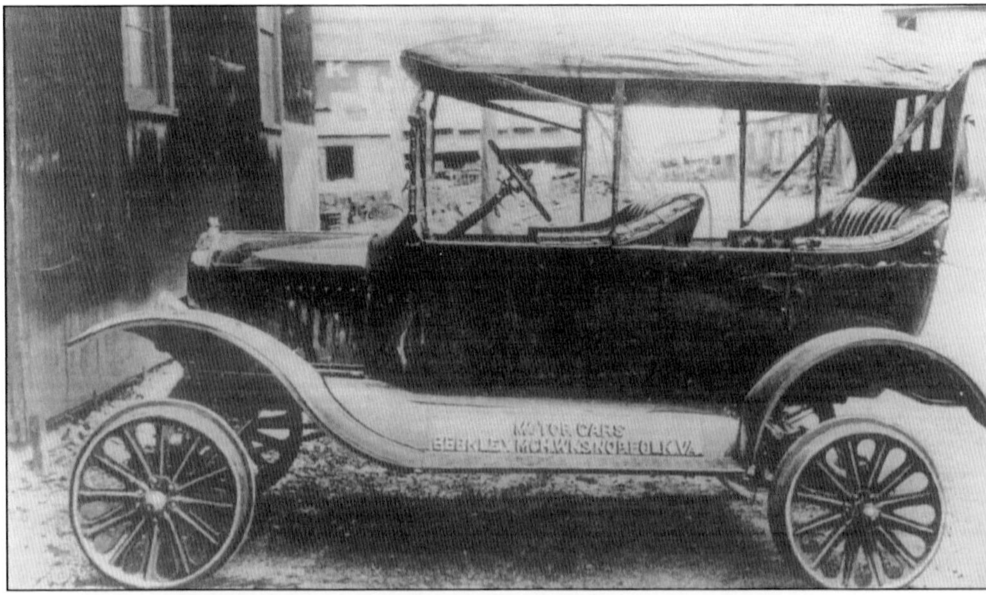

The Berkley Machine Works, a manufacturer of motorcars, built this modern vehicle in Berkley, Virginia. The wheels appear to consist of metal rims with wooden spokes.

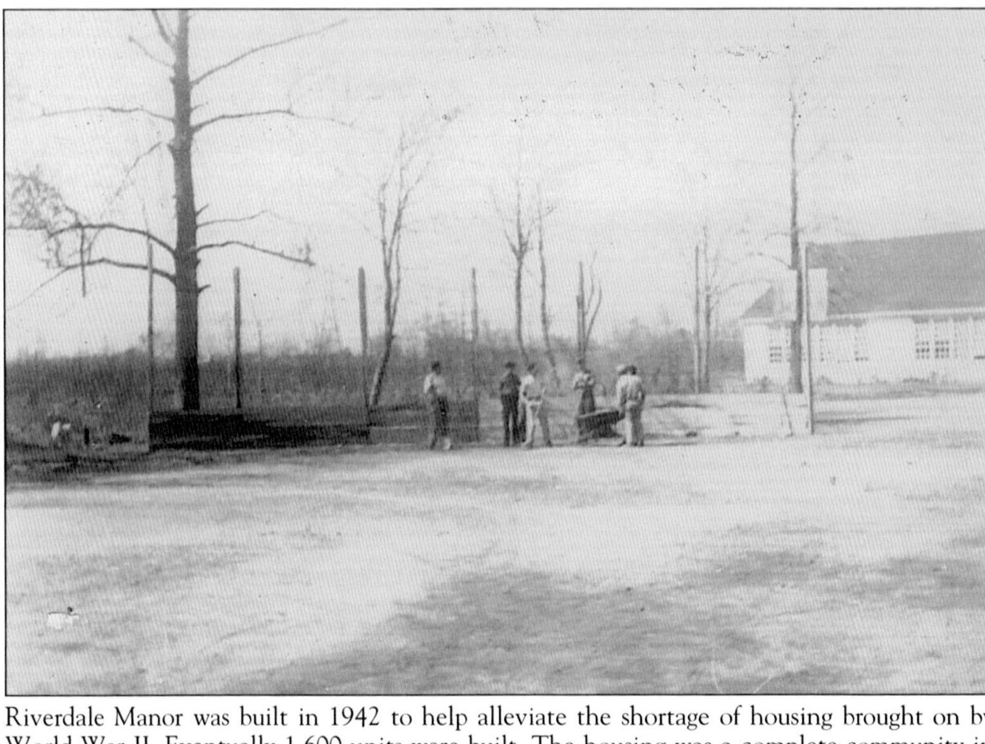

Riverdale Manor was built in 1942 to help alleviate the shortage of housing brought on by World War II. Eventually 1,600 units were built. The housing was a complete community in that it had grocery stores, a school, a drugstore, a gas station, a garage, a theatre, and ball teams. In this early-1940s picture, a group of men work on the athletic field.

A familiar sight during the summer months was the ice cream vendor who peddled his cart through the streets of Riverdale. In this photograph, he is making a sale to Ms. Vivian Frascini.

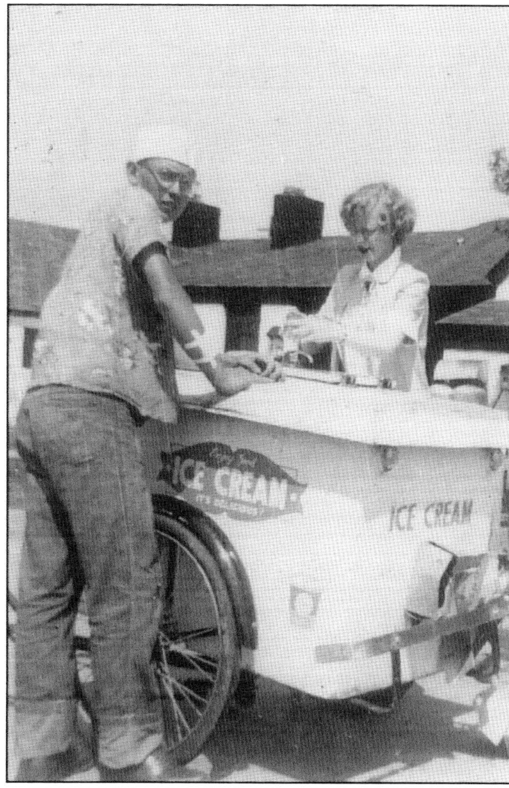

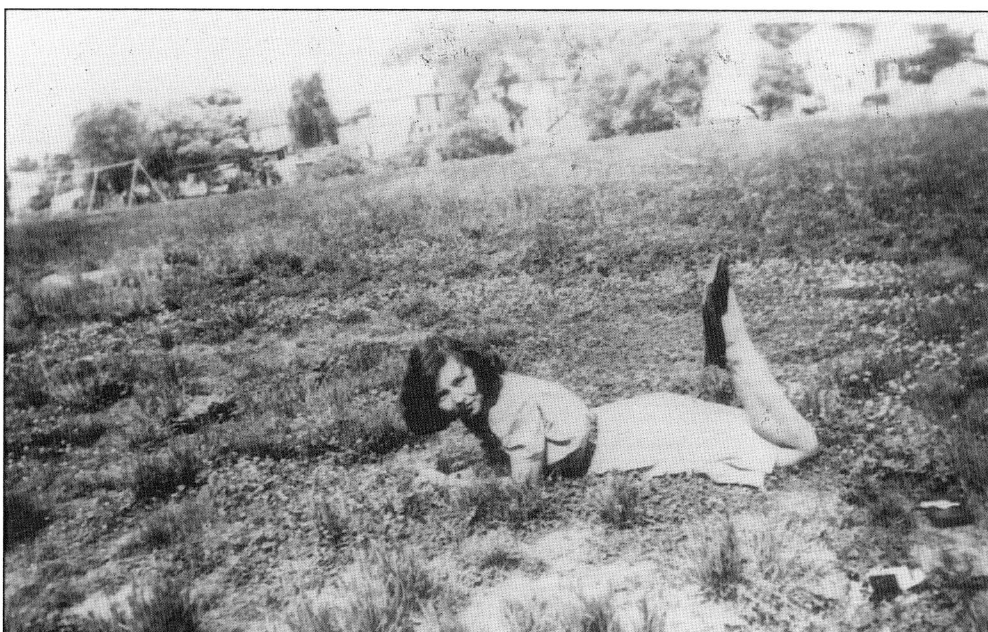

The weather is nice and it's a beautiful day. The lovely Ms. Edwards is enjoying a day in the Riverdale Park, *c.* 1947.

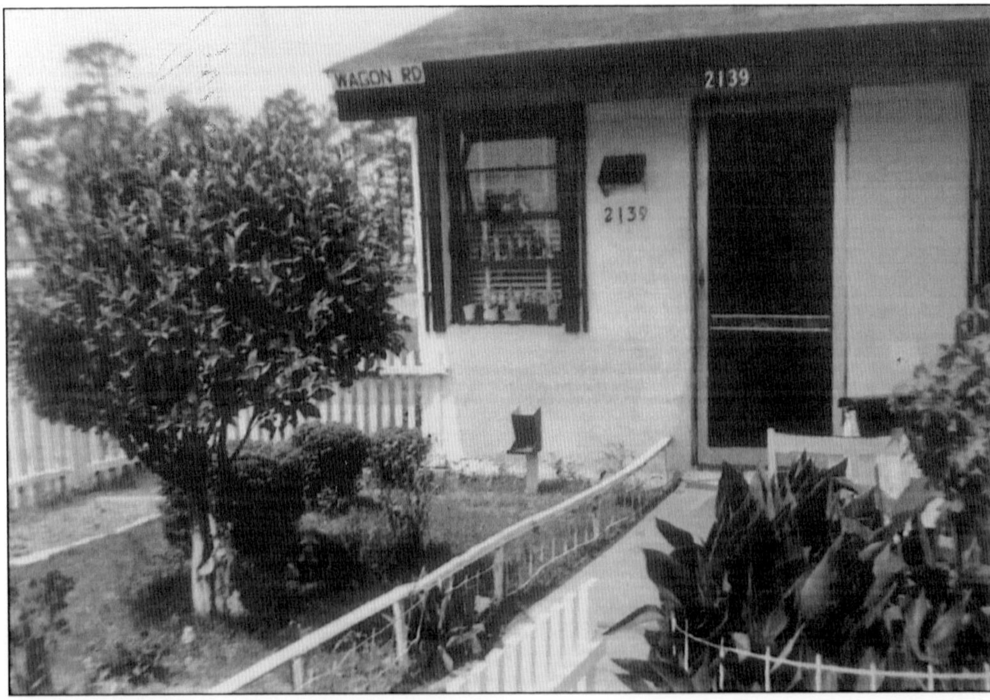

This was the home of the Fuller family at 2139 Wagon Road in Riverdale Manor. As can be seen by this 1949 picture, the yard was well kept and gave visitors a feeling of being welcome to the home.

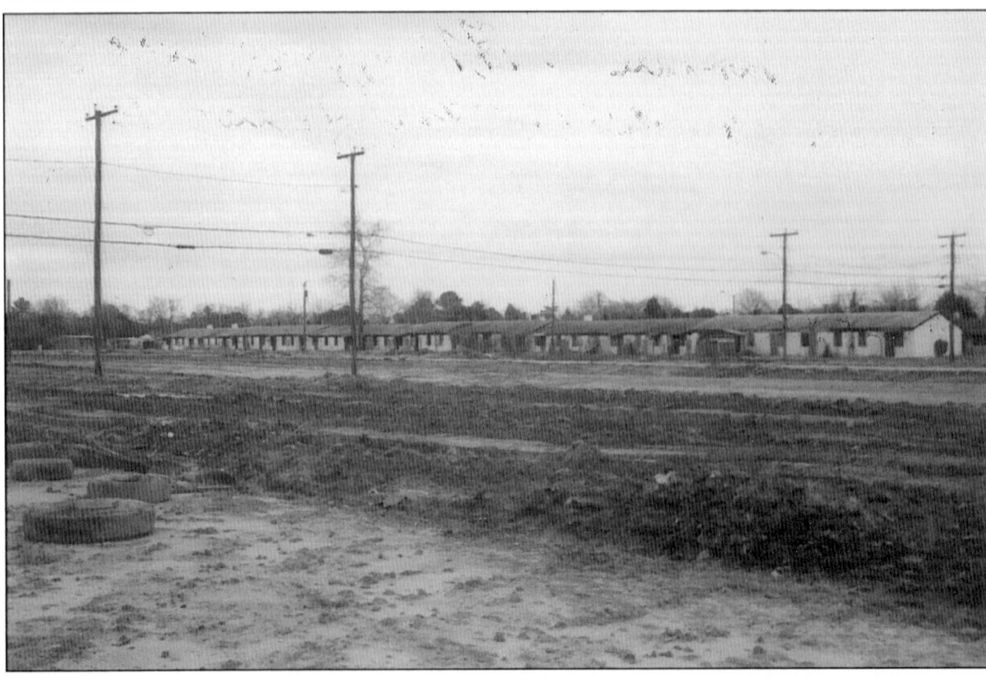

This photograph, taken in 1997, shows the recent demolition of Riverdale Manor. This row of houses on Pond Lane was all that remained of the original 1,600 units. Campostella Square now occupies the site.

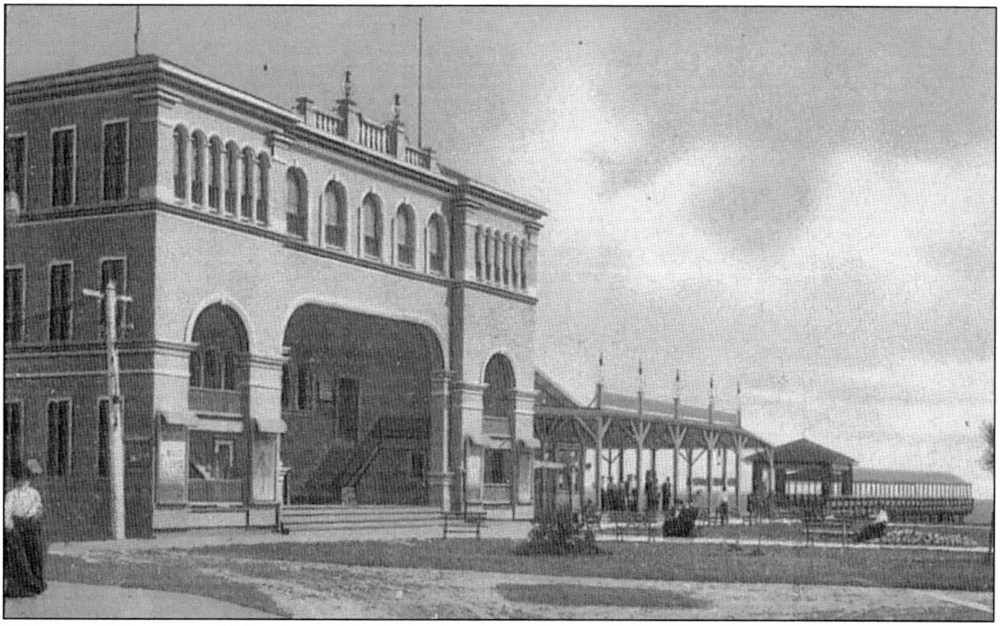

This c. 1907 image of the casino and pavilion at Ocean View, Virginia, is one of several taken from the collection of Ms. Ella Mae Simpson.

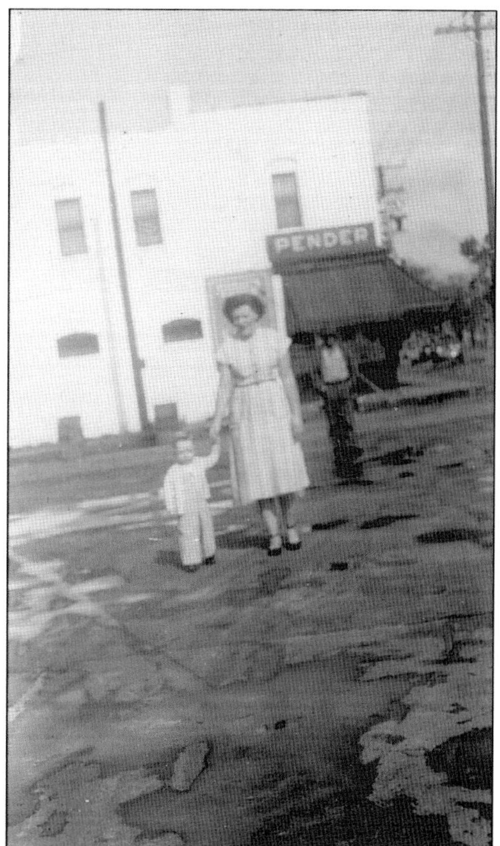

This c. 1947 picture was taken when the Pender grocery store was located at the corner of Bainbridge Boulevard and Freeman Avenue. The area, which was in Norfolk County, became a town in 1948 and three years later was annexed by the City of South Norfolk. Mrs. Vernell Milteer and her son Richard are on their way to visit Mr. Milteer at his service station.

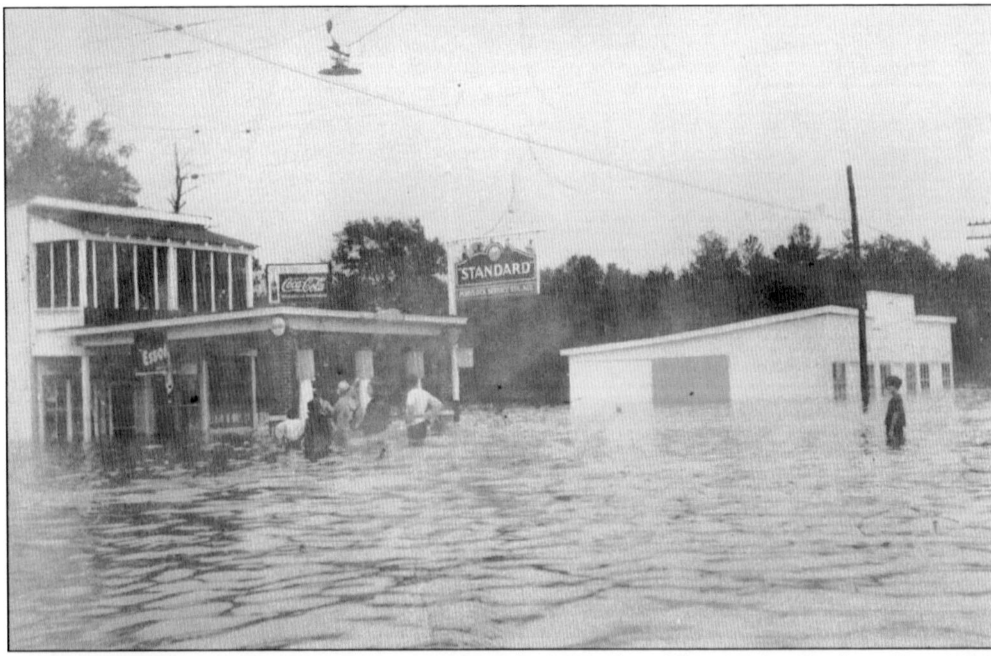

This photograph was taken at the corner of Portlock Road and Bainbridge Boulevard in 1932. The flooding was the result of a hurricane that hit the area the day before. The building on the left is the Portlock Service Station and Market, and there are three Esso gas pumps in front of the building.

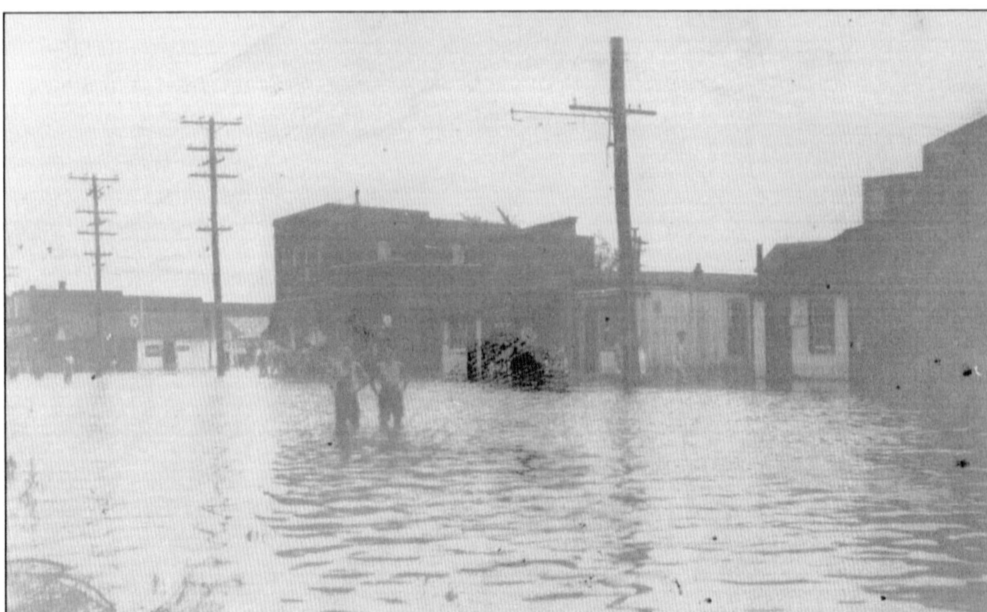

The flooding seen here was also caused by the 1932 hurricane. This picture was taken along Bainbridge Boulevard near Freeman Avenue. The Texaco station at the corner of these streets can be seen in the left background.

The Portsmouth Light Artillery was organized before the War of 1812 between the United States and England. One of its main engagements was the battle of Craney Island in 1814, when it forced the British to retreat to the Lynnhaven River. This image of the Portsmouth Light Artillery monument was taken from the postcard collection of Ella Mae Simpson.

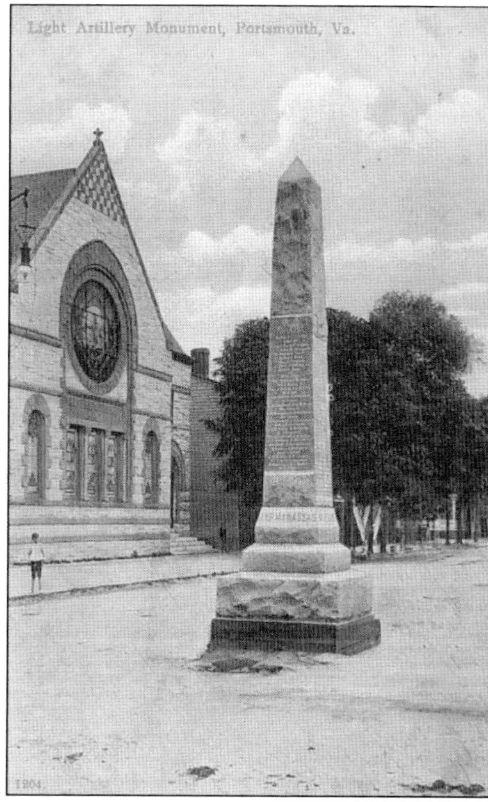

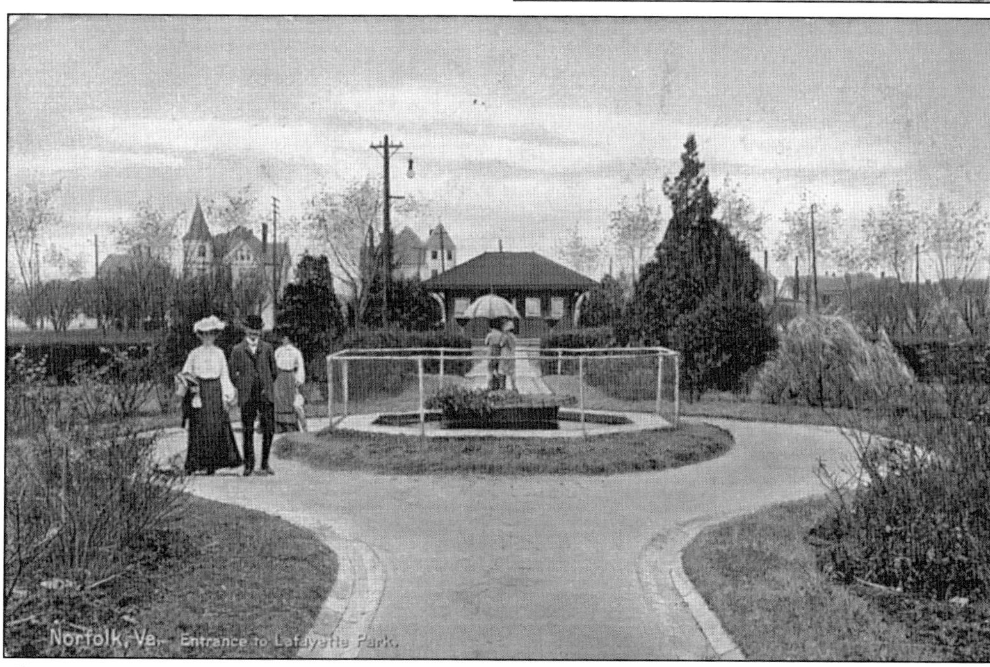

The entrance to the Lafayette Park in Norfolk looks quite different than that of today. Several of the large homes of the period are visible in the background. This postcard is one of many collected by Miss Simpson in the early 1900s.

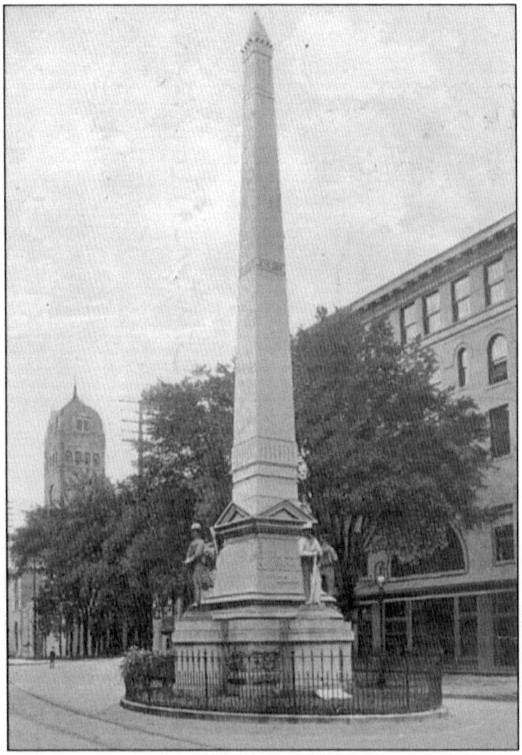

This postcard shows the Confederate Monument, which was erected in Portsmouth, Virginia, in the early part of the twentieth century. There are two postmarks on the reverse side: one was stamped in Berkley on December 11th and the other in South Norfolk on December 14th. It took all of three days to travel about 2 miles.

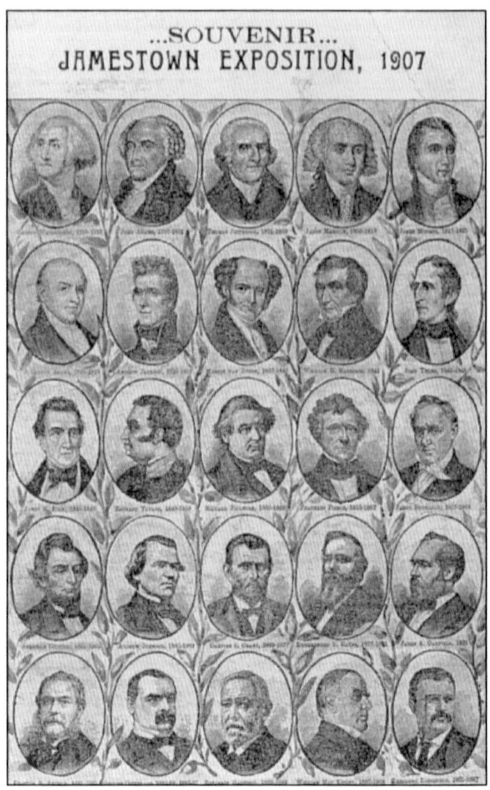

This postcard of "our presidents" was acquired at the Jamestown Exposition in 1907. At that time, Theodore Roosevelt was in office. For those who do not remember their high school history, it is interesting to note that Grover Cleveland served two non-consecutive terms as president of the United States.

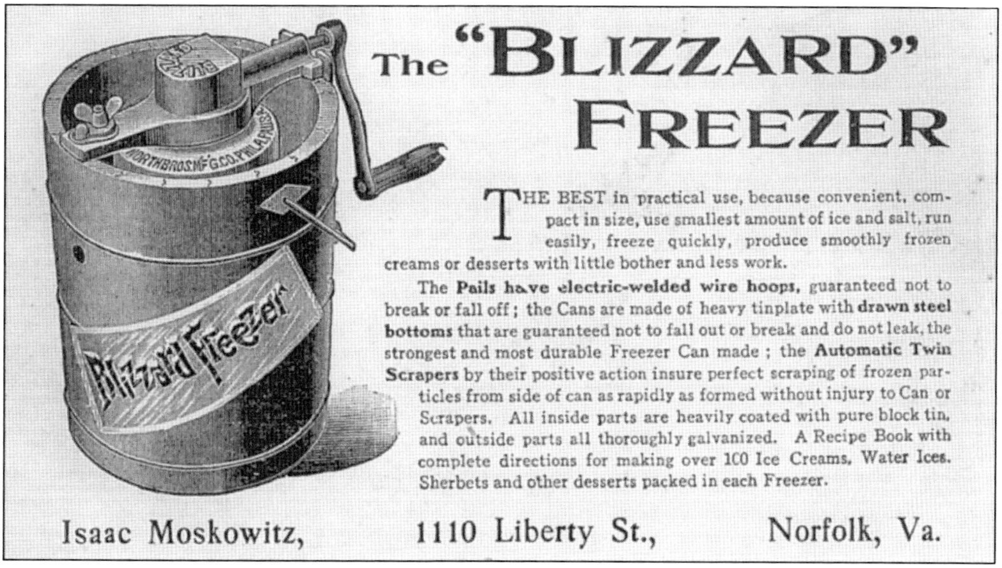

Here is an advertisement for the "Blizzard" Freezer, which was sold by Isaac Moskowitz at 1110 Liberty Street. The freezer was advertised as being practical, using only small amounts of salt and ice, and producing smooth frozen deserts with little bother and less work. Those words were written by a marketing specialist, because if you have ever cranked one of those contraptions, then you know how hard it is. However, it did have its reward. Usually the person that did the cranking got to lick the paddles. This freezer came with a recipe book with directions for making over 100 ice creams, water ices, sherberts, and other desserts.

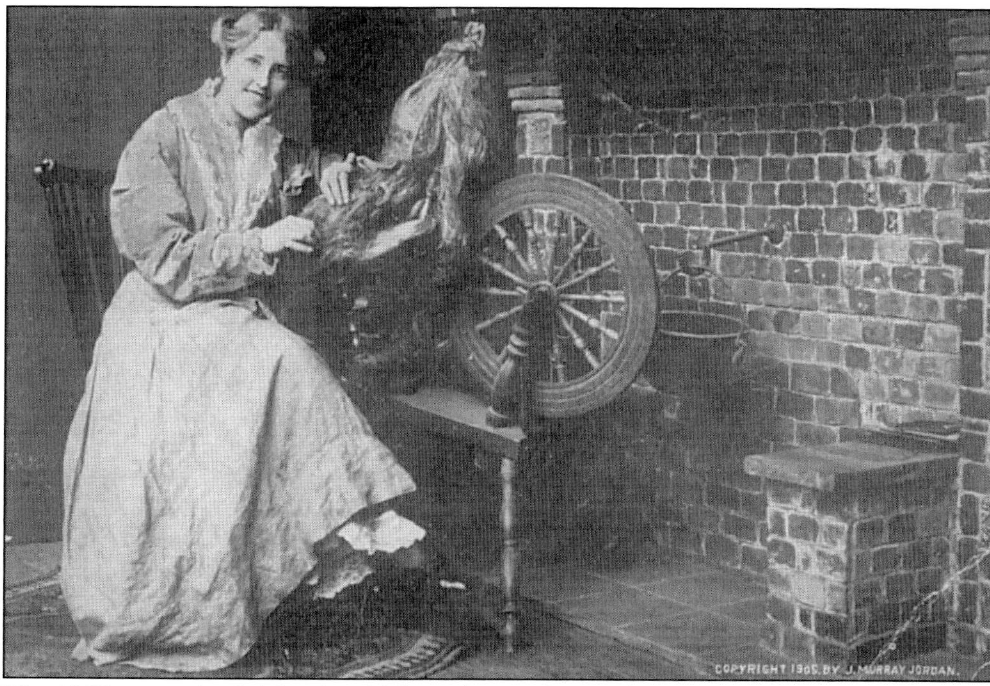

This 1905 postcard titled "in the old days" shows a beautiful young lady demonstrating the use of a spinning wheel. This device was used for spinning wool or flax into yarn or thread. The large wheel was usually operated by a foot pedal.

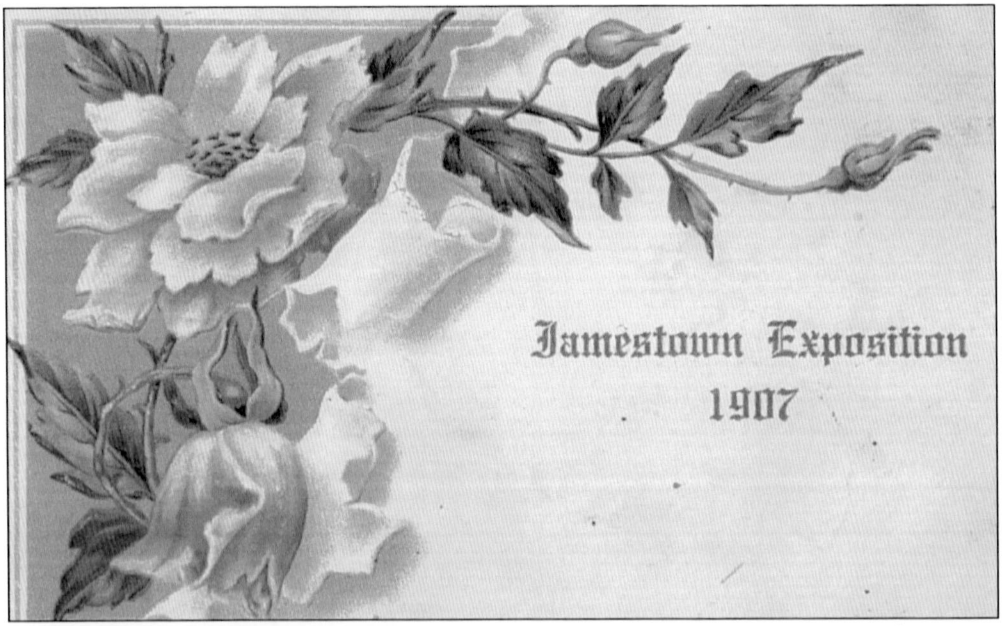

Many souvenirs were produced during the Jamestown Exposition of 1907. Among them were a collection of postcards, some of which are presented in this book. The exposition was held at Sewell's Point on land that is now used by the U.S. Navy. At the time, this area was part of Norfolk County.

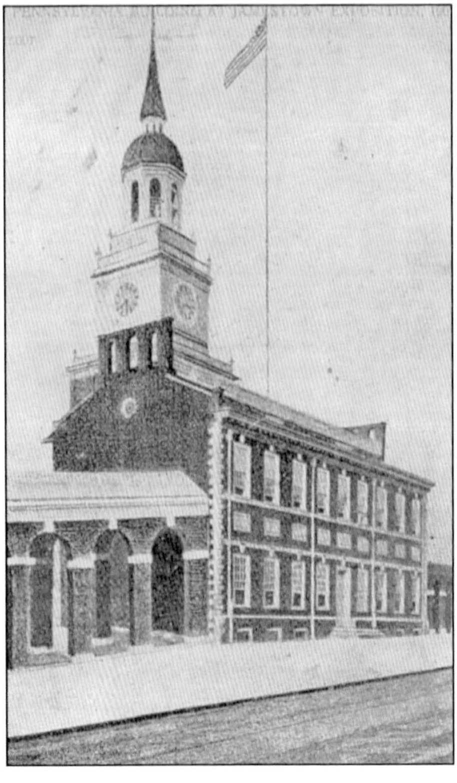

This is the Pennsylvania building, which is a reproduction of Independence Hall in Philadelphia. It later served as the officer's club, where this author spent more than a few hours.

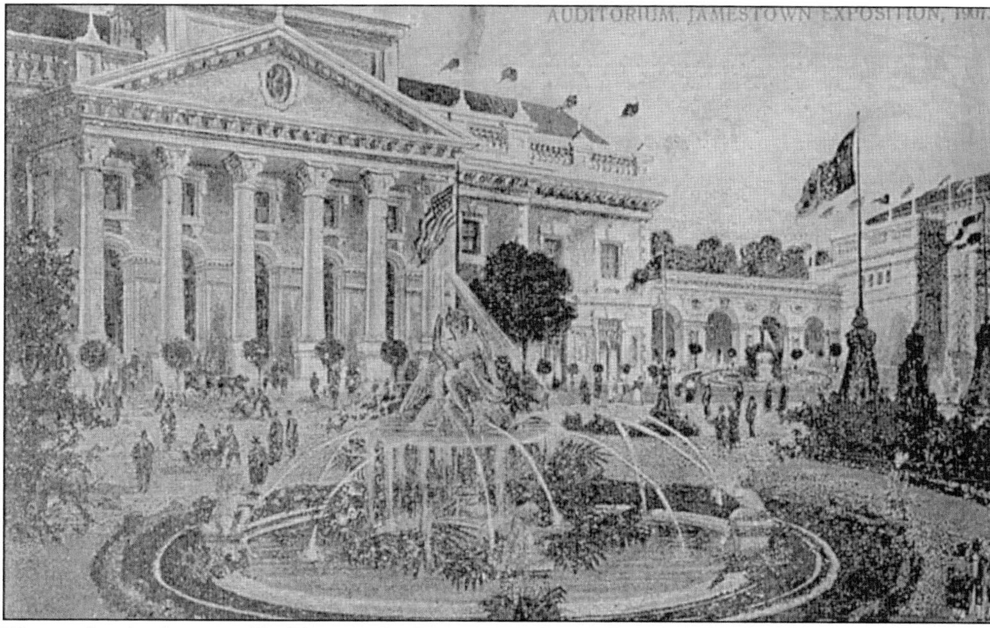

This is the Auditorium Building at the Jamestown Exposition in 1907.

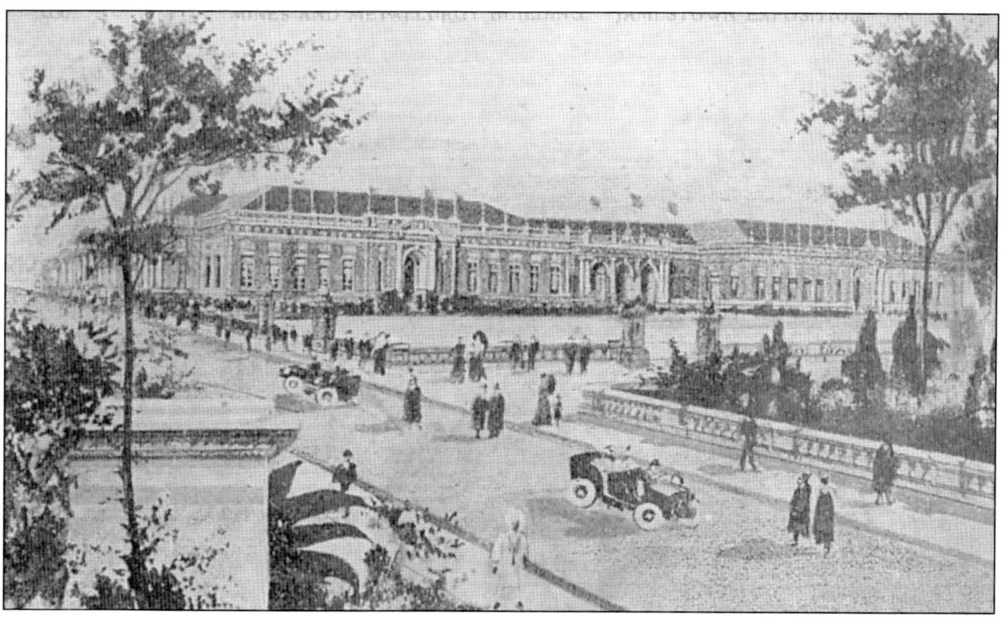

This postcard depicts the Mines and Metallurgy Building at the Jamestown Exposition.

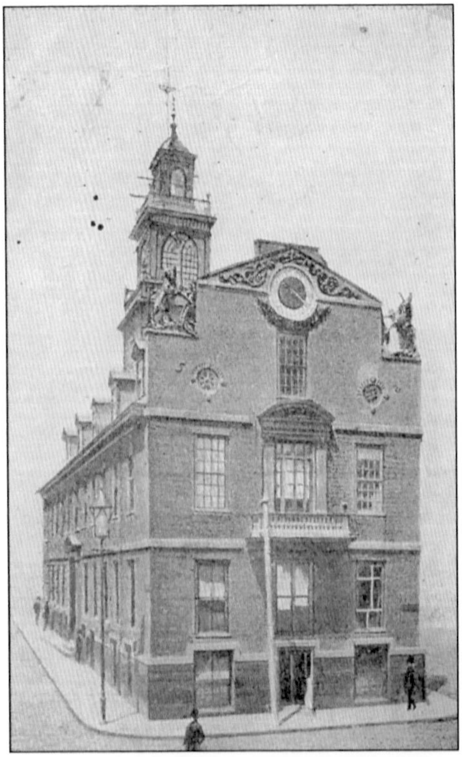

This is an end view of the Massachusetts State Building as it appeared at the Jamestown Exposition.

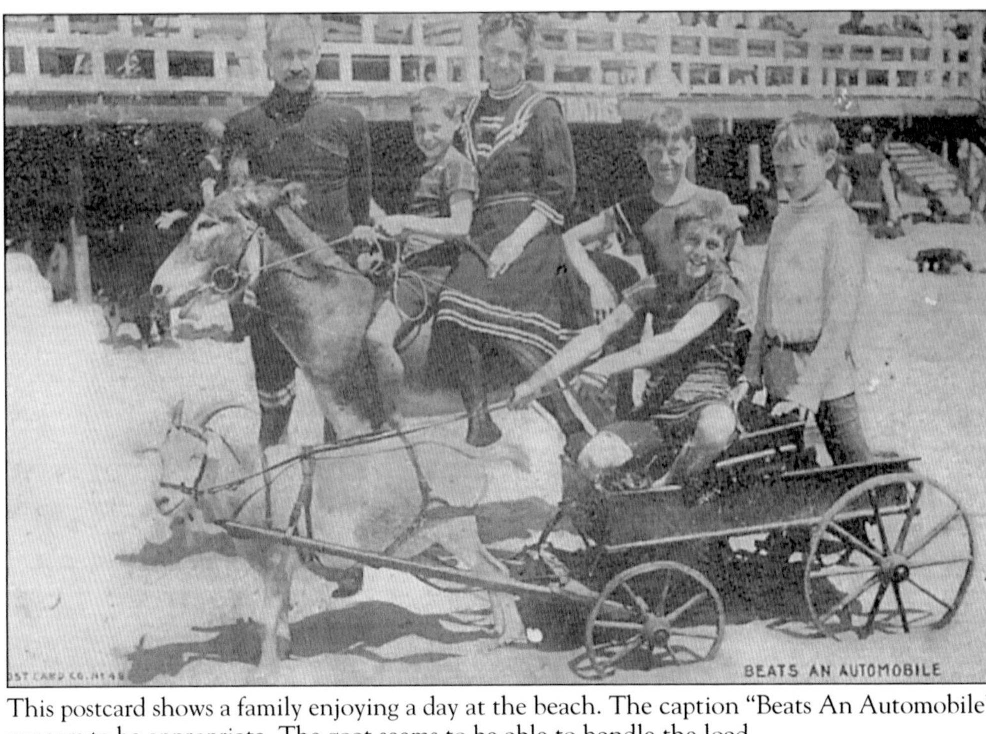

This postcard shows a family enjoying a day at the beach. The caption "Beats An Automobile" appears to be appropriate. The goat seems to be able to handle the load.

Three

EDUCATION IN NORFOLK COUNTY

It was in 1796 that Thomas Jefferson introduced his plan for the "General Diffusion of Knowledge" for Virginia. Through his influence and suggestion, on December 22, 1796, the General Assembly of Virginia enacted a school law entitled "An Act to Establish Schools." Two years later, Norfolk County adopted Jefferson's plan and put into operation a system of public education.

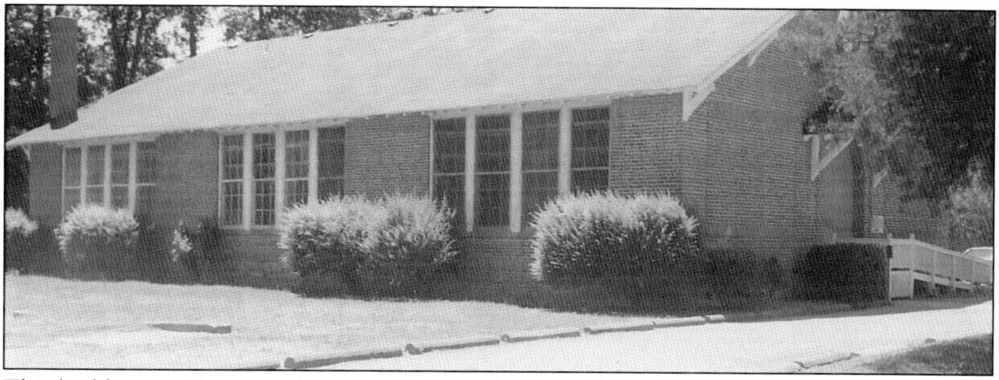

This building on Homestead Road, which was built in 1922, once served as the Sunray school and later was used as a post office. The community of Sunray was founded in the latter 1800s by a group of Polish Americans.

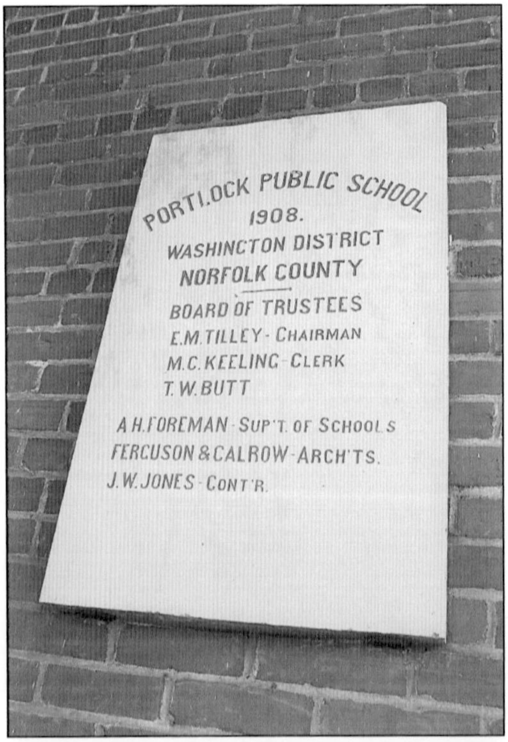

This self-explanatory sign is mounted near the front entrance of Chesapeake's Museum and Information Center at 3815 Bainbridge Boulevard. It was installed in 1908 when the small four-room schoolhouse was built.

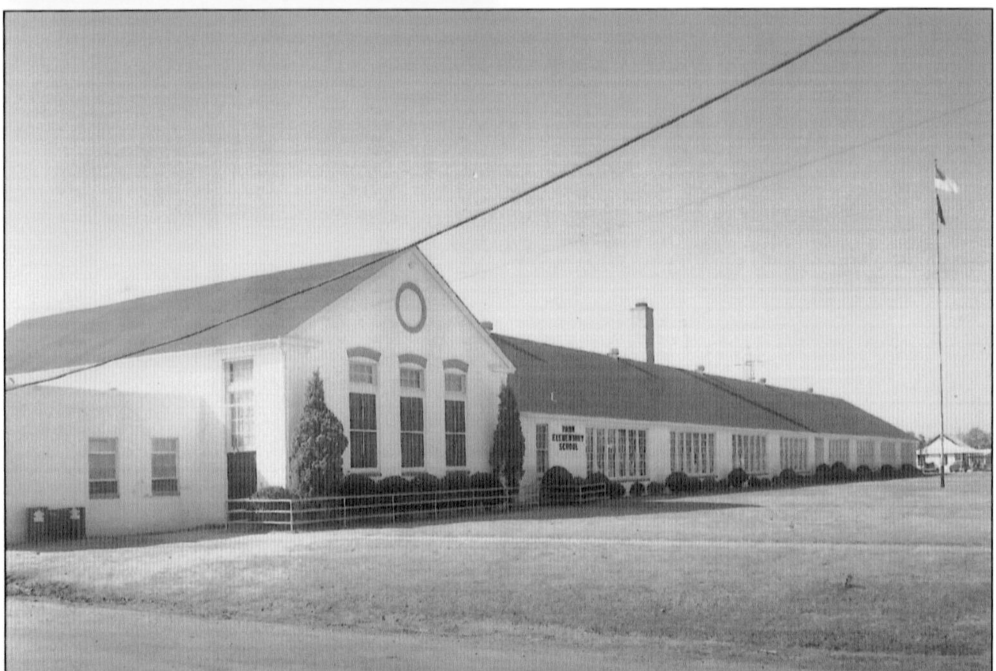

The first school in Riverdale Manor was held in one of the vacant units. In 1943, the Riverdale Elementary School was built. Later the name of the community was changed to Foundation Park, and the school seen in this picture became known as the Park Elementary School.

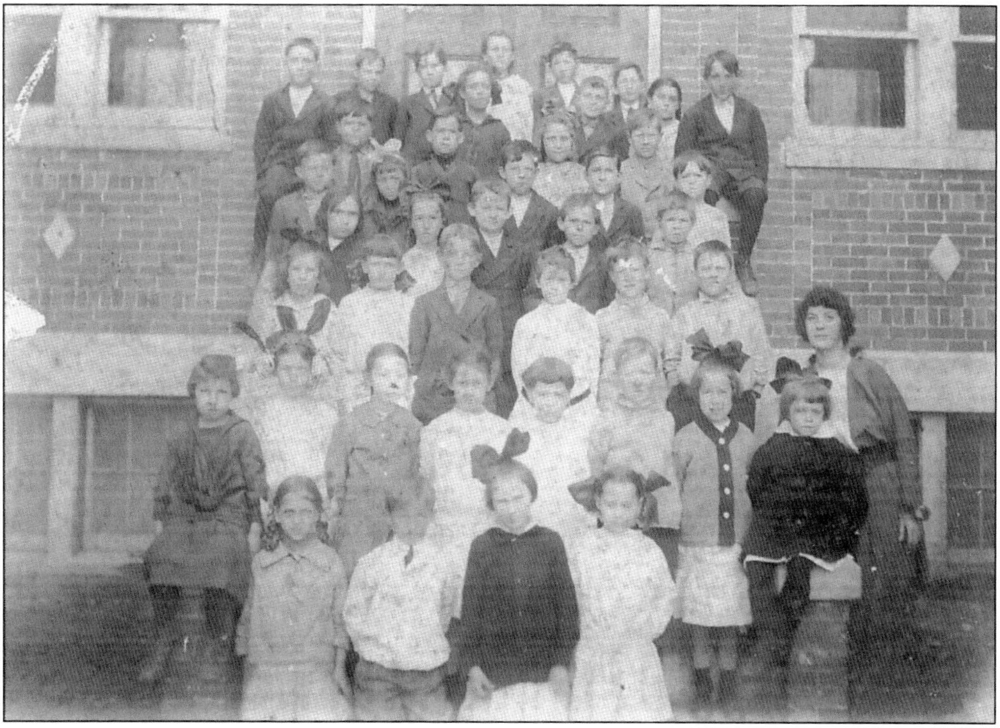

This picture was taken at the South Norfolk Grammar School on February 5, 1914. Miss Eugenia Portlock appears in the second row, second from the right, with a large bow in her hair.

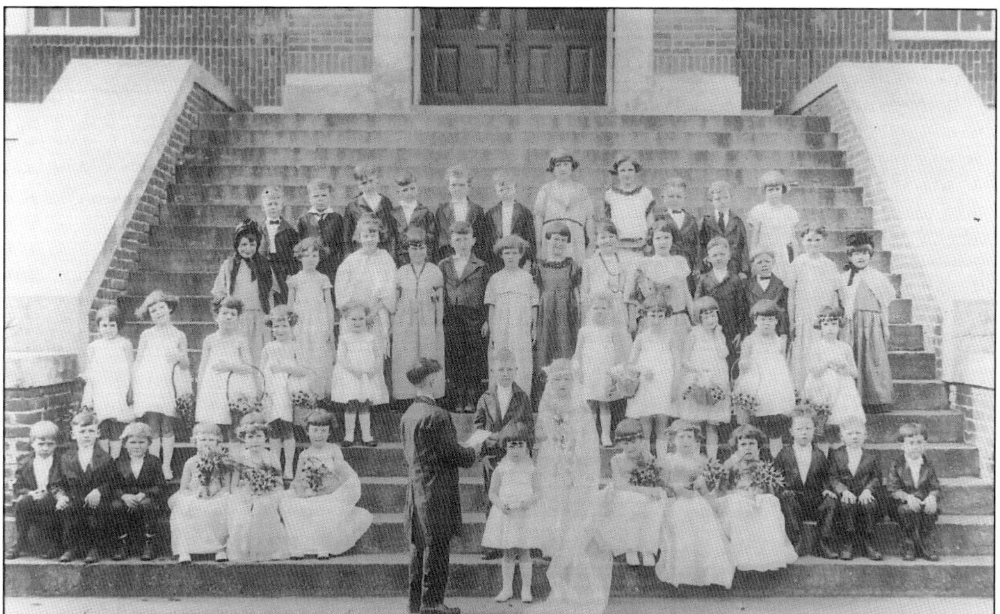

This group of schoolchildren participates in a Lilliputian wedding. Most of their names have faded into the past, but a few are identifiable. The preacher is Jerry Bray, the bride is Anna Lindsey, William Consolvo is the first boy on the left in the back row, and his brother, Frederic E. Jr., is sixth from the left.

1940

First Music Festival

PRESENTED BY

Norview-Portlock-Hickory-Great Bridge

NORFOLK COUNTY SCHOOLS

Direction, JOHN H. BUTCHER, Director of Music

NORVIEW HIGH SCHOOL

Friday, April 26th, 1940, 8 o'clock p. m.

Program

INTRODUCTION

Mr. H. C. Barnes........*Principal Norview School*

Orchestra—(a) "Marching Feet"........*DeLamater*
(b) "Campus Pride"........*DeLamater*
JOHN H. BUTCHER, Director

Norview School Toy Symphony—(a) "Welcome Sweet Springtime"
(b) "In An Old Dutch Garden"
MISS ABBIE MAE EDWARDS, Director

Portlock Glee Club—(a) "Song of the Danube"........*Strauss*
(b) The Lord's Prayer........*Malotte*
MISS MARY STONE, Director

Orchestra—(a) Barcarolle, from "Tales of Hoffmann"........*Offenbach*
(b) Elves Dance, from "Nut Cracker Suite"..*Tschaikowsky*
JOHN H. BUTCHER, Director

Vocal Solo—"The Kiss Waltz"........*Ronell*
MISS LENA GOSMAN (Portlock School)
MISS IMOGENE KITTS, Accompanist

Piano Solo—"Valse Caprice"........*Newland*
MISS JUNE McNEAL (Norview School)

Great Bridge Glee Club—(a) "Carmena"........*Wilson*
(b) "Calm as the Night"........*Bohm*
MISS FRANCIS SIFFORD, Director

Orchestra—(a) "Hungarian Dance" No. 5........*Brahms*
(b) "Tschaikowsky Overture"........*Tschaikowsky*
(Based on his Themes)
JOHN H. BUTCHER, Director

Norview Glee Club—(a) "A Dream Boat Passes By"........*Lemare*
(b) Barcarolle,
from "Tales of Hoffmann"........*Offenbach*
MISS BEVERLY M. STONE, Director

Trio—Clarinet, Saxophone, Piano—"Moonbeams"........*McCaughley*
ELIZABETH HARRISON, LLOYD HARRISON, BEVERLY JENNINGS (Hickory School)

Drum Corps—"A Parade Routine"
Norview and Portlock Combined Units
JOHN H. BUTCHER, Director

FINALE — TAPS

NOTE:—The Orchestra Group consists of selected pupils from the four above schools.

The First Music Festival of Norfolk County schools was presented by Norview, Portlock, Hickory, and Great Bridge schools on Friday, April 26, 1940, at the Norview High School.

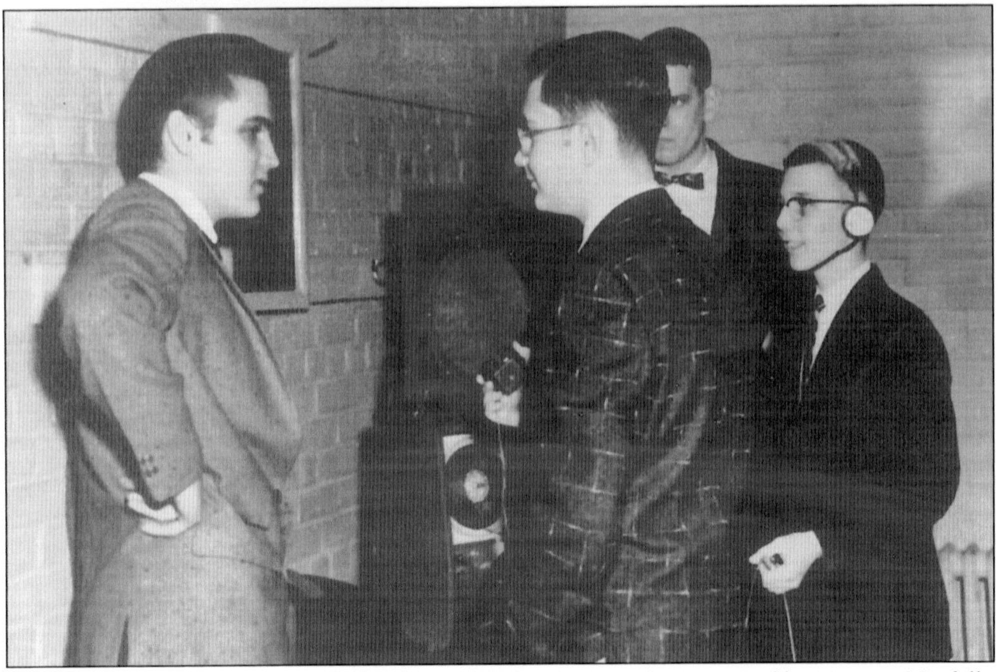

A surprise visit by the "King," Elvis Aaron Presley, was made on one of his trips to Norfolk, when he decided to call on the students at radio station WFOS. From left to right are Elvis, Ray Pulley, Mike Carter, and Steve Jones.

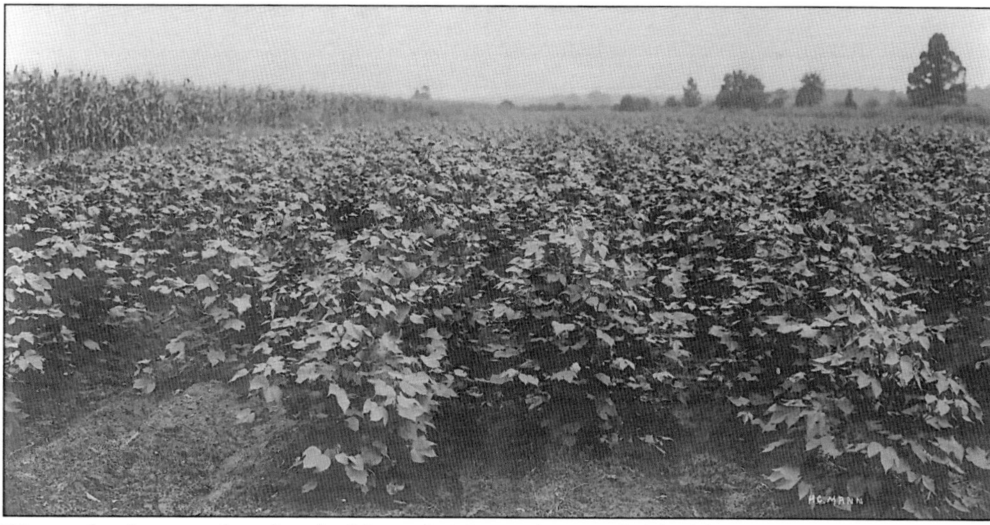

This early photograph, taken by Harry C. Mann, shows a field of demonstration cotton at the Cumberland Farm in Grassfield. Judging by the height of the corn to the left of the cotton, the picture was probably taken in the month of July.

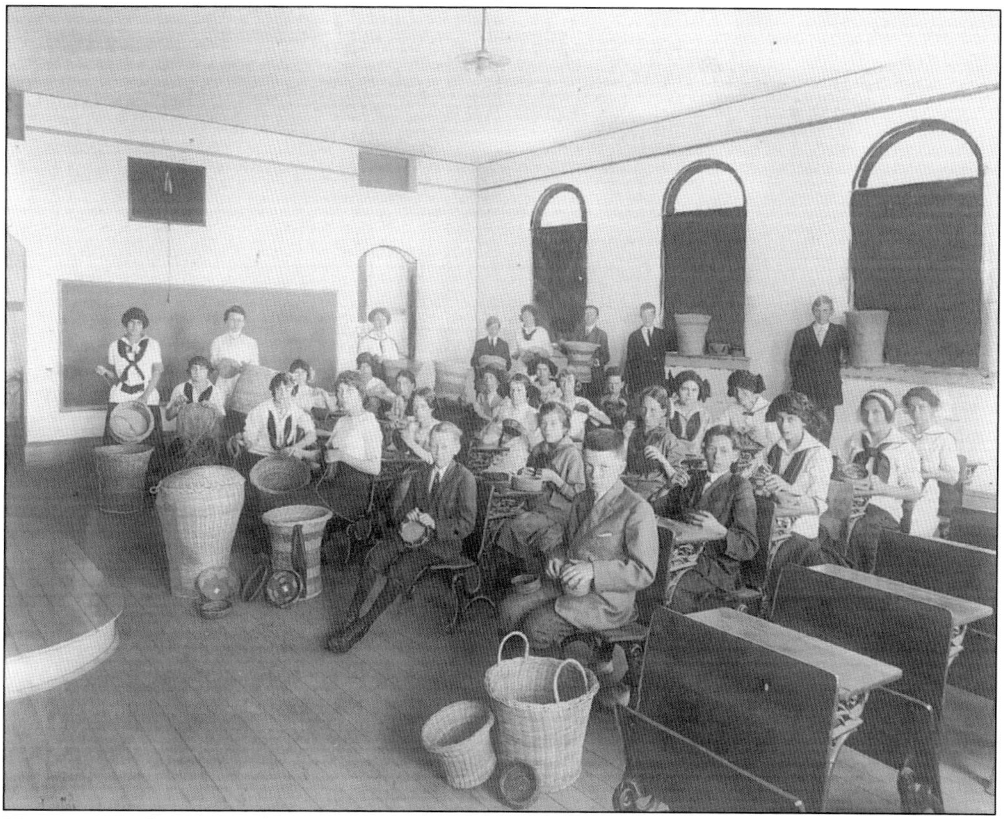

Here is an early-twentieth-century picture of the manual training class at the Lafayette School. The class appears to be one in basket weaving. Note the modern light in the top center of this view—it has four bulbs mounted on a reflective surface with a pull string connected to the on-off switch.

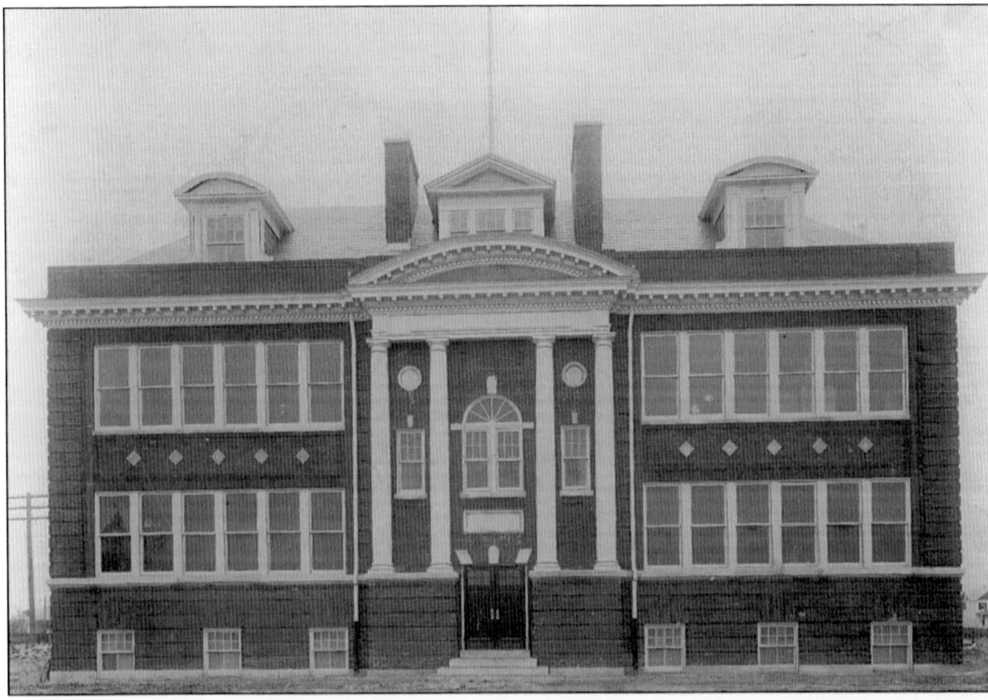

The Lafayette High and Grammar School was located in the Tanner's Creek District. It began as a grammar school in Norfolk County in 1905 and was enlarged to accommodate the high school in 1910. A very close look reveals two children peering out the lower right windows.

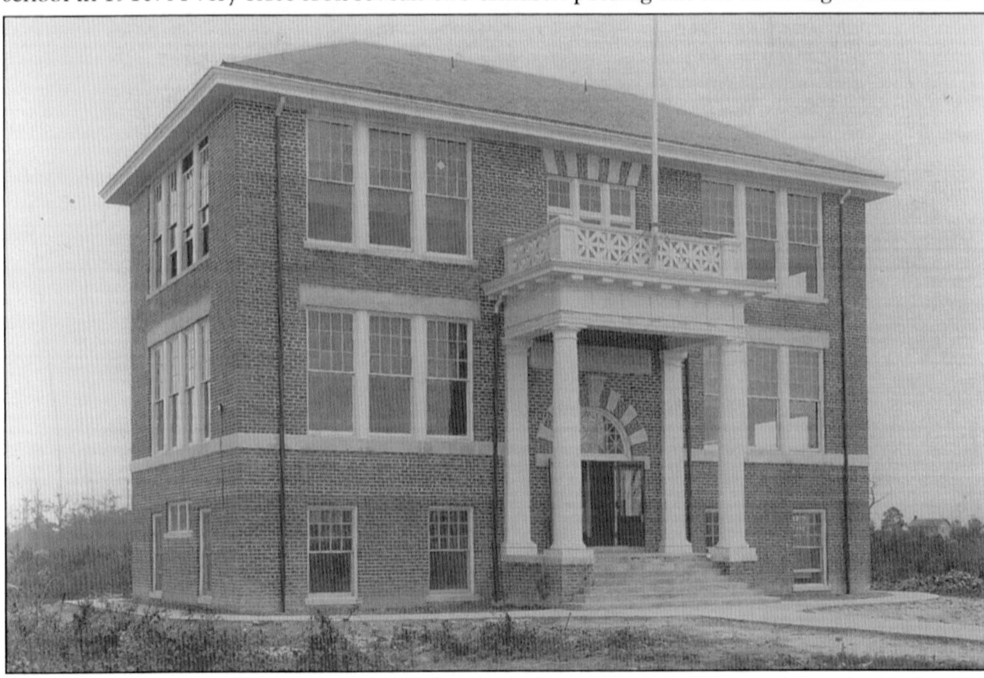

Here is the new Sewell's Point School shortly before its occupancy in the early 1900s. The surrounding yard is filled with debris that was probably removed before the children enrolled. (Harry C. Mann, photographer.)

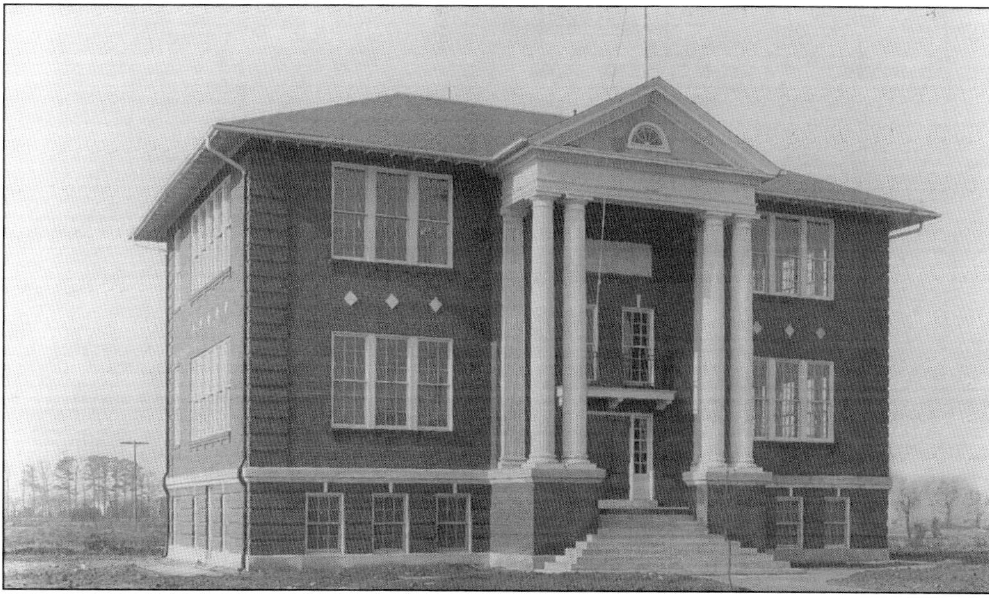

Construction on the new Norfolk County public school in Larchmont was begun in 1912, and it opened on January 2, 1913.The school had four rooms and was constructed so that four more could be added without detracting from the architectural beauty of the structure. It served as a grammar school in which the branches of all seven elementary grades in the Norfolk County curriculum were taught. Mrs. Jessie Heath was the first principal and Miss Mildred Alexander was the assistant. The building cost about $13,000 and was constructed under the supervision of Superintendent A.H. Foreman of the Norfolk County public schools, and the Tanner's Creek District School Board, composed of J.D. Guy, chairman; B.F. Cartwright, and George G. Martin.

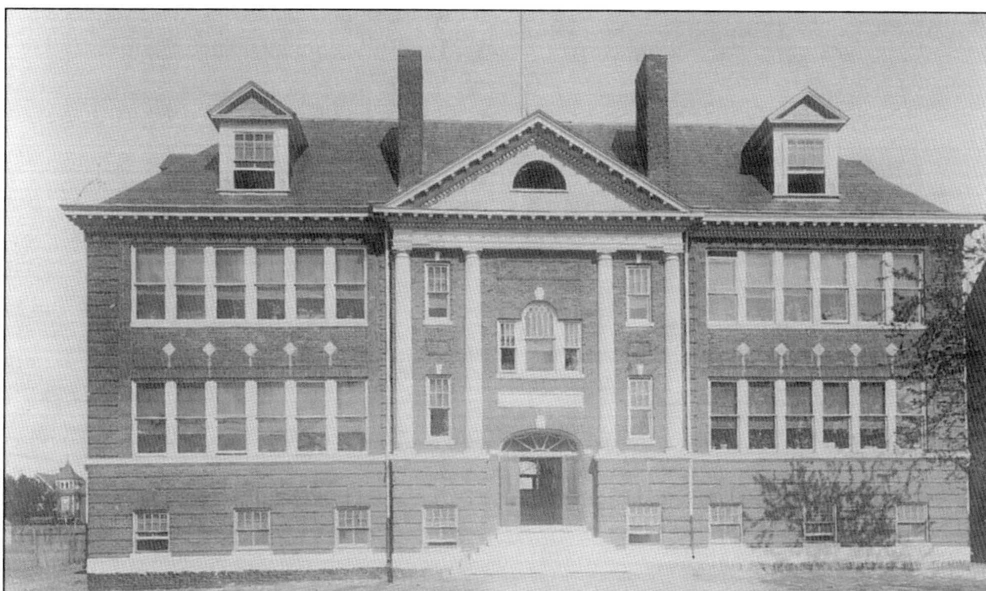

This is an early photograph of the Prentis Park School. A close look at the windows reveals a variety of potted plants. A beautiful three-story home can be seen in the left background.

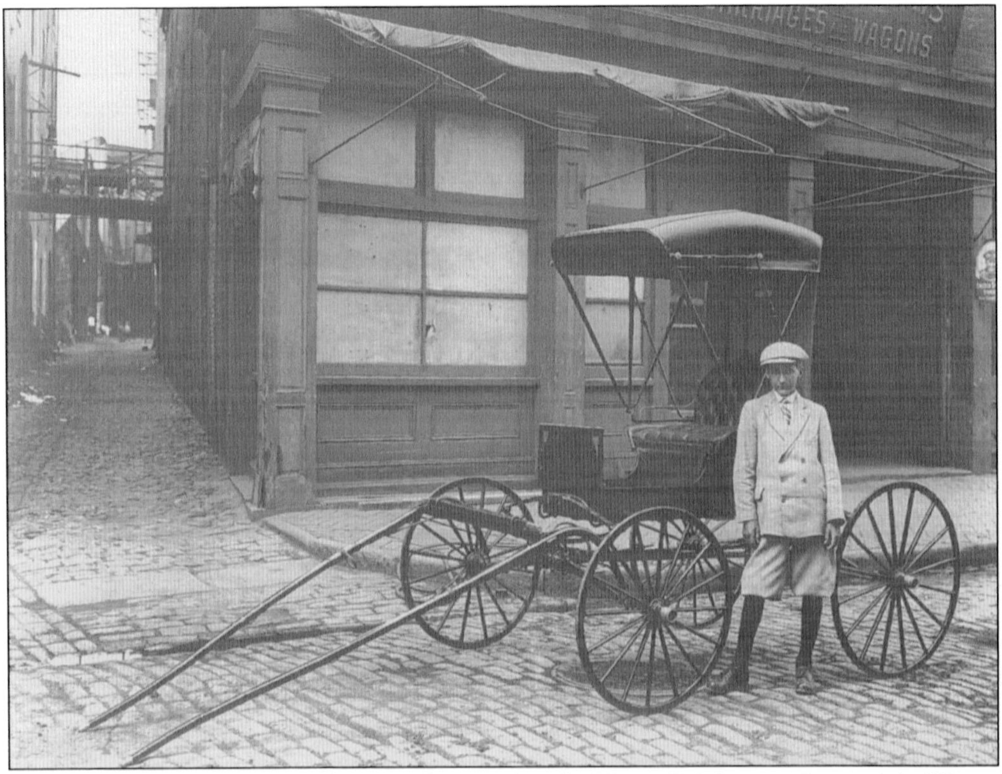

This early-twentieth-century photograph was taken by Harry C. Mann in front of A. Wrenn & Sons, a maker of carriages and wagons. Wrenn started the business in 1852. The young man, Garland Bell, is dressed in his finest suit with knickers, long socks, and highly polished shoes. He poses beside a new carriage that has just been completed and rolled out on the cobblestone street. Young Mr. Bell was awarded first prize at the Second Congressional District Fair for raising the greatest number of bushels of corn per acre.

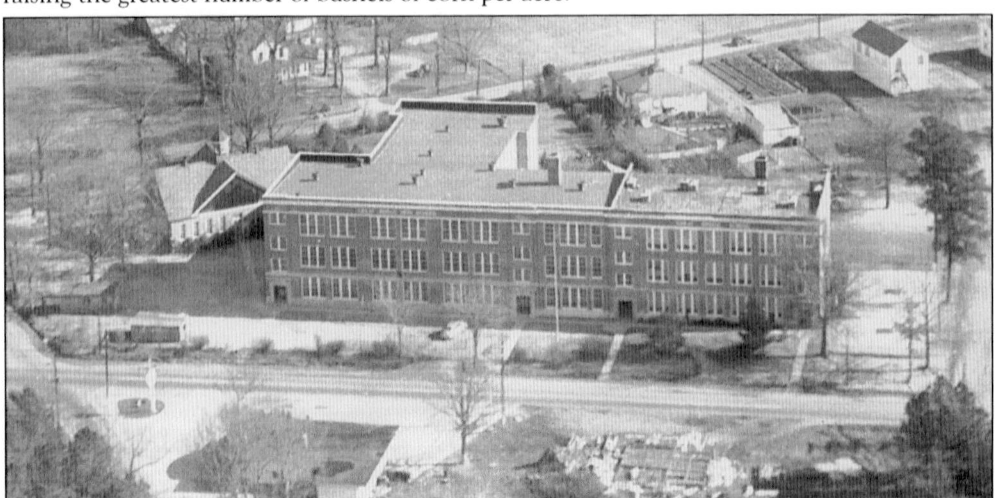

This is the Great Bridge High School around 1922. It fronted on what was known as the Great Road, which led from Norfolk to Great Bridge. The building now faces Battlefield Boulevard at the corner of Johnstown Road. The road behind the school is Mount Pleasant.

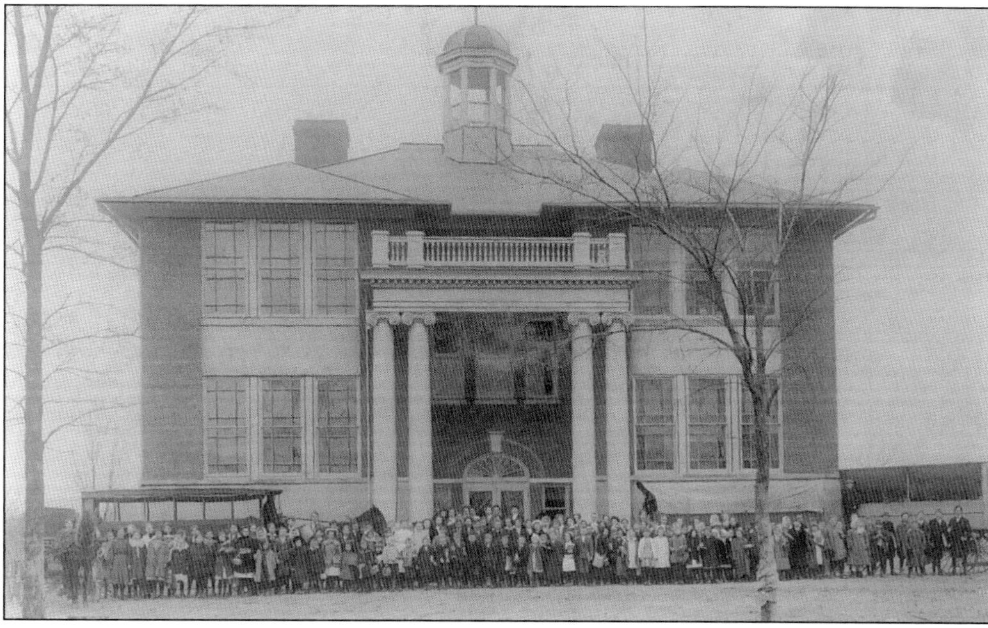

In 1910, this beautiful new building housed both the Deep Creek Grammar and High School students. The dress of the children and the buds on the young trees indicate that this photograph was possibly taken around March. The wet ground is due to a recent rain or melting snow. Transportation to and from school was furnished by horse-driven school buses and wagons equipped with roll canvas curtains that provided shelter during inclement weather.

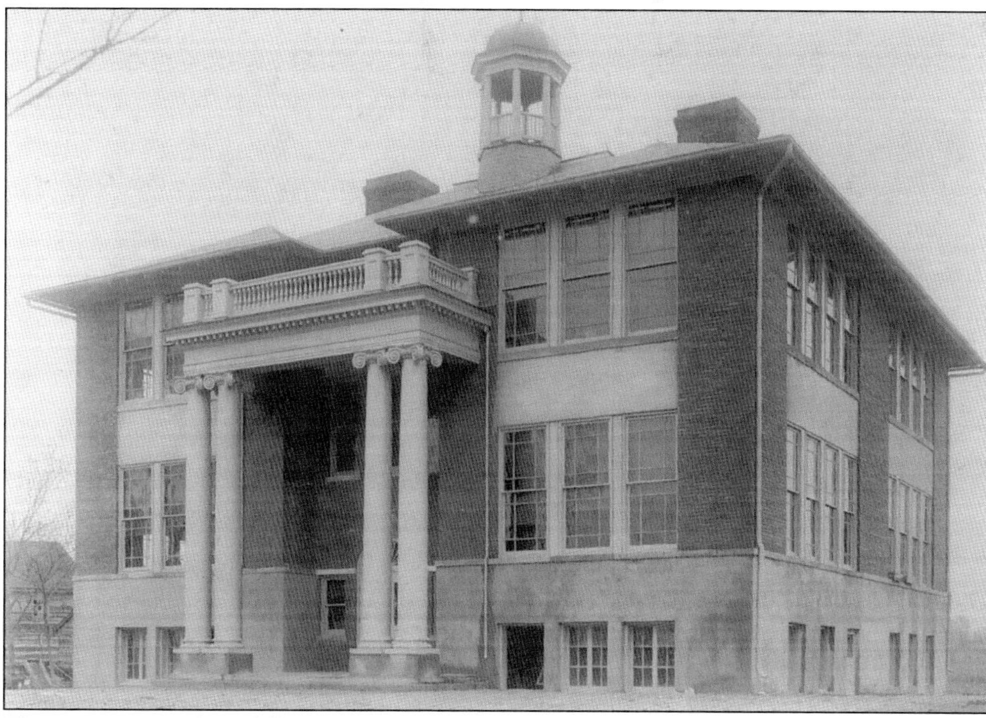

This picture provides a different view of the Deep Creek School in 1910. A dilapidated building can be seen to the left of the school.

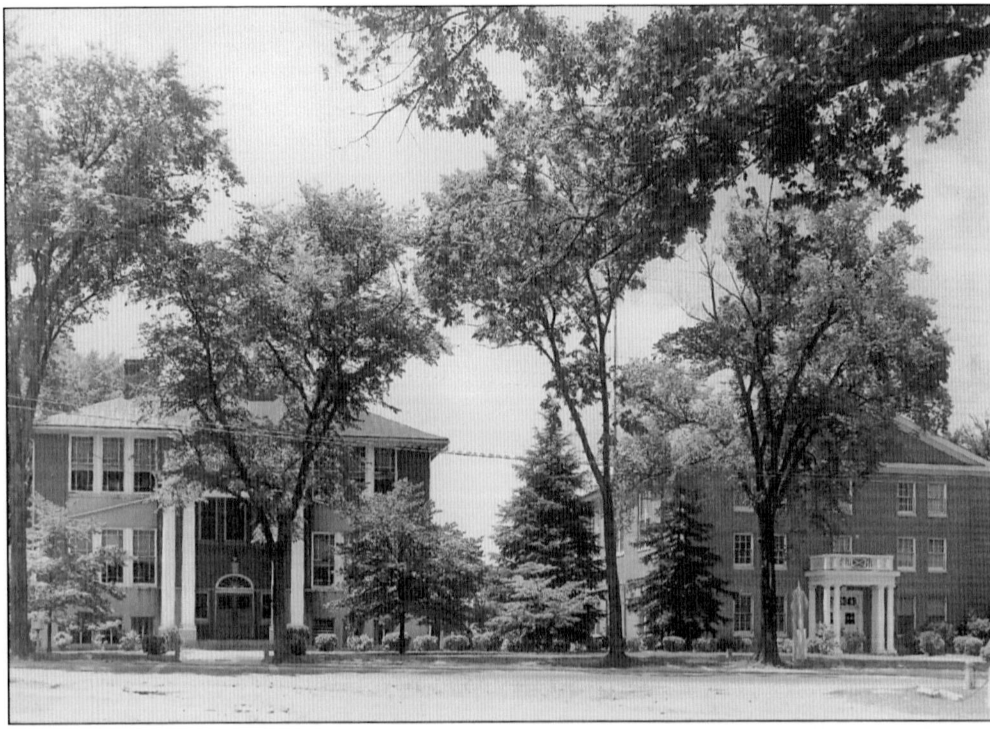

In this *c.* 1955 photograph of the Deep Creek School, trees, shrubbery, and an additional building have been added. When this picture was taken, the two buildings served as the elementary school.

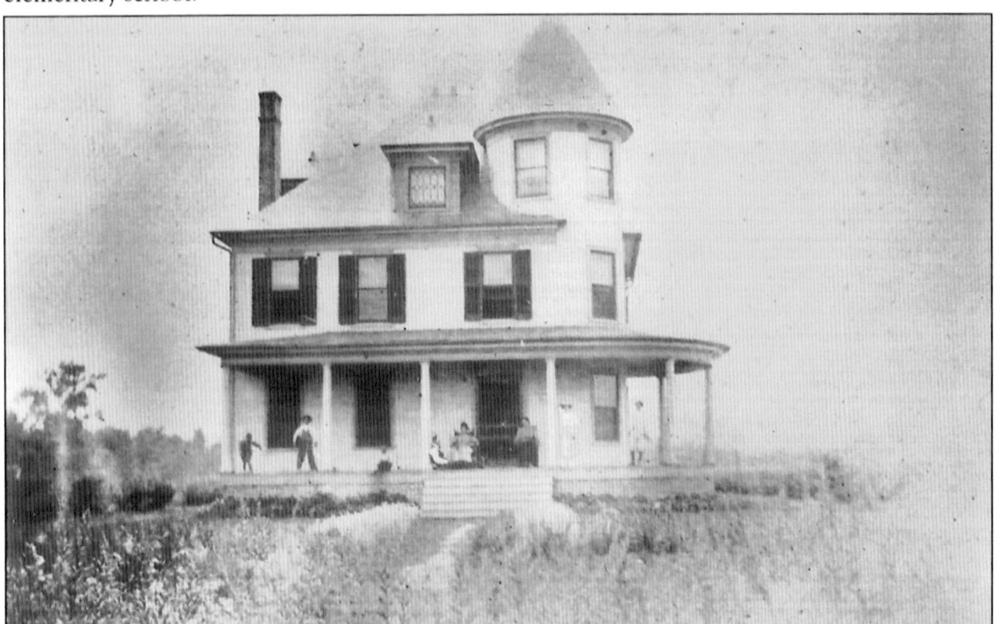

The Harlowe House, a large two-story farmhouse, served as the first Norview school building in 1921. The Norview Middle School now occupies this site. Two girls who transferred from Maury High School in 1924 became Norview's first graduating class.

Four

Great Bridge, Deep Creek, and Surroundings

The area of Great Bridge has been mostly remembered for the Chapel of Ease, which was located there in 1701, and for the Battle of Great Bridge, which took place during the Revolutionary War. It was also known for its agricultural impact on Norfolk County. The Dismal Swamp was, at one time, part of the area that Chief Powhatan controlled. The tribes to the north and west congregated in the area now called Deep Creek. In the eighteenth century, early settlers became aware of the value of timber growing in the Dismal Swamp and began cutting it for shingles and lumber. In 1650, William Drummond, the first governor of North Carolina, discovered a large lake in the middle of the swamp. This later became known as Lake Drummond.

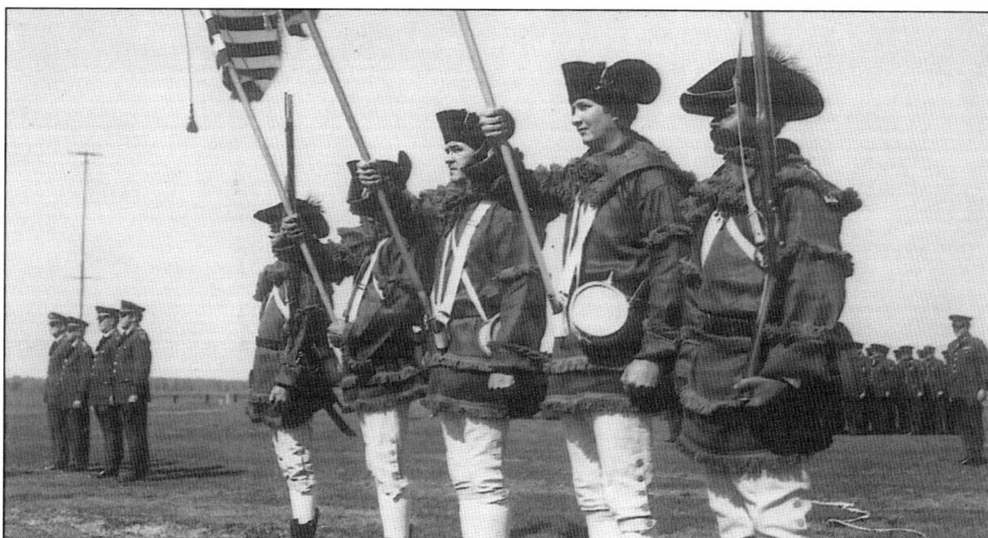

Members of the Great Bridge Patriots' Color Guard performed at many community functions. Pictured are, from left to right, SSG Guy L. Respass, SFC Harry D. Fuller, SSG Hurley R. Gough, SP4 Joseph Outlaw, and SP5 Johnnie L. Mosley.

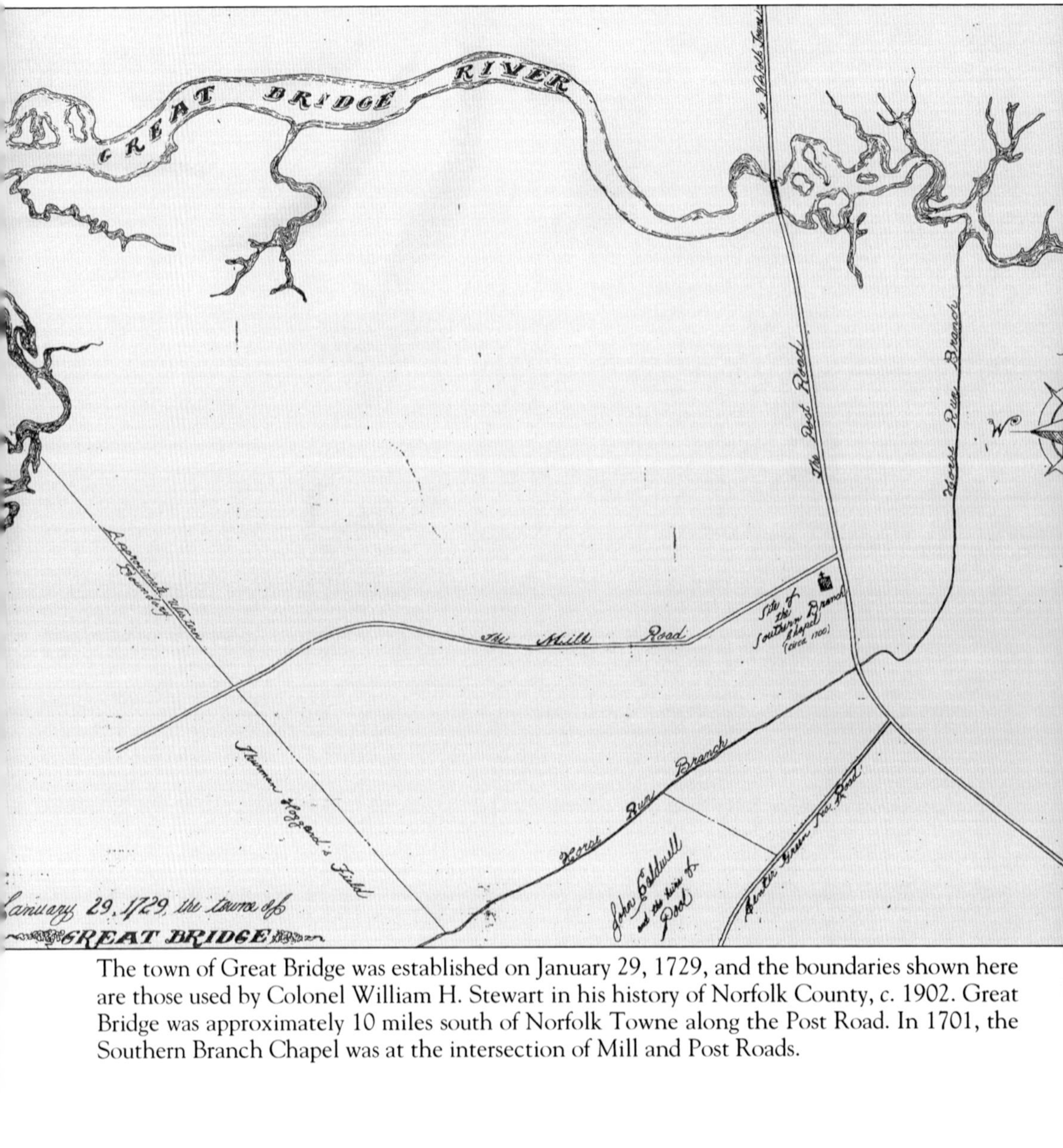

The town of Great Bridge was established on January 29, 1729, and the boundaries shown here are those used by Colonel William H. Stewart in his history of Norfolk County, *c.* 1902. Great Bridge was approximately 10 miles south of Norfolk Towne along the Post Road. In 1701, the Southern Branch Chapel was at the intersection of Mill and Post Roads.

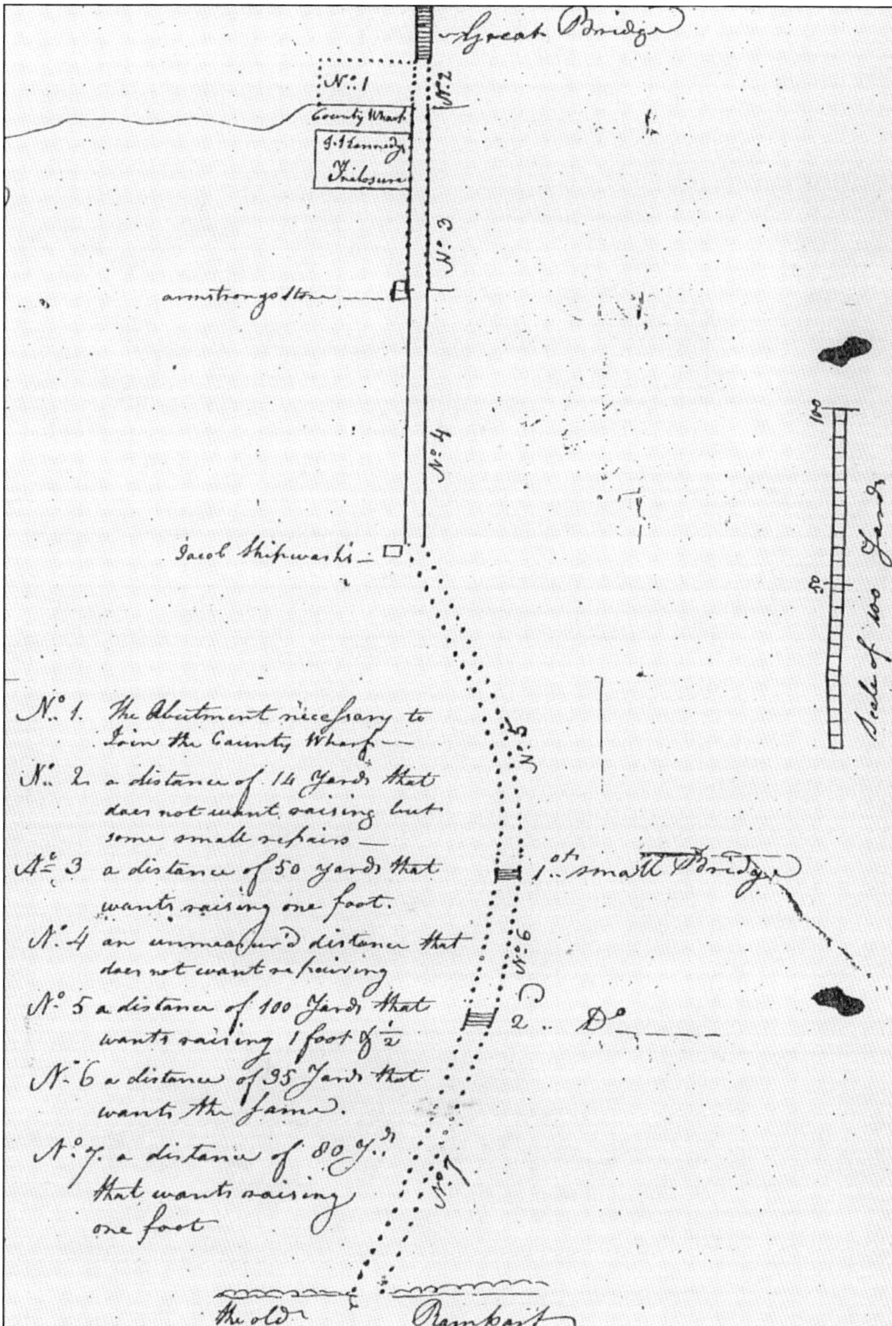

In June 1787, John Portlock and John Nash were ordered by the Norfolk County Court to inspect the causeway adjoining the Great Bridge and to report their findings of repairs needed at that time. On July 18, 1787, they submitted their report along with this sketch. Their explanation of possible cost was as follows: "The expense of these repairs is not easily ascertained, we cannot however suppose it would be much less than eighty pounds. But with great definition we recommend the worshipful court may order it be let to the lowest bidder for ready money which may be an inducement to make the undertaken work cheap."

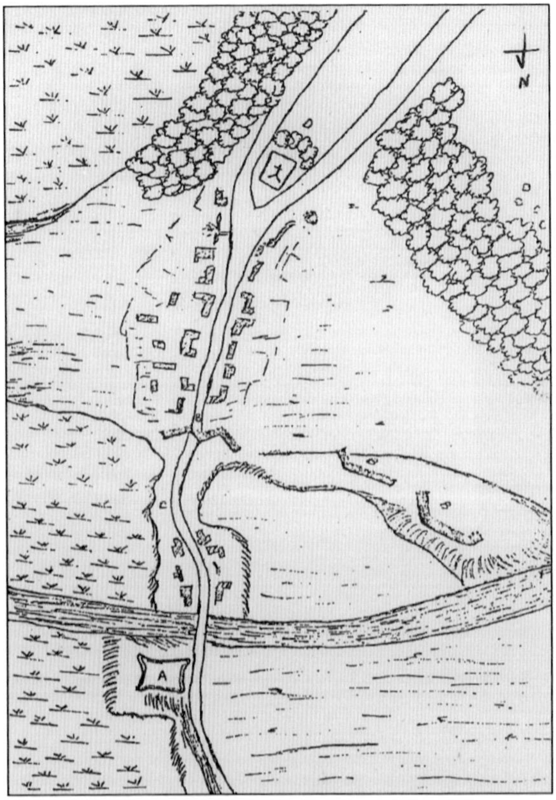

This map of Great Bridge shows the area as it appeared at the time of the battle. The lower portion is north. "A" is the fort built by Lord Dunmore's troops; "B" indicates the fortifications erected by the Americans; "C" identifies the causeway across the swamp; and "D" is the Southern Branch Chapel. The Great Bridge across the Southern Branch is directly in front of the British fort.

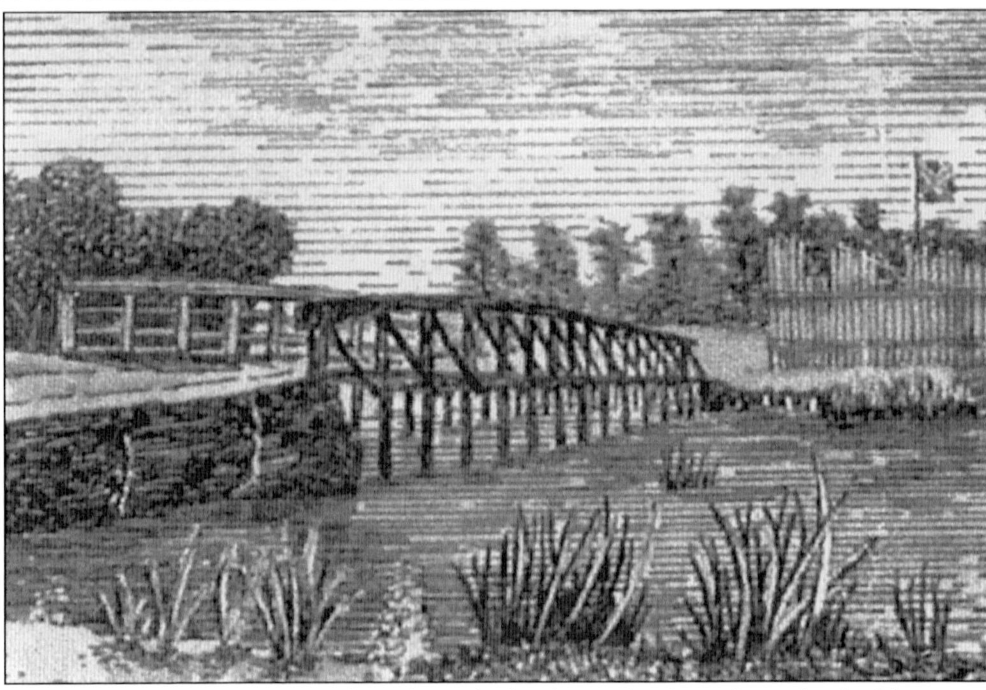

This image shows the Great Bridge, where the battle was fought and won by the Virginians. The British fort, erected in 1775, can be seen in the right background.

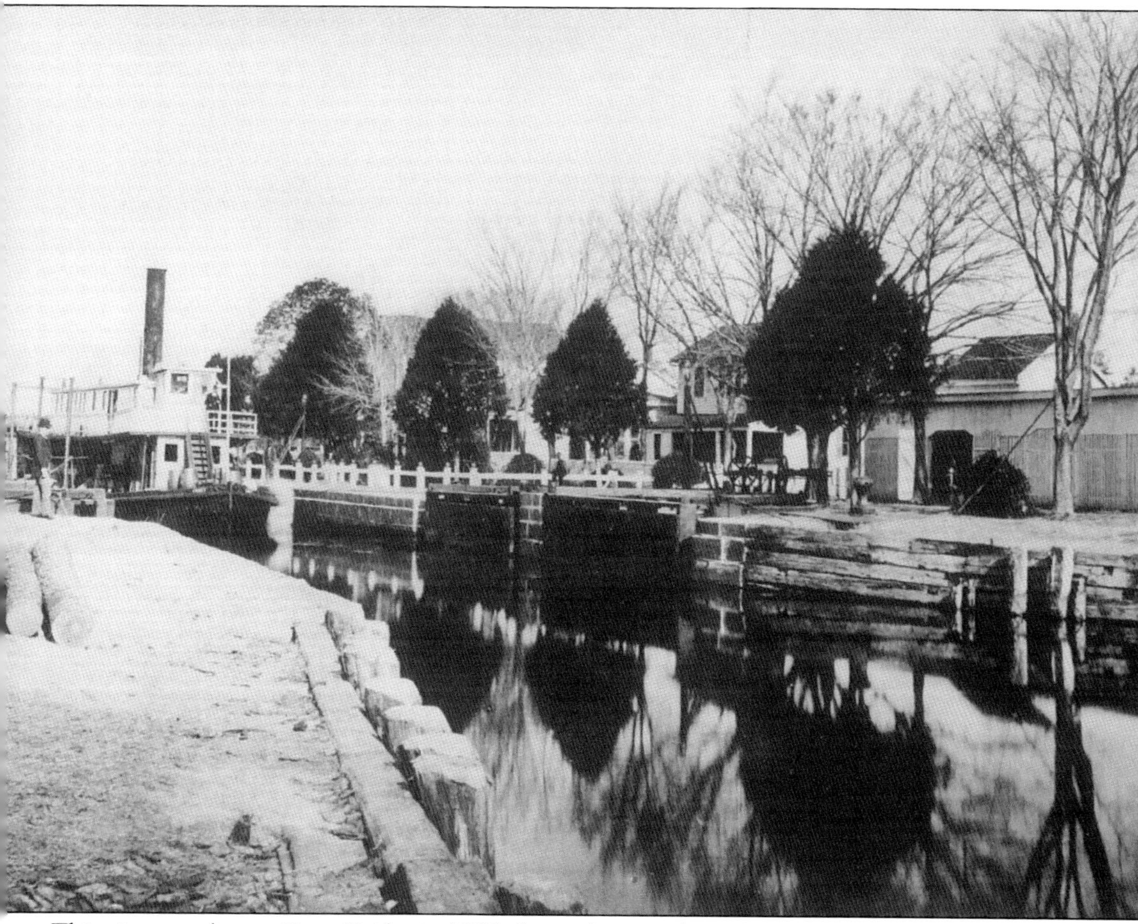

This picture, taken at Great Bridge in 1895, shows the steamboat *Comet* exiting the locks of the Chesapeake and Albemarle Canal. The canal was originally planned and surveyed during the Colonial period but was not built until much later. It opened in 1859 and was acquired by the federal government in 1913. The canal is 70 miles long and runs from the Elizabeth River in Virginia to the North River and Albemarle Sound in North Carolina.

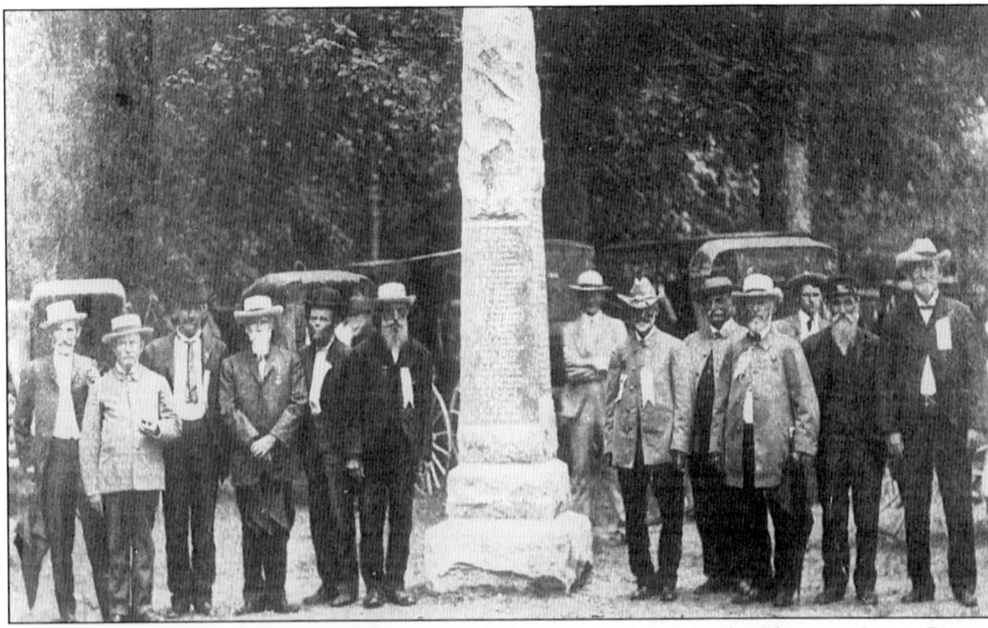

This picture was taken in 1905 when the Confederate monument at the Pleasant Grove Baptist Church in Hickory was unveiled. The men seen here are members of Jackson Grey's regiment from lower Norfolk County, which was organized on July 1, 1861, and named for James P. Jackson. From left to right are Dr. H.S. Etheridge, Carey Foreman, J.N. Wood, W.A. West, J.W. Creekmore, Alex Lee, Leroy West, Captain William H. Stewart, Tom West, Caleb Hodges, and unidentified. Captain Stewart was eventually promoted to lieutenant colonel.

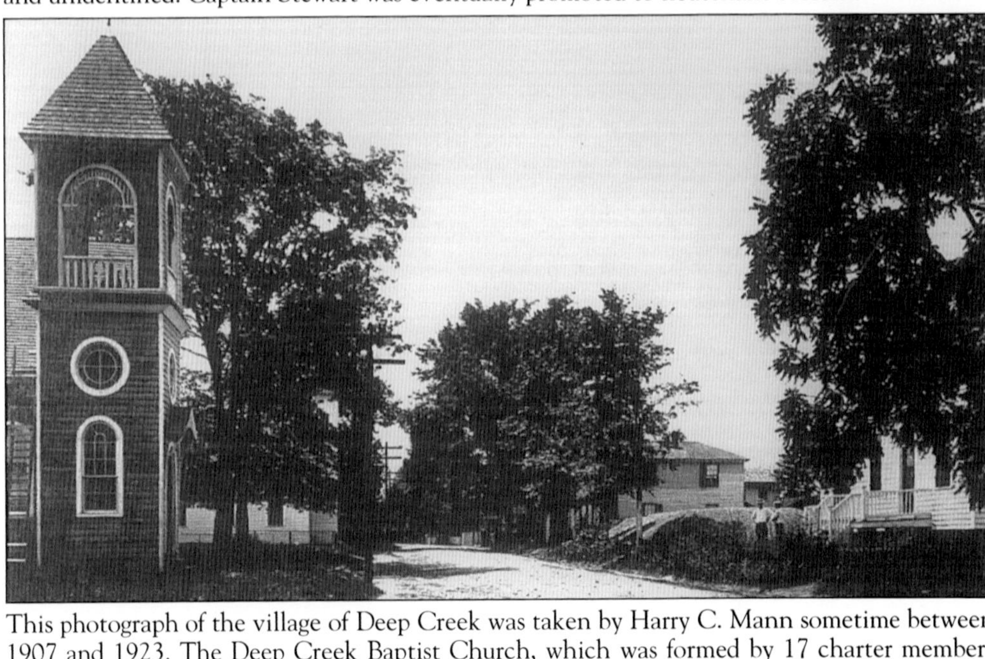

This photograph of the village of Deep Creek was taken by Harry C. Mann sometime between 1907 and 1923. The Deep Creek Baptist Church, which was formed by 17 charter members on August 29, 1869, stands to the left of the main road. In April 1870, the Reverend A. Paul Repiton began serving as the first minister at a salary of $150 per annum. Many of the early members of the church were baptized in the waters of the Deep Creek in Norfolk County.

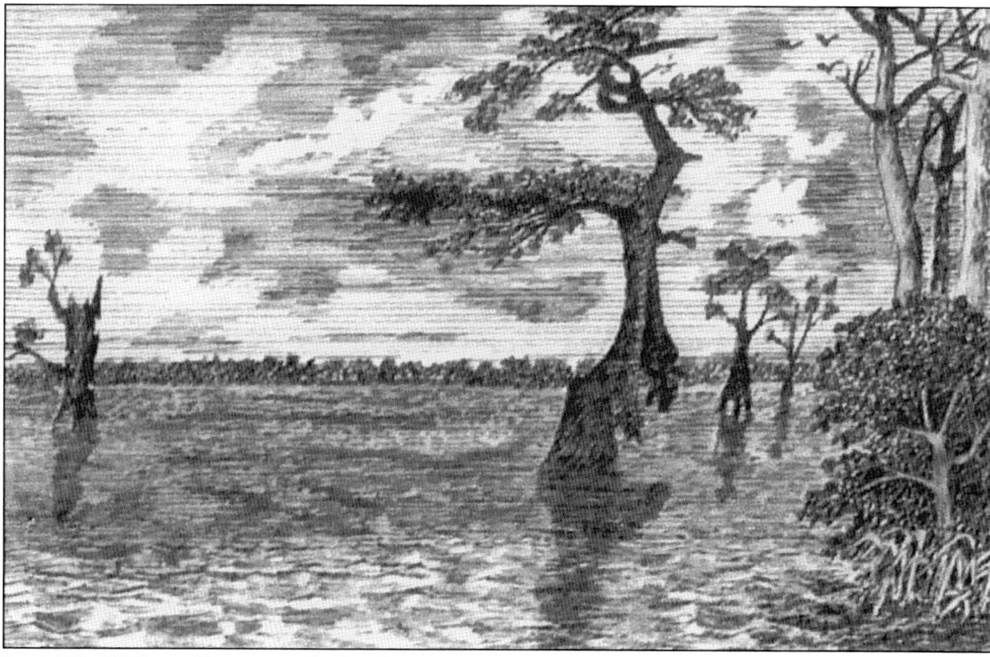

In 1650, William Drummond, the first governor of North Carolina (1663–1667), discovered a large lake in the middle of the Dismal Swamp. It would later be known as Lake Drummond. This image shows a portion of the lake.

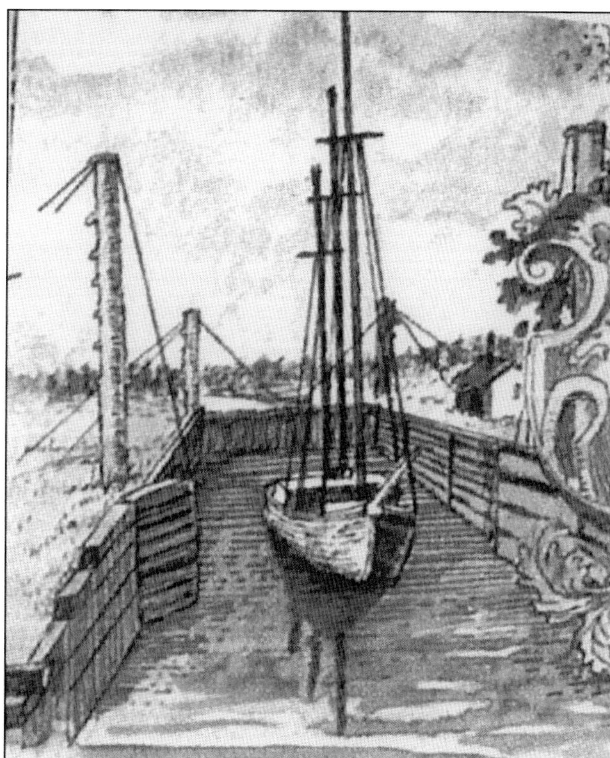

Pictured here is a drawing of the Deep Creek locks. In 1933–1934, new drawbridges were built at Deep Creek and South Mills. In 1940–1941, new locks were again constructed at Deep Creek and South Mills.

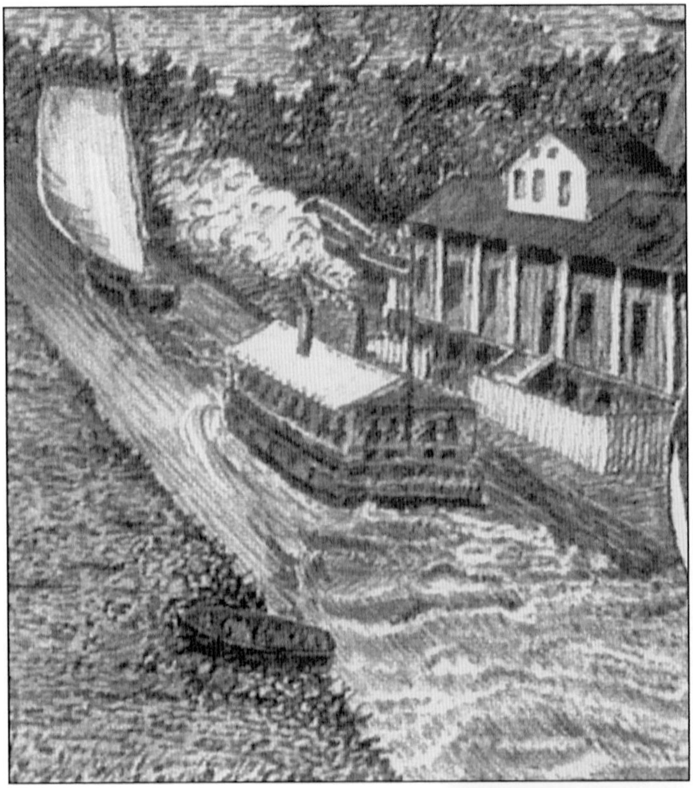

This image shows the Lake Drummond Hotel, also known as the "halfway house." It was built in 1830 and was located on the Dismal Swamp Canal near the Virginia-North Carolina line.

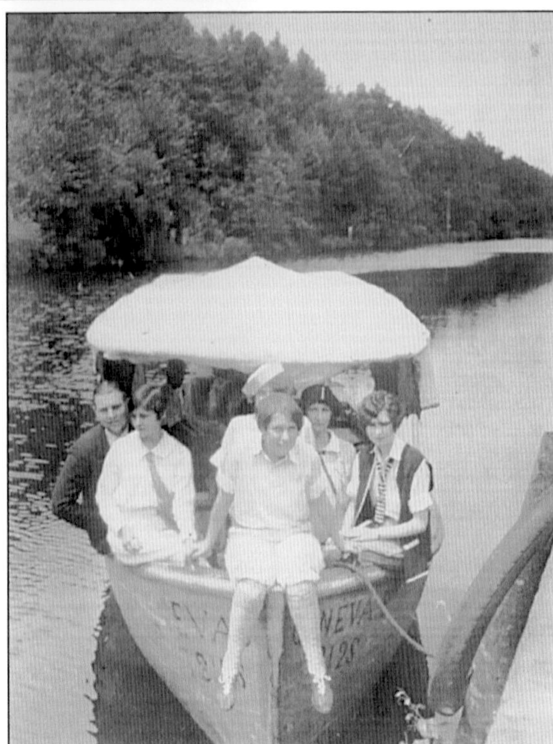

Here is a photograph of Frank Portlock and a group of lovely ladies making preparations for a trip to Lake Drummond.

On the trip to Lake Drummond, one of the ladies decides to lend a hand. A close look reveals several 5-gallon cans and a fire extinguisher on board the boat. Most likely, the operator was carrying extra fuel.

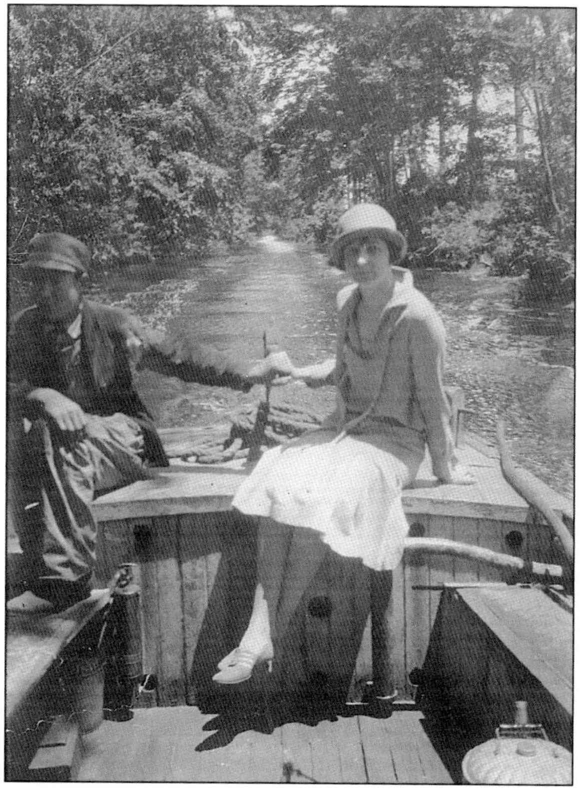

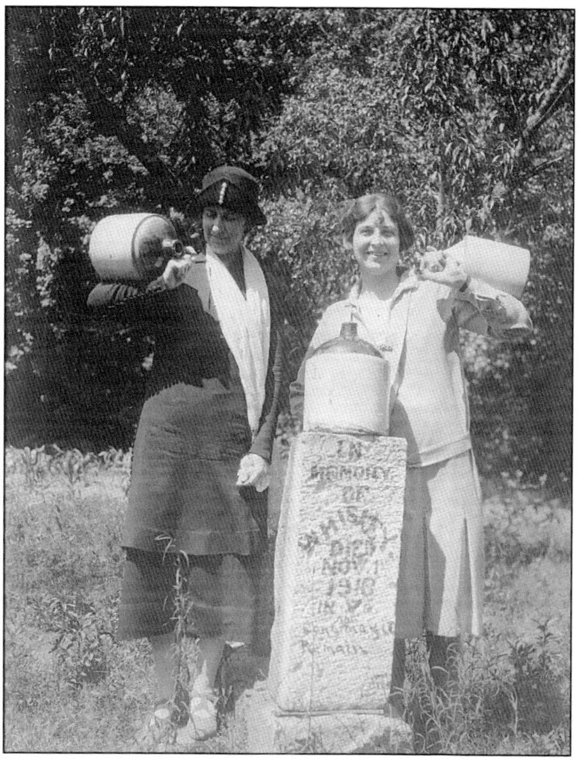

This monument, which was placed on the banks of the canal, reads as follows: "In memory of Whiskey died Nov. 1, 1916, in Va. Gone and may it remain." These ladies are going through the motions of emptying jugs of whiskey.

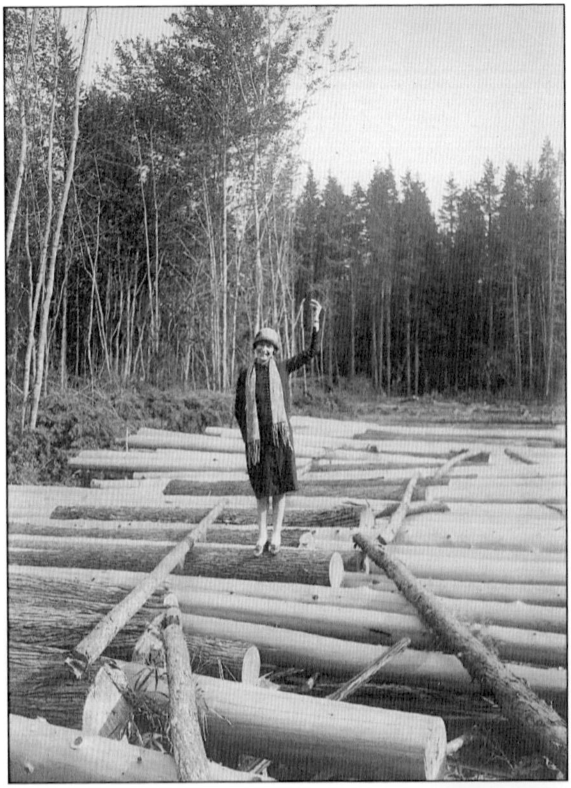

This picture of a lady standing on a log is indicative of the timber business that was carried on in the Dismal Swamp.

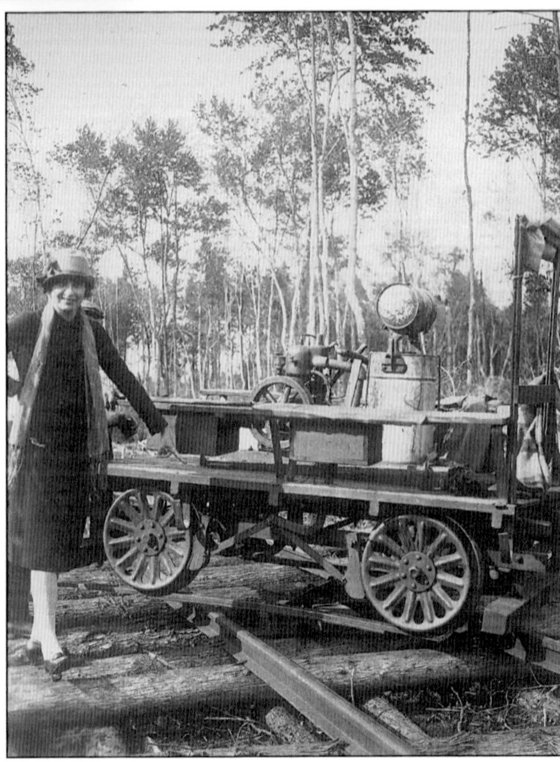

This photograph shows the railroad tracks and a piece of equipment used in the timber business in the Dismal Swamp, as well as one of the young ladies that made the trip to Lake Drummond.

Five

DOWN ON THE FARM

A large part of Norfolk County was devoted to agriculture and dairy farming. The area where K-Mart is located on Military Highway was once dairy land, as was Georgetown, Edmonds Corner, Princeton Halls, the land where Walmart and Sam's Club sit, Clearfield, parts of Indian River, Great Bridge, Saint Brides, and other areas. There were so many dairies, it's a wonder that any of them were able to survive. However, there were times when one could not produce enough to supply their customers and had to buy milk from one of the others. Some of the local dairies were White and Jernigan, B.M. Williams, Curling/Colonial, Darden/Lakeside, Westmoreland/Todd, Beech Grove, Coleman, and Gray.

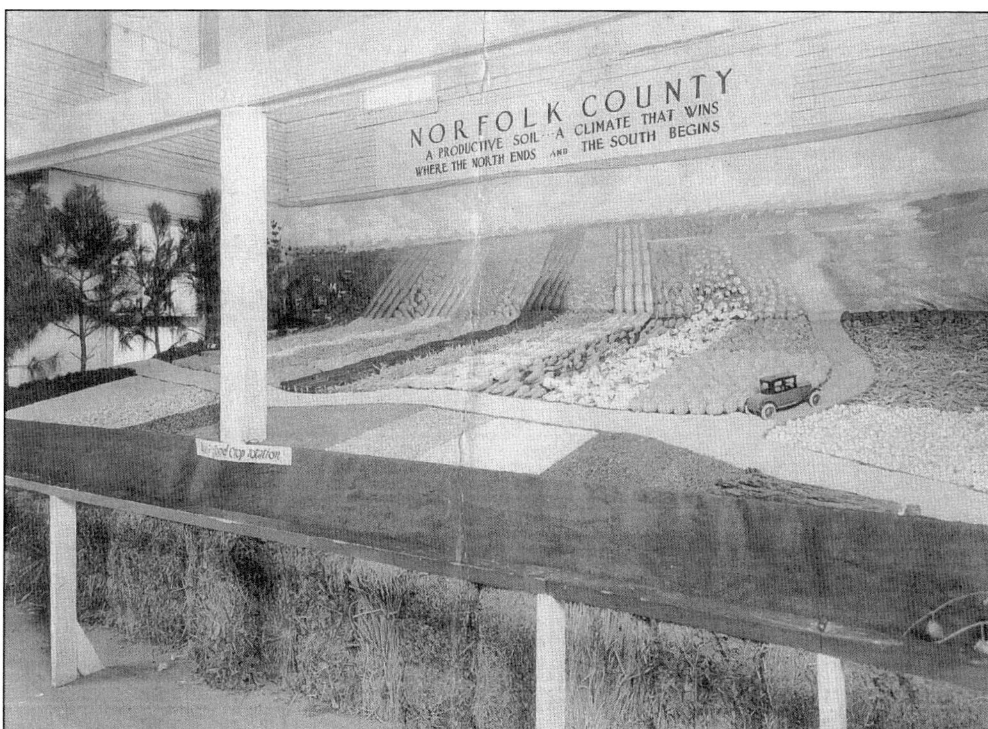

This was one of many exhibits at the Norfolk County Fair in 1923. The display, which teaches the importance of crop rotation, was furnished by the Metropolitan Engraving Company of Richmond, Virginia.

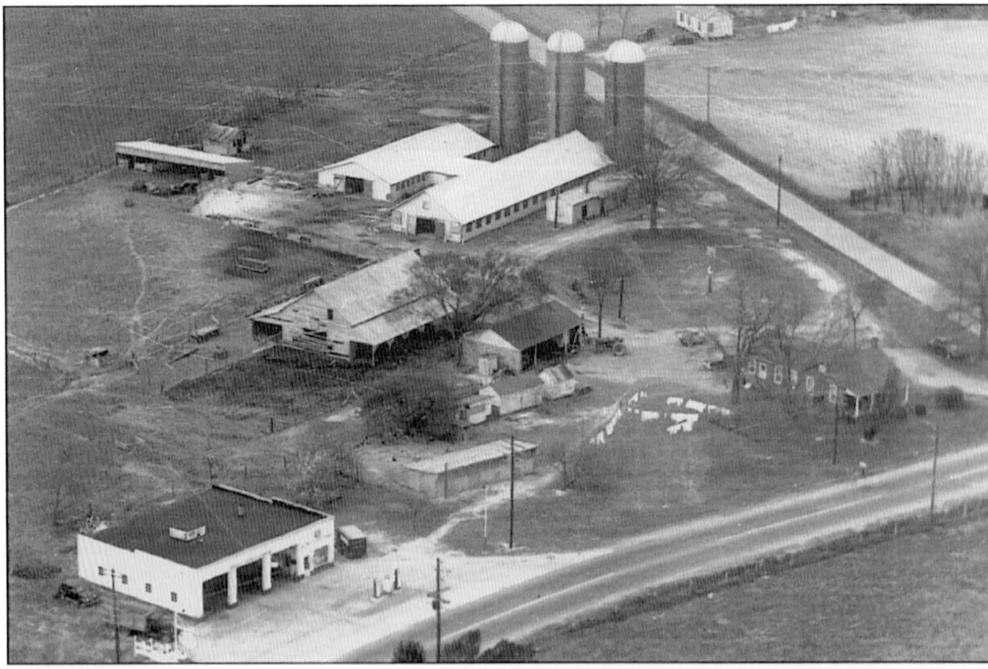

Occasionally, one of the pilots from the old South Norfolk airport would fly over and snap pictures of some of the farms. This aerial view shows part of the Curling/Colonial Dairy. The house, barns, Mr. Curling's Esso station, and other buildings can be seen. It must have been wash day because a close look near the right center of the picture reveals clothes hanging on the lines.

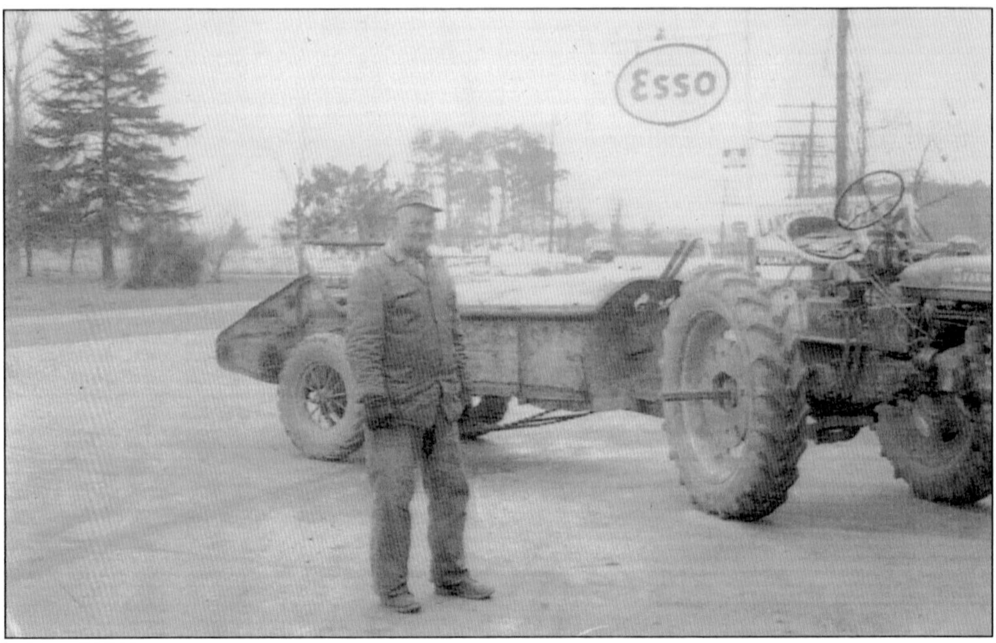

Here is Mr. John D. Curling, who has pulled his manure spreader into the Esso station. He had to fill the tank before getting down to serious work. The billboard behind Mr. Curling's Farmall Tractor advertises Lakeside Dairy.

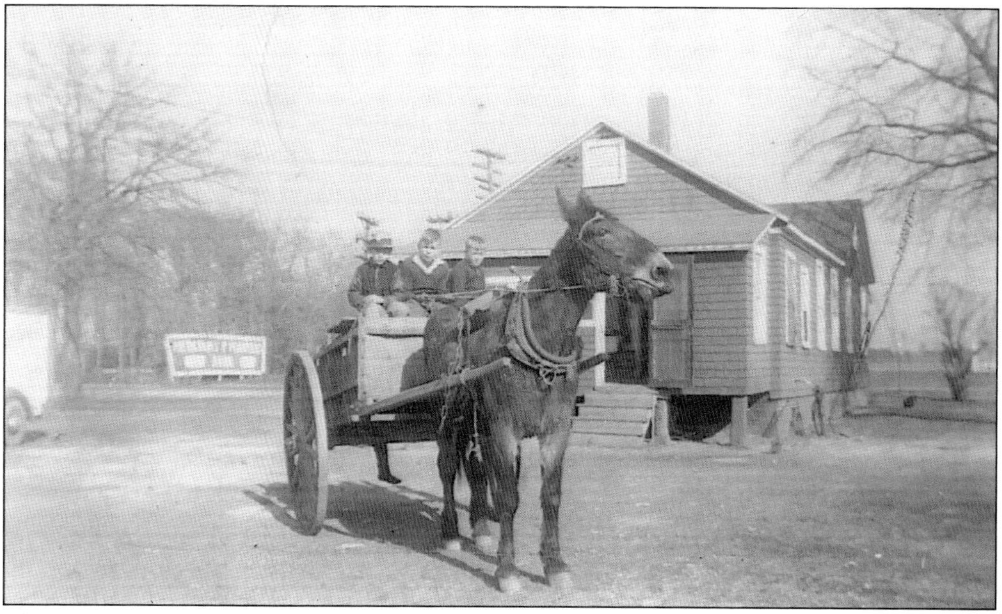

This photograph shows "Biggie," the mule, hooked up to a cart full of children. The children are, from left to right, as follows: Durwood Curling, John Beverly Curling, and Earl Pangle. The leg hanging off the back of the cart belongs to Doris Curling. The background includes a farmhouse, the back end of a milk truck, and a billboard advertising the Merchant and Planters Bank.

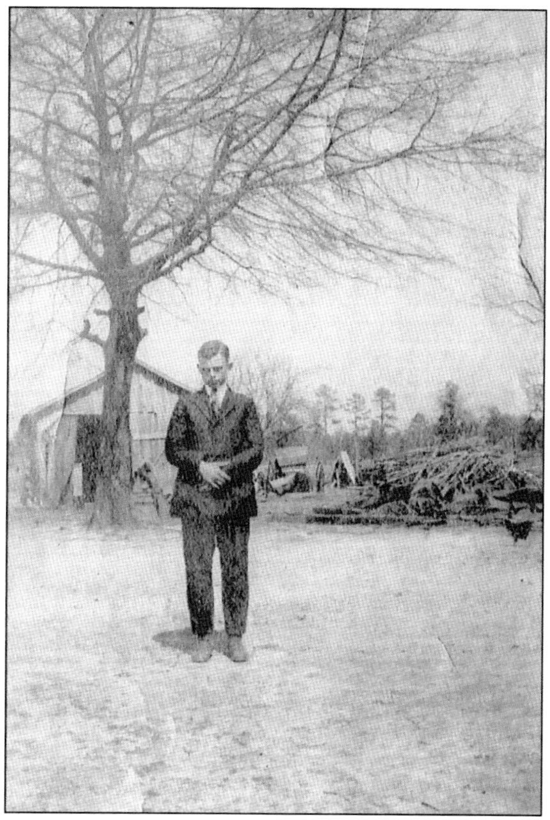

Pictured here is Mr. John Debaum Curling at age 22. He was born in 1902 and later worked on the farm with his father, Frank L. Curling.

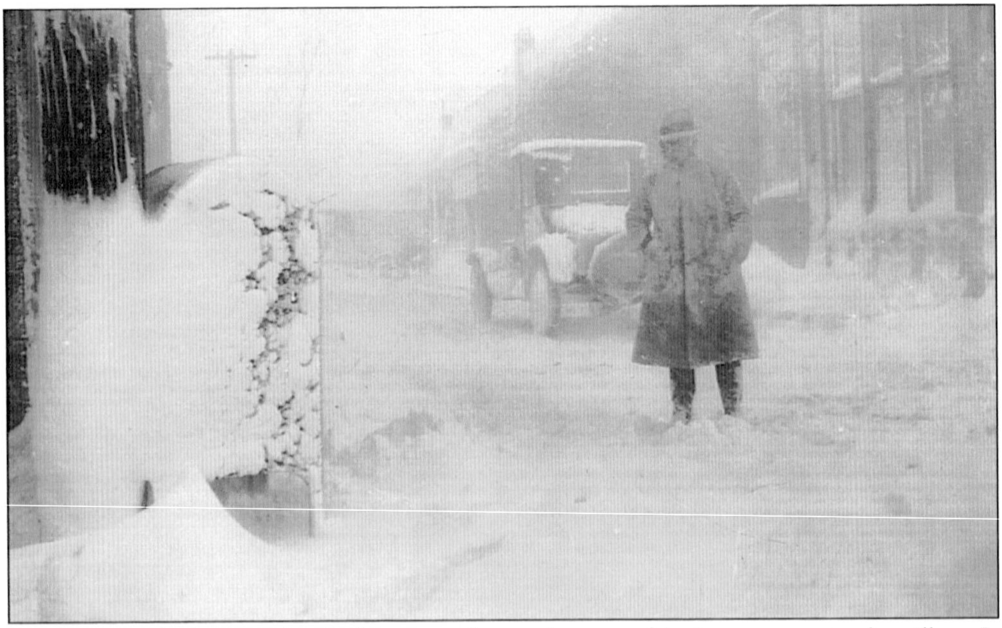

This picture of Mr. Frank L. Curling was taken as he approached a snow-covered mailbox. It was taken in South Norfolk in 1927.

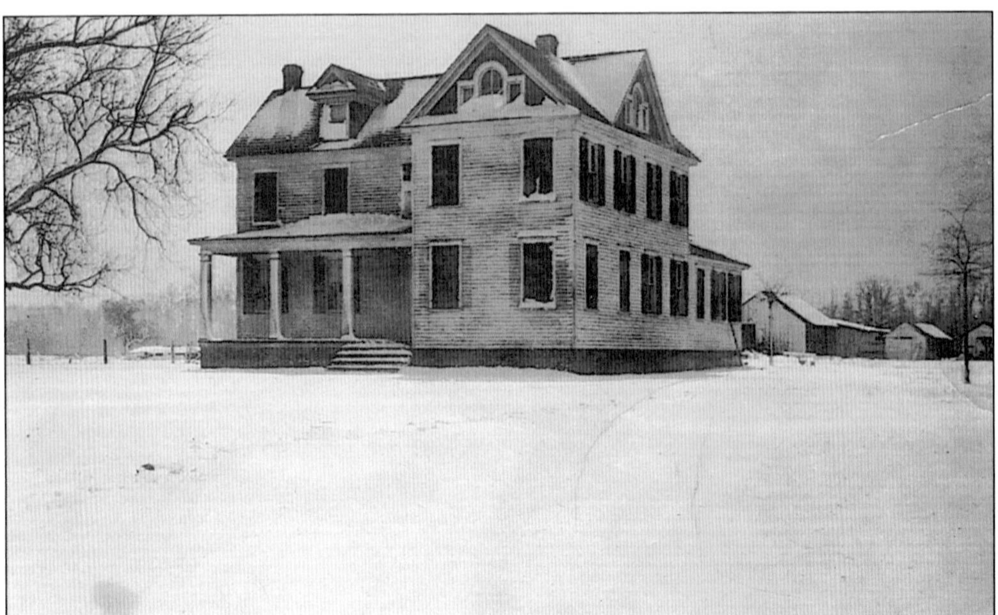

This farmhouse was the Stewart home and was built *c.* 1914 at Mount Pleasant and Hillwell Roads. This is now the location of Great Bridge Gardens.

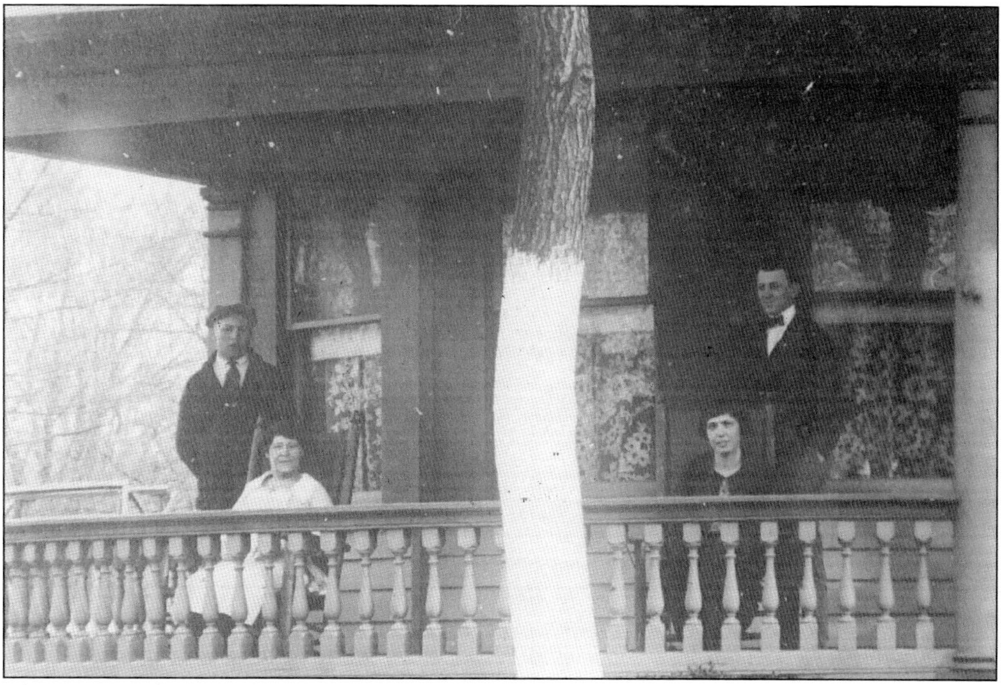

This c. 1922 photograph was taken on the porch of the Sam Wilson home in South Norfolk. Those relaxing are, from left to right, Lutton (standing behind his mother), Jennie Wilson, and Bill Darden (standing behind Christine Wilson). Mr. Bill Darden and Miss Christine Wilson married and produced two daughters, Jane and Betty. Mr. Darden helped his father run Darden/ Lakeside Dairy Farms and eventually became the owner.

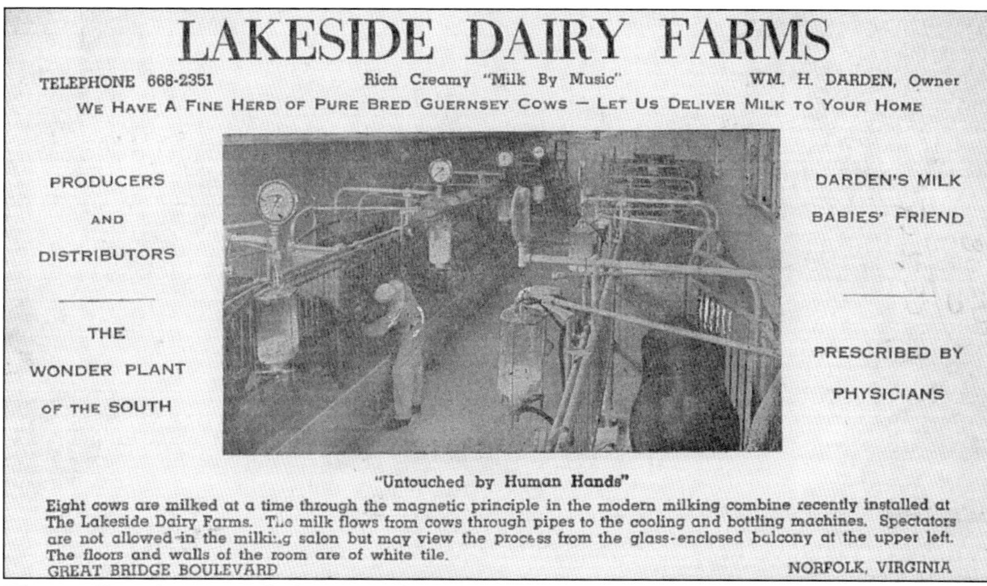

This small card contained advertising for Lakeside Dairy, owned by William H. Darden. It states that Darden's milk was "babies' friend," was prescribed by physicians, and that the cows were "milked by music." The dairy was located on Great Bridge Boulevard, which is now Battlefield Boulevard, in the vicinity of Walmart and Sam's Club.

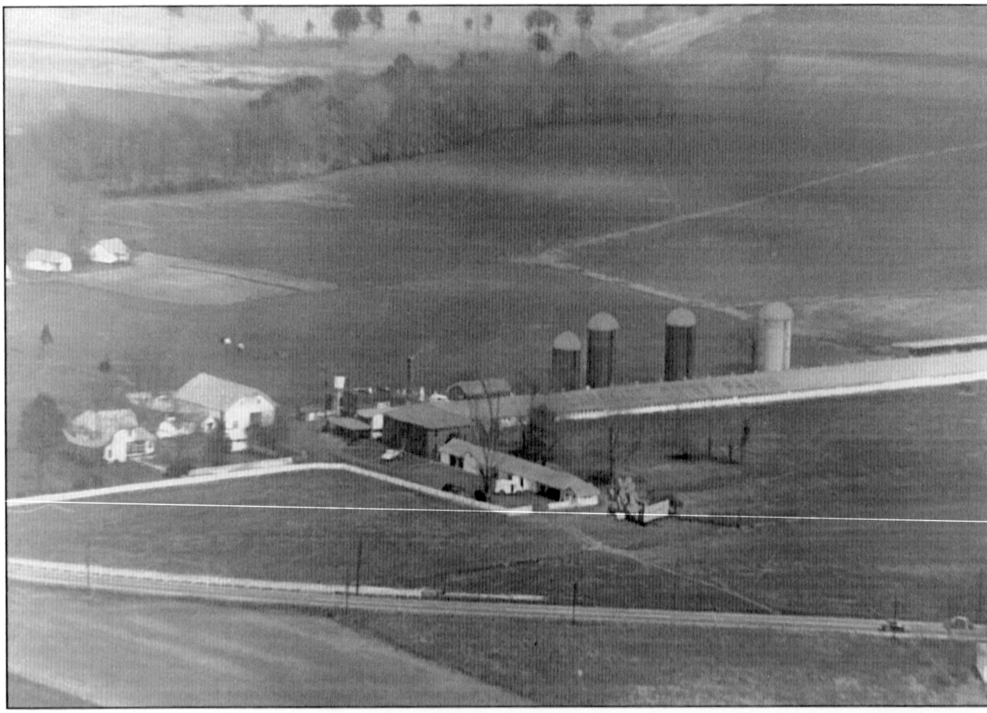

This is an aerial view of Darden's Lakeside Dairy Farms. The dairy was the producer and distributor of rich creamy milk from contented cows.

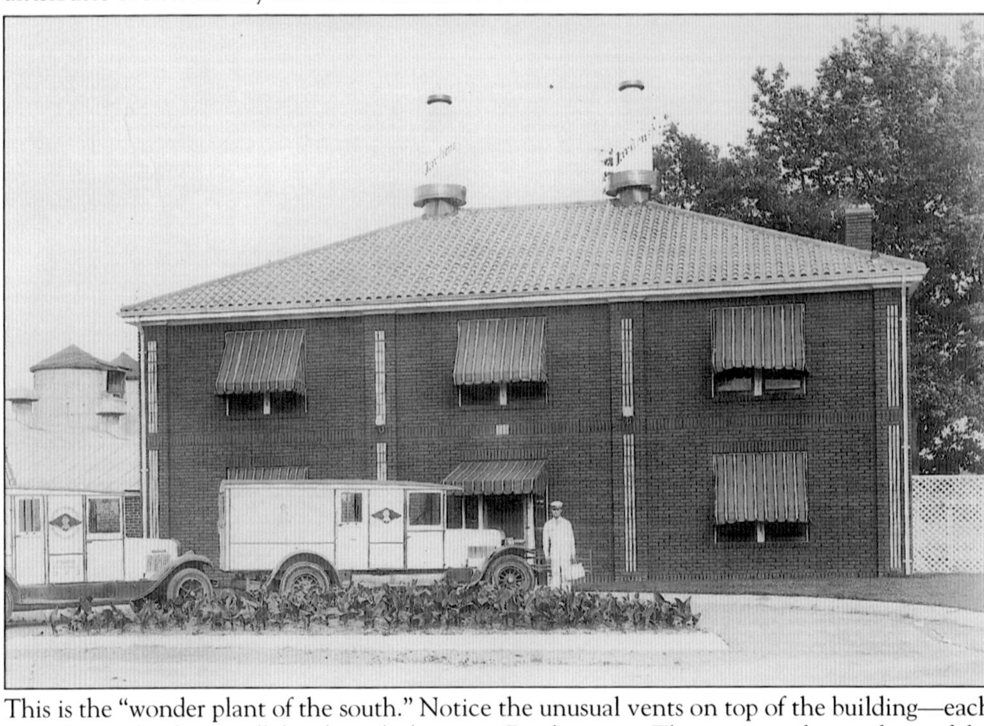

This is the "wonder plant of the south." Notice the unusual vents on top of the building—each is capped with a large milk bottle with the name Darden on it. The man standing in front of the milk truck is ready to make his deliveries.

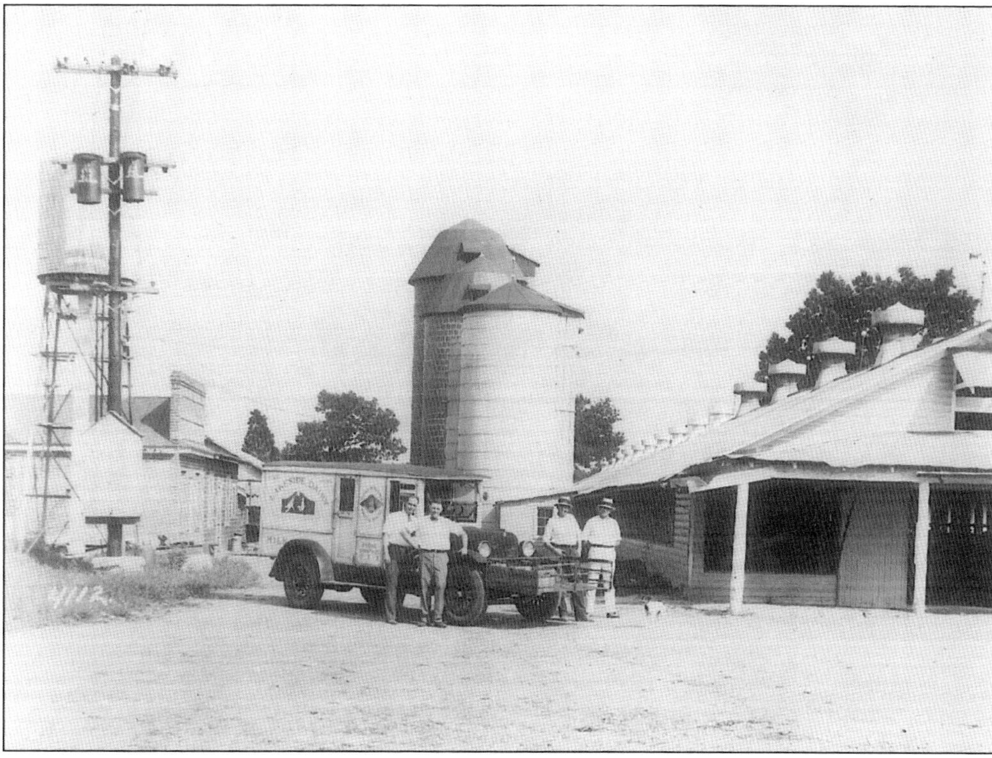

The milk truck has a rack on the front that was probably used to carry empty bottles picked up from customers. At the dairy, eight cows were milked at a time, and the milk flowed through pipes to the cooling and bottling machines. The floors and walls of the room were covered with white tiles.

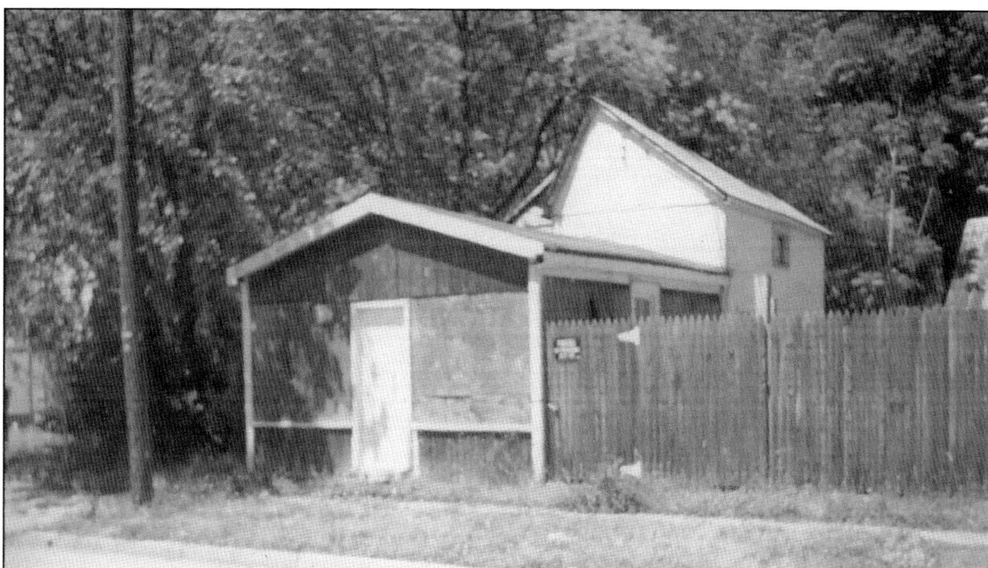

This old building, which still stands on Jefferson Street in South Norfolk, was Mr. John White's first dairy. In the 1920s, he owned four cows, and his entire operation was carried on in the two small buildings shown here.

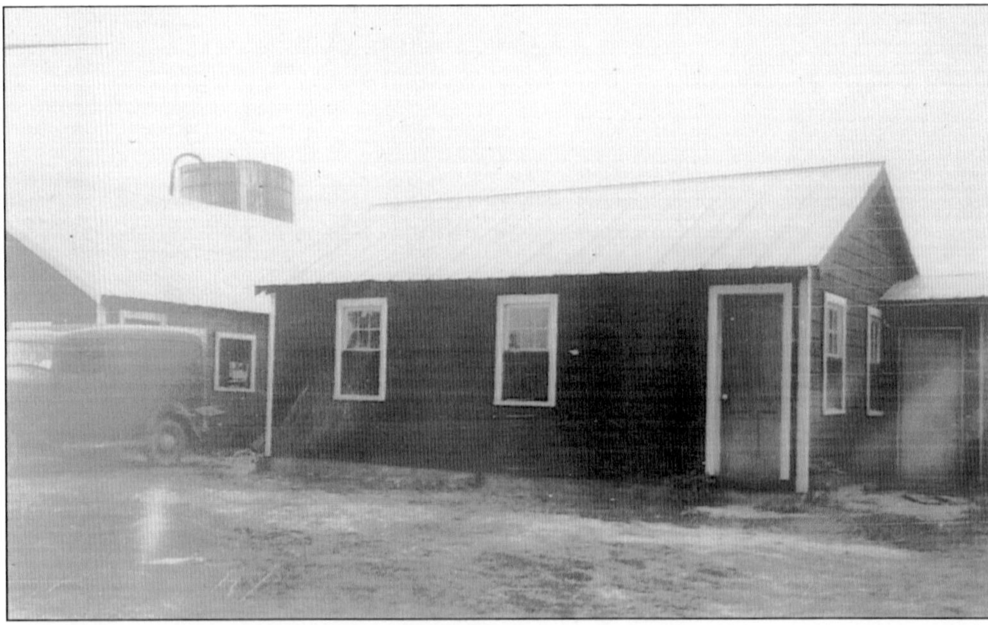

This picture includes the silo, barn, milk truck, wash room, and cold storage building used by the White and Jernigan Dairy at the Butt farm on Clearfield Road.

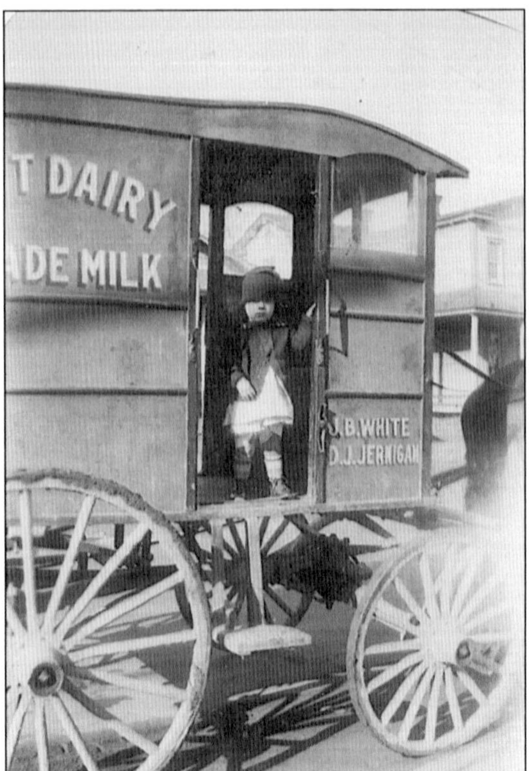

This happy-go-lucky child seems to be enjoying her trip aboard White and Jernigan's horse-drawn milk wagon.

This picture was taken at the Gray Farm, located at Edmond 's Corner. Mr. David Smithson has the chore of feeding the chickens.

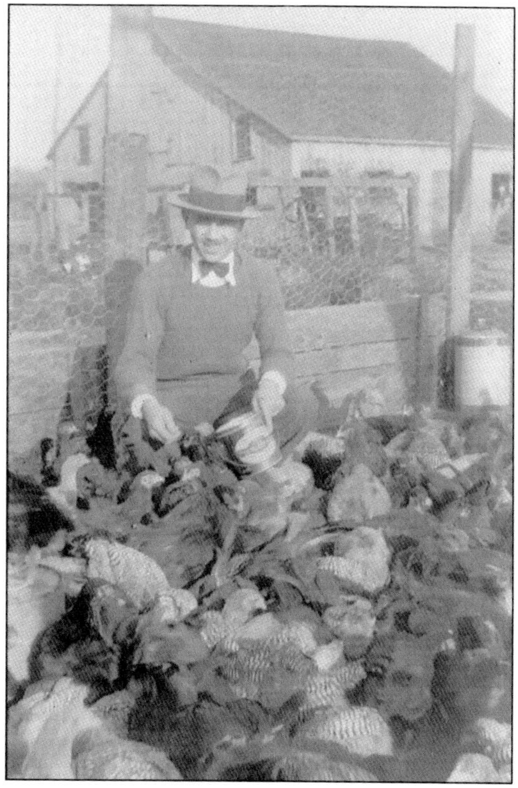

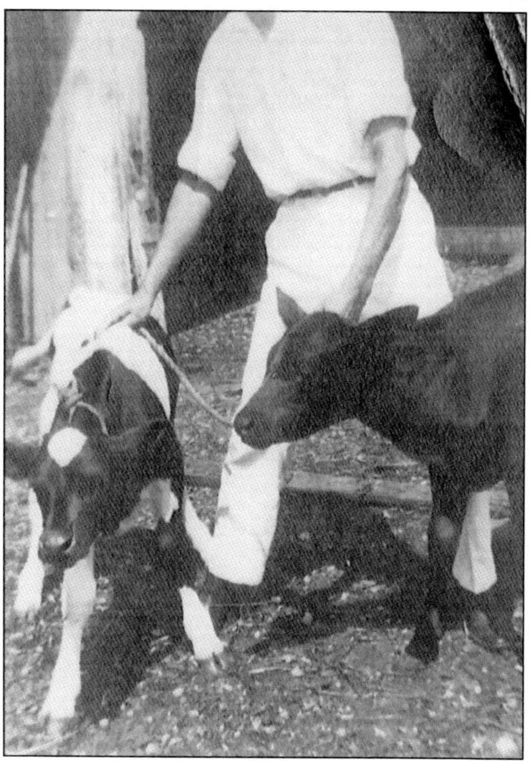

When this photograph was taken, David Smithson lost his head while trying to handle two calves.

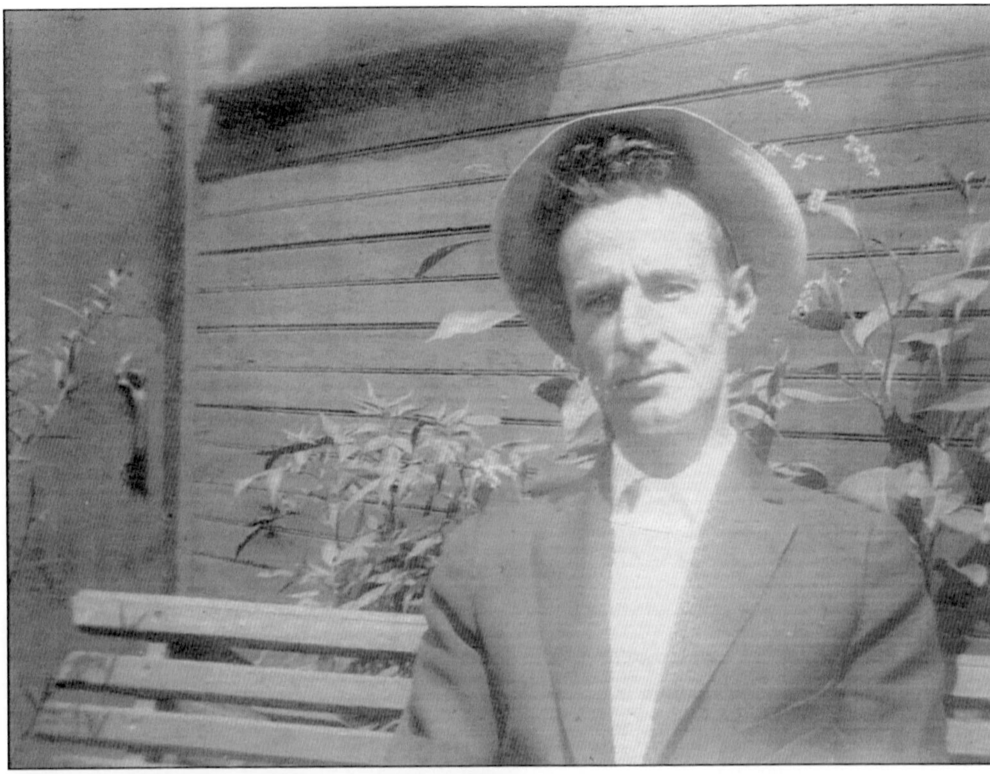

This is a picture of Bert White of White and Jernigan Dairy as a young man.

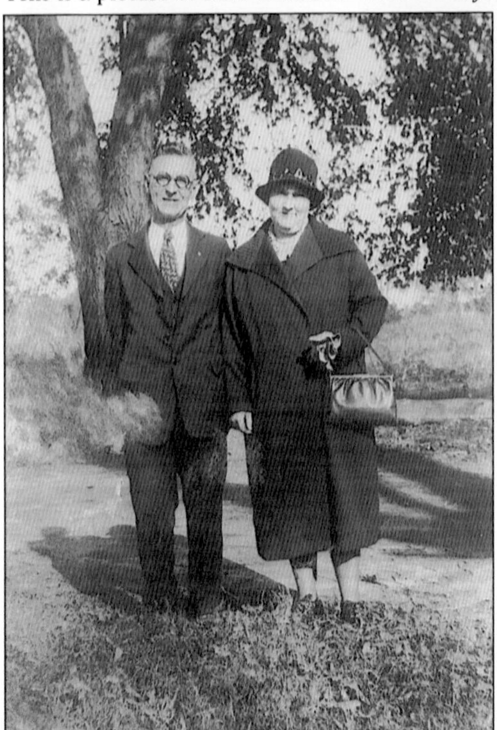

Here is Bert White with his wife, Lettie, on the Gray Farm at Edmond's Corner.

This image of D.R. Smithson and an unknown child was taken at the White and Jernigan Dairy at the Butt Farm on Clearfield Road. The farmhouse appears in the background.

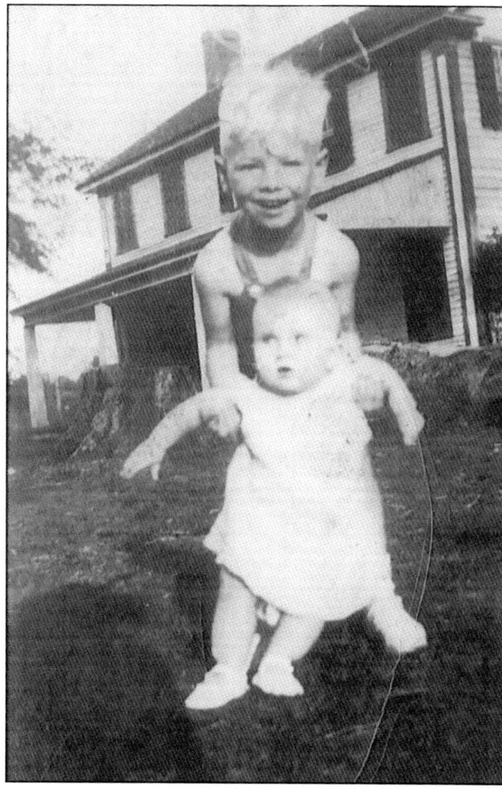

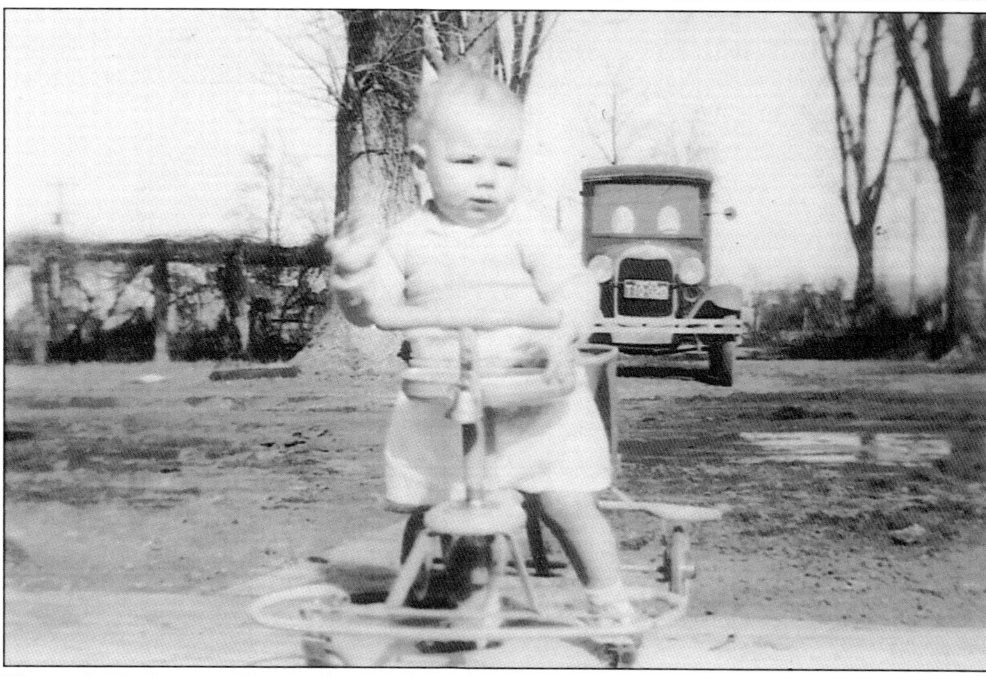

This *c.* 1930 photograph was taken at the White and Jernigan Dairy when it was located at the Gray Farm in Edmond's Corner. A milk truck can be seen in the background. The young man in the picture was a nine-months-old D.R. Smithson.

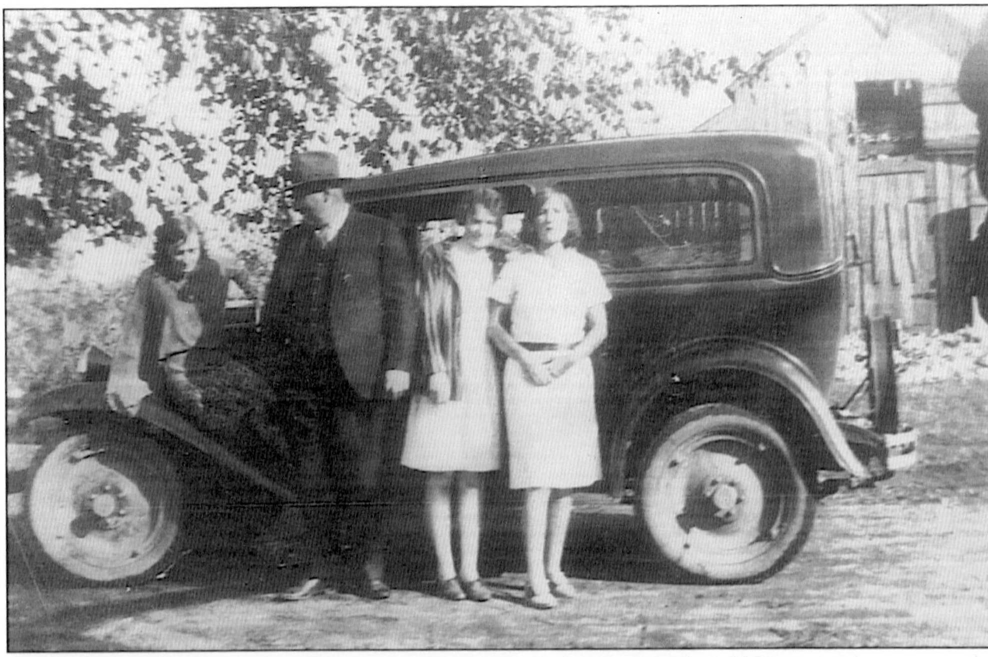

The title of this picture should be "Sunday down on the farm." The old barn can be seen in the background, and the well-dressed people are, from left to right, Catherine White, Bea White, Margaret Smithson, and D.J. (Donnie) Jernigan.

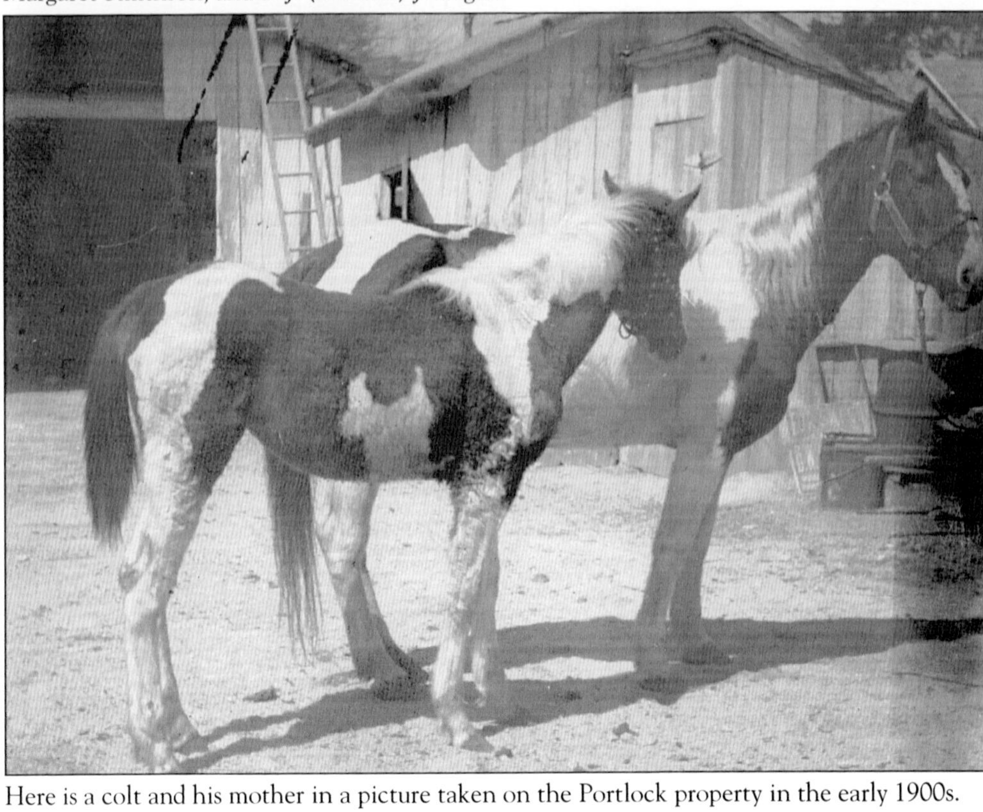

Here is a colt and his mother in a picture taken on the Portlock property in the early 1900s.

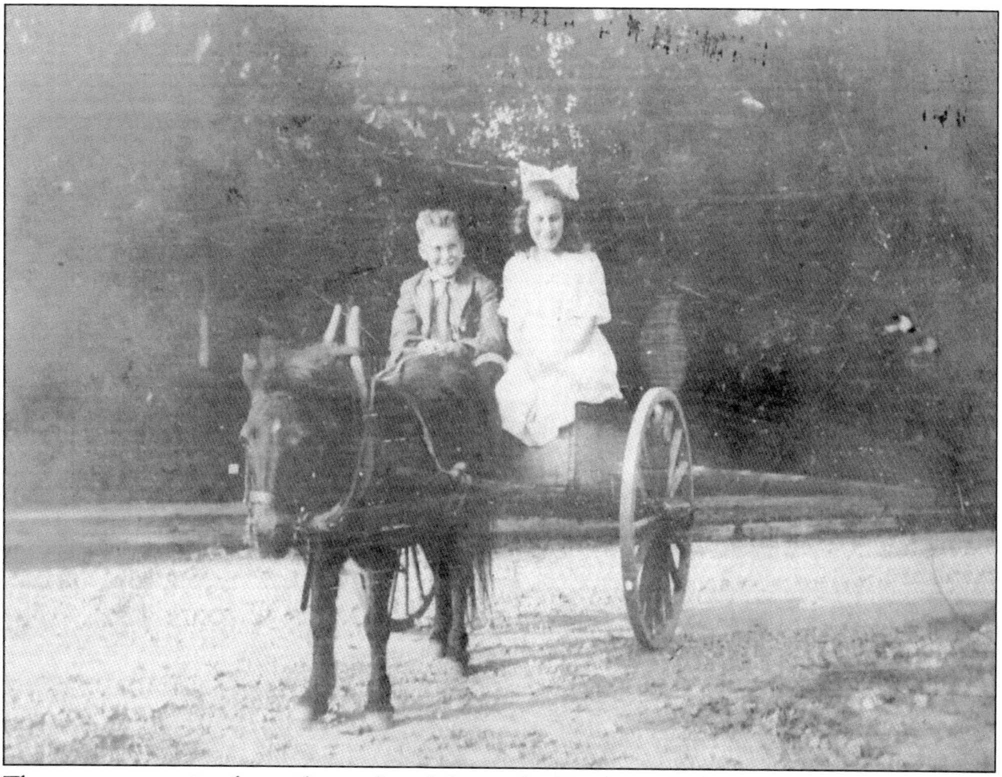

The youngsters going for a ride are, from left to right, Frank Portlock and his sister Eugenia. The wagon was pulled by "Pet."

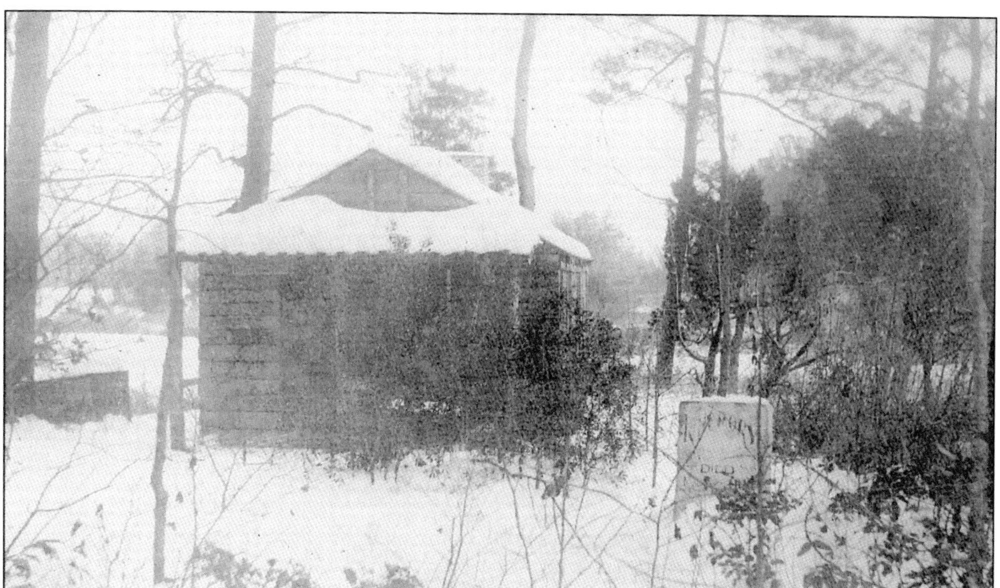

This snow-covered cabin and the surrounding area made up the camp of Frank Portlock. The tombstone on the right is unreadable and was most likely part of an old family burying ground.

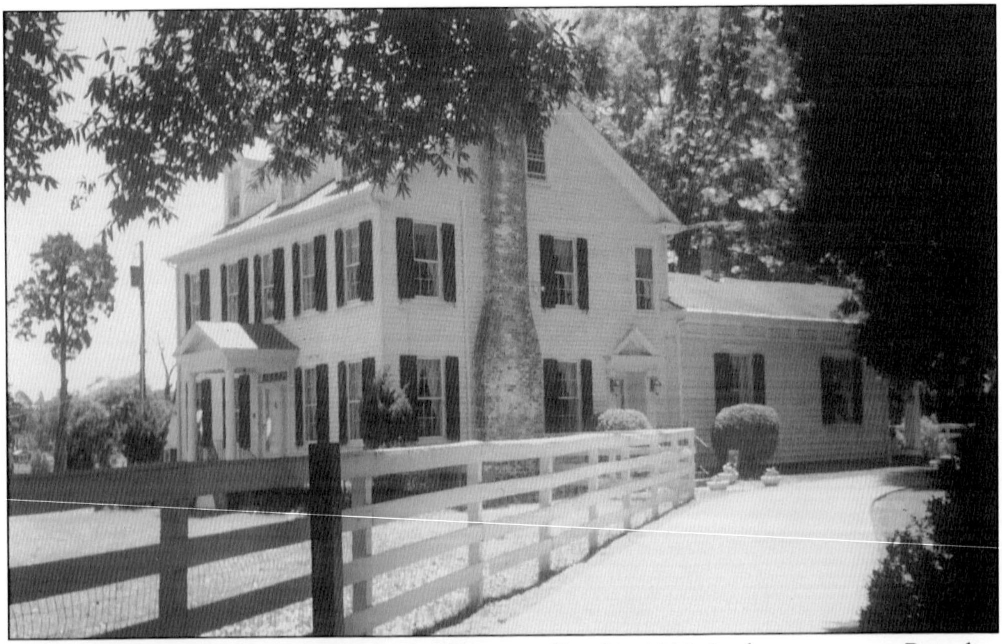

This is "Wildwood," which was built on 100 acres of land in 1812. Its first owner was Brigadier General John Hodges. The original farmhouse has received many additions and renovations in the years since. It now faces Portsmouth Boulevard.

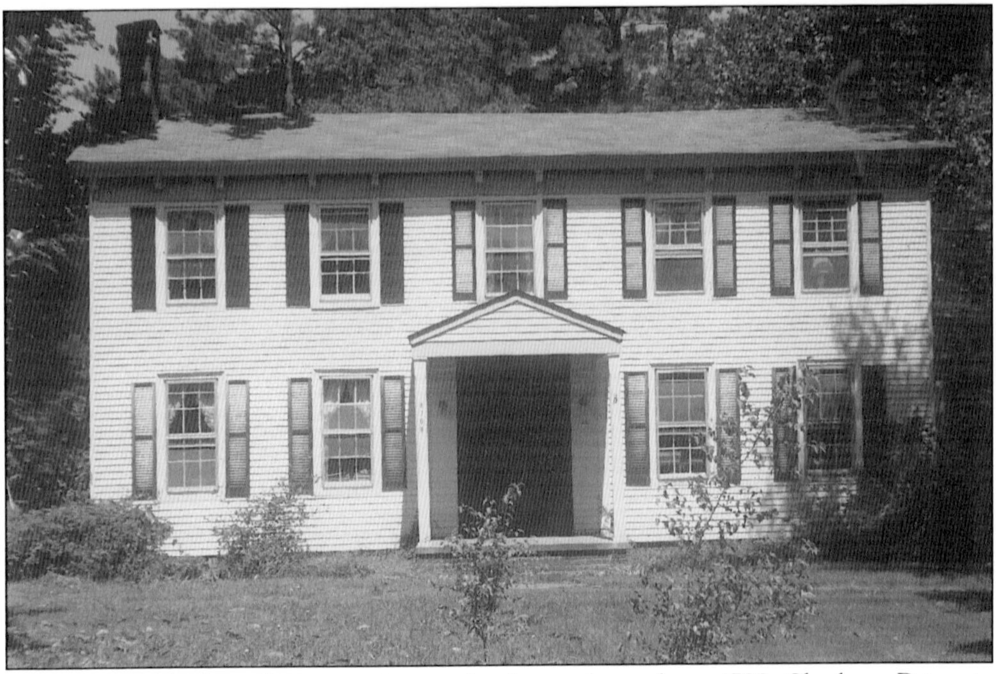

This is the Charlton House, a former farmhouse located at 4708 Charlton Drive in Western Branch.

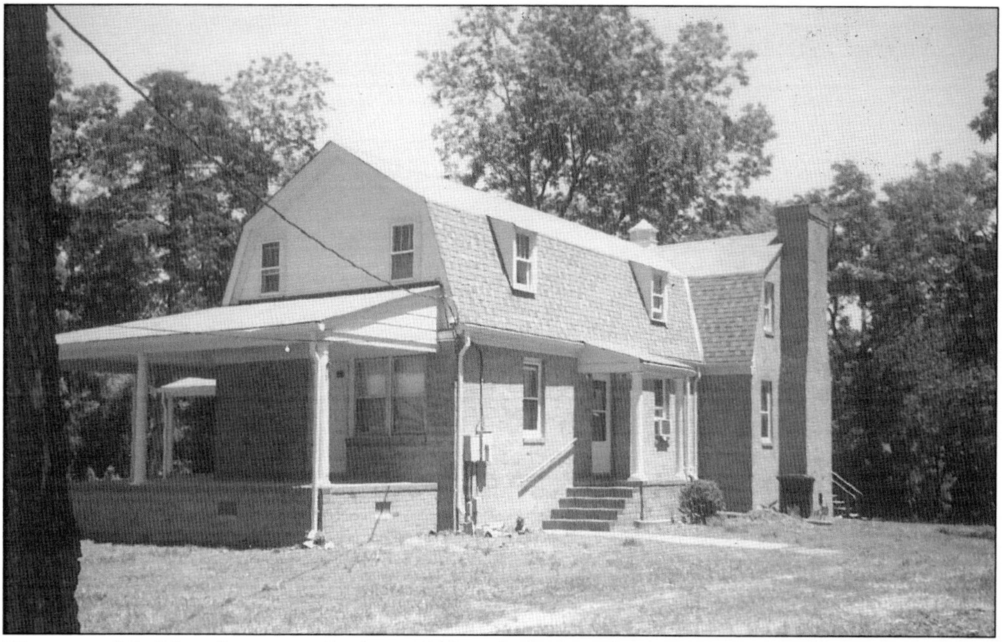

This remodeled farmhouse was built in 1900 with Gothic elements and is located at 3332 Taylor Road in Western Branch.

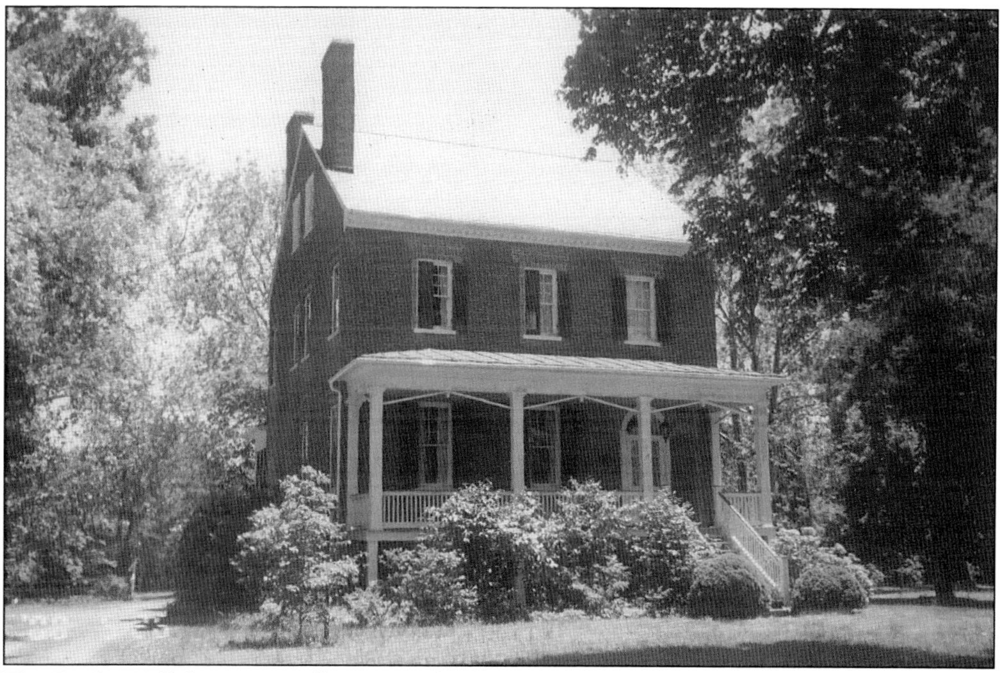

The Poplar Hill farm originally consisted of 172 acres, but by the mid-1930s, the owner lost most of it. The house, which was built of handmade clay bricks in 1806, is located at 208 Poplar Hill Road in Western Branch. The house now sits on a 25-acre parcel.

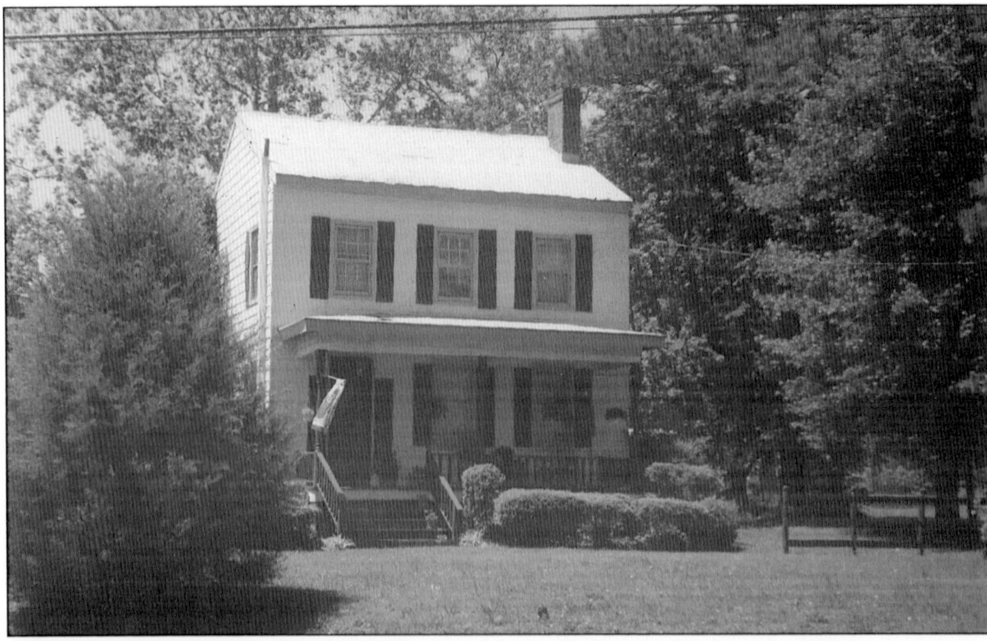

This former farmhouse at 1404 Jolliff Road in Western Branch was built in 1880.

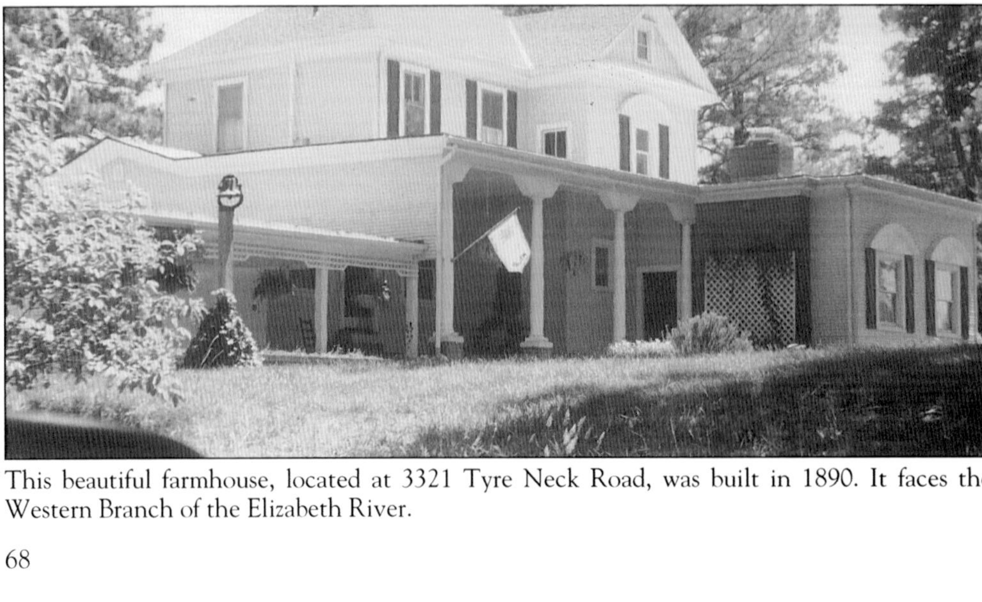

This beautiful farmhouse, located at 3321 Tyre Neck Road, was built in 1890. It faces the Western Branch of the Elizabeth River.

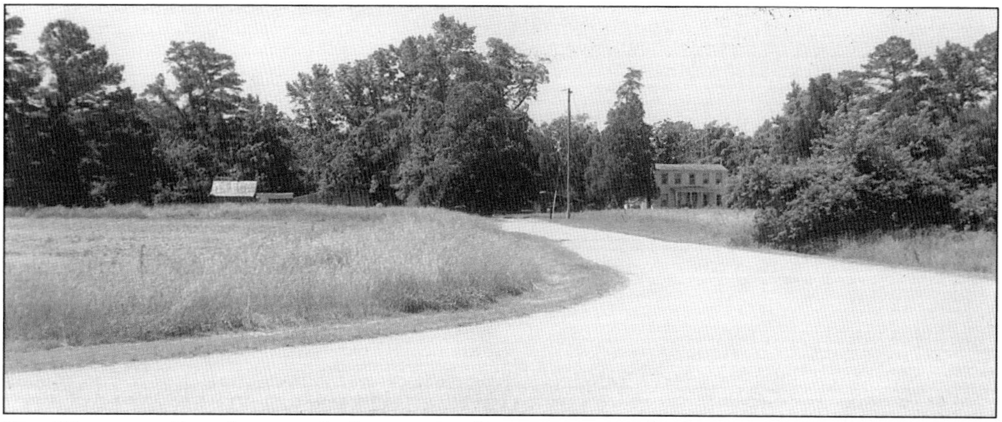

The Glemming Farm house, which contains 38 windows, was built in 1872 at what is now 4255 Dock Landing Road in Western Branch. Brick for the house was made from clay from the farm and many bricks have signatures on them. A brick foundation, which may have been from an earlier house, was uncovered some time ago. There is an elm tree in the yard that is said to be 17 feet in circumference and probably dates back to the seventeenth century.

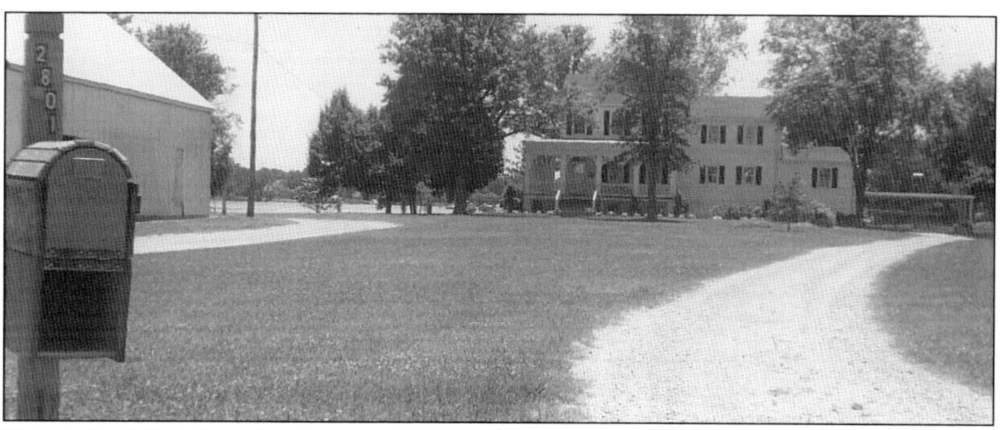

This is the Lilly's Lane farmhouse, which was built in the mid-1800s. This beautiful dwelling faces the water.

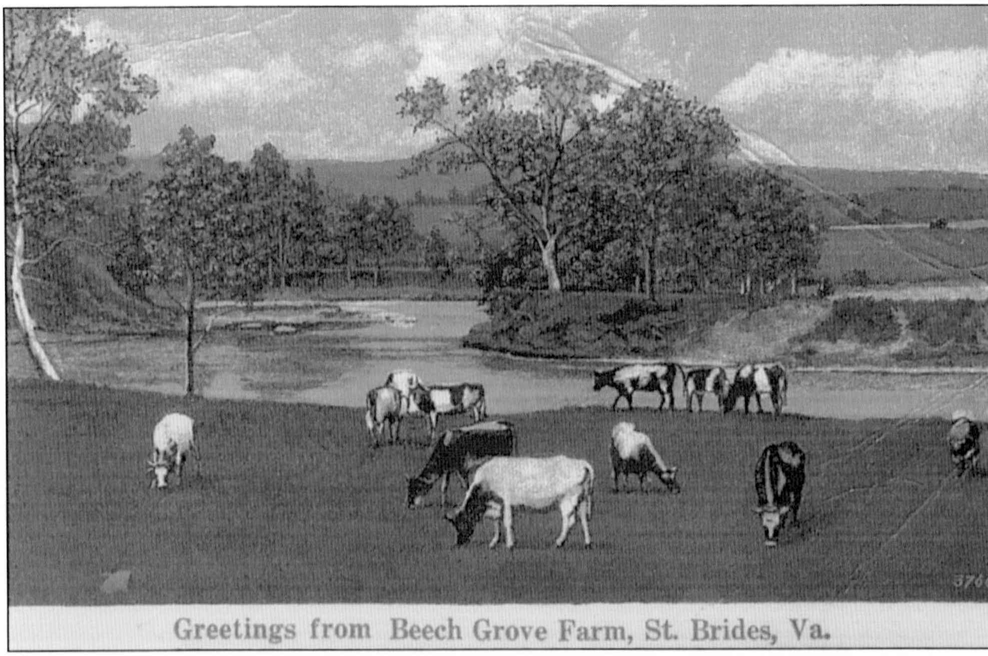

This postcard sends its recipient greetings from the Beech Grove farm in St. Brides, Virginia.

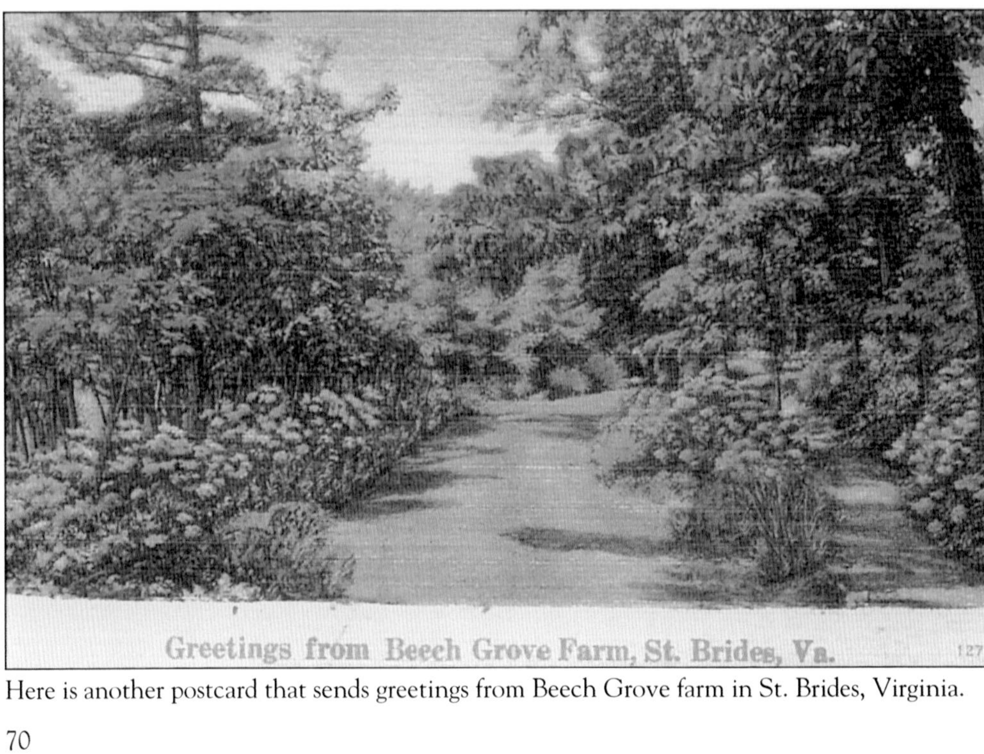

Here is another postcard that sends greetings from Beech Grove farm in St. Brides, Virginia.

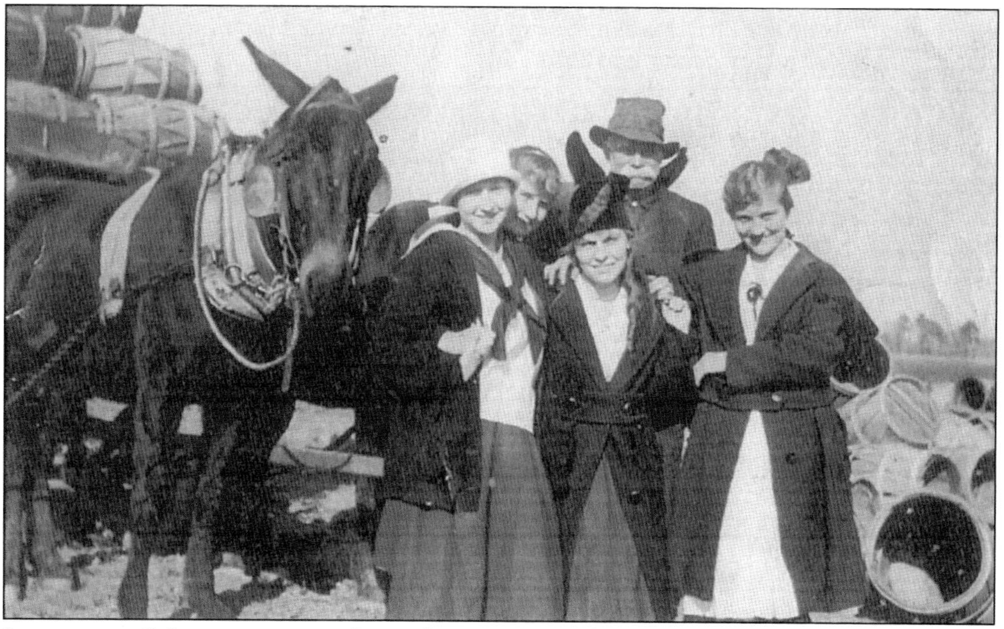

It appears as if this picture was taken at harvest time—the wagon is full of baskets and the old mule is ready to go. The ladies are, from left to right, Vera ?, Rosa ?, Ethel ?, and Helen ?. The man is Mr. J. Halstead.

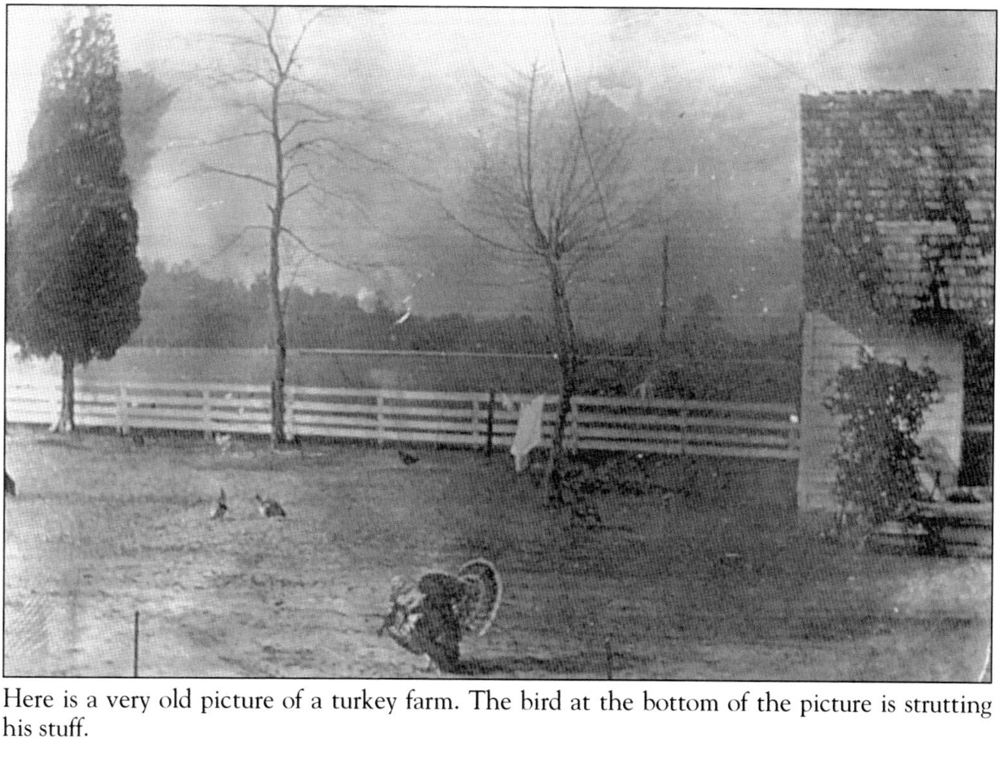

Here is a very old picture of a turkey farm. The bird at the bottom of the picture is strutting his stuff.

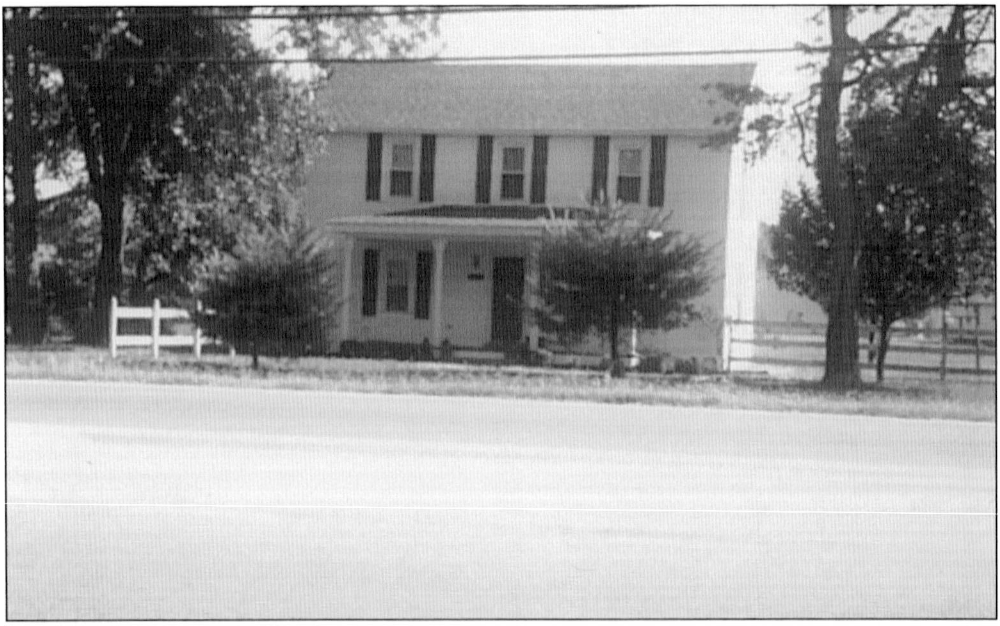

This property at 737 Great Bridge Boulevard has been in the Kilian family since November 23, 1900, when it was purchased by Mike Kilian. The farm contained 40 acres—about half was cleared and half was wooded. One of Mike's main crops was blackberries, which he used to make blackberry wine. He also produced barrels of pickles and sauerkraut, which he used for the family. Mike was a full-time farmer, and he and his wife raised four children. On Saturdays they left home very early, went to Norfolk to sell products from the farm, and returned home very late. Eventually Mike's two sons, William and Frederick, took over the farm and expanded it to approximately 200 acres. Upon William's death, his son Leonard took over his father's part of the farm. Leonard retired from the farm in February 1994, thus ending 94 years of farming by the Kilian family. However, members of the family still reside there.

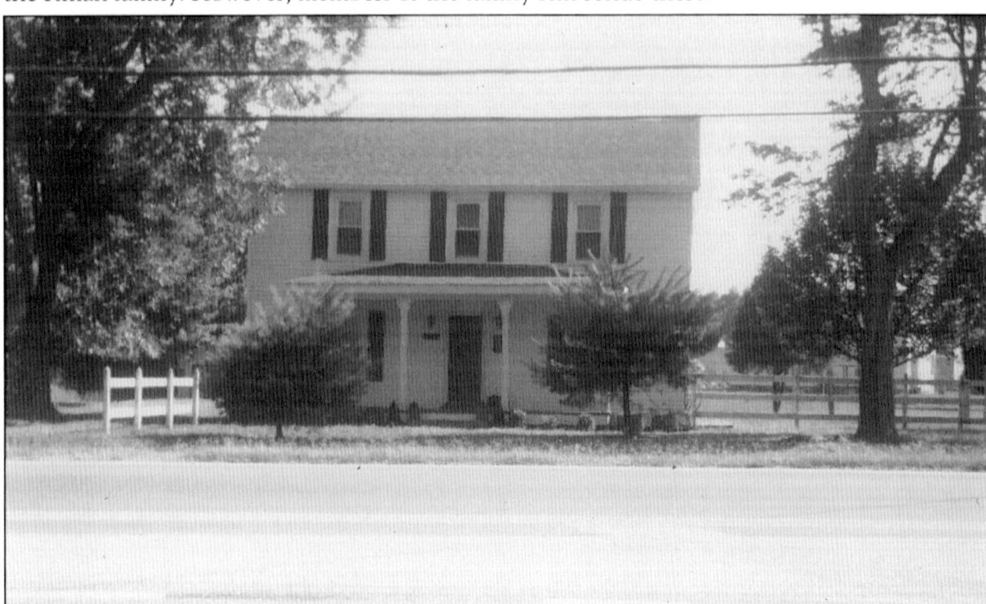

Six

Favorite Pastimes

This chapter could just as well be titled sports, as it includes football, baseball, and bowling teams as well as views of hunting and ice skating. The names of most of the individuals in this chapter have long since slipped away or were never known, but the author thanks them for their participation in their favorite pastime.

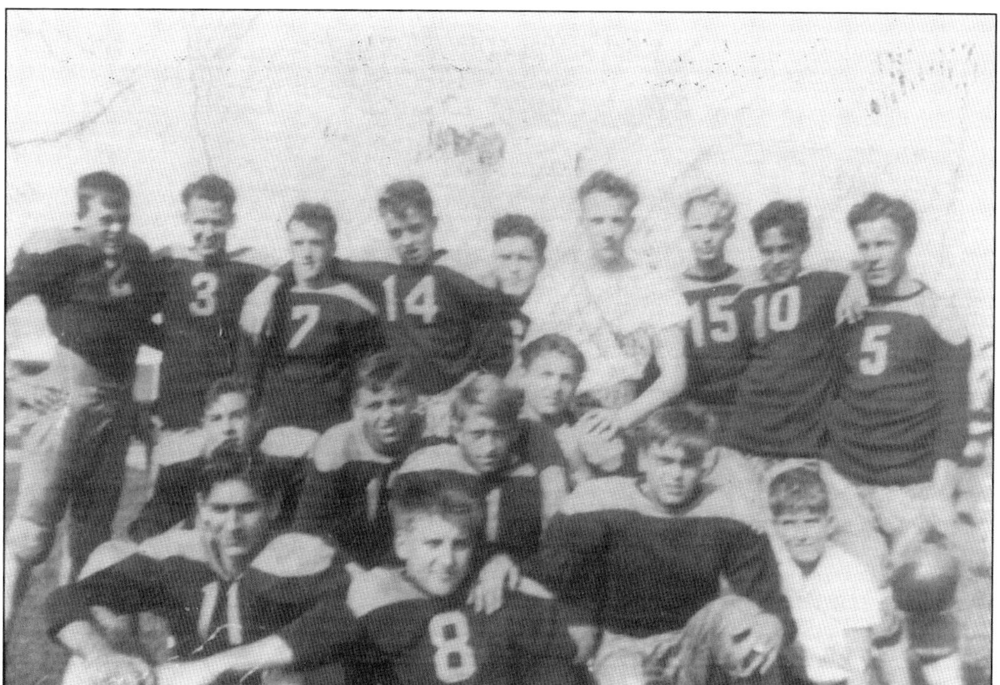

This is the 1947 Riverdale community football team, better known as the Steelers. The contributor of this picture, Harry D. Fuller, wearing the number 11 jersey, is the first man on the left in the front row. The names of the other players are unknown.

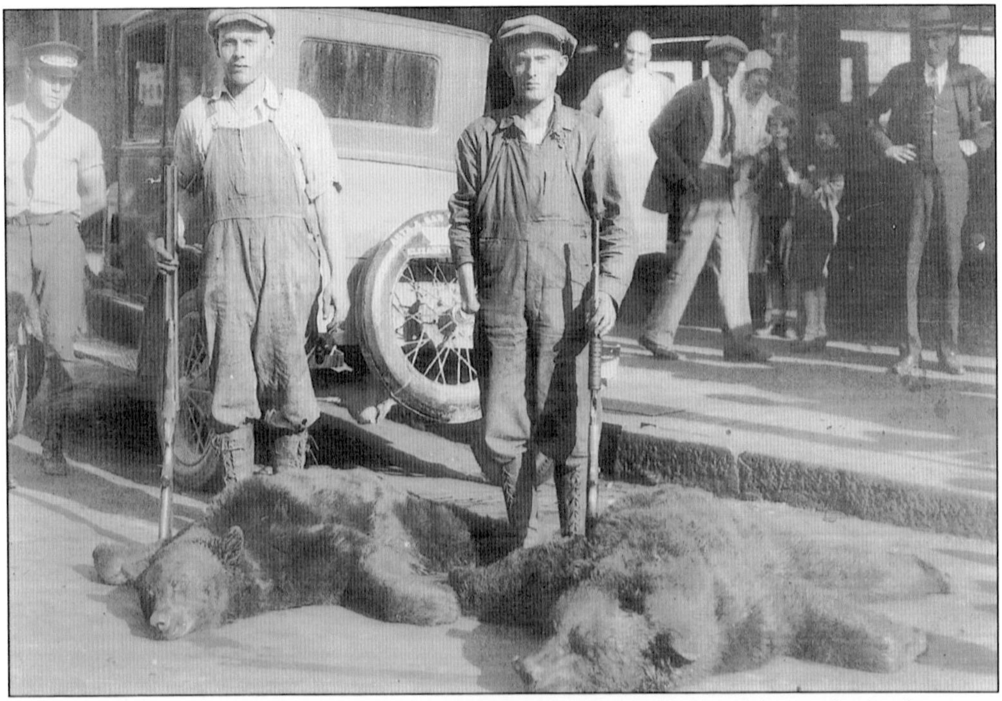

Here are a couple of bear hunters from North Carolina. By the looks of their vehicle, this scene probably took place in the early 1920s or earlier. The man on the left works for Western Union; he rides a bicycle and delivers telegrams.

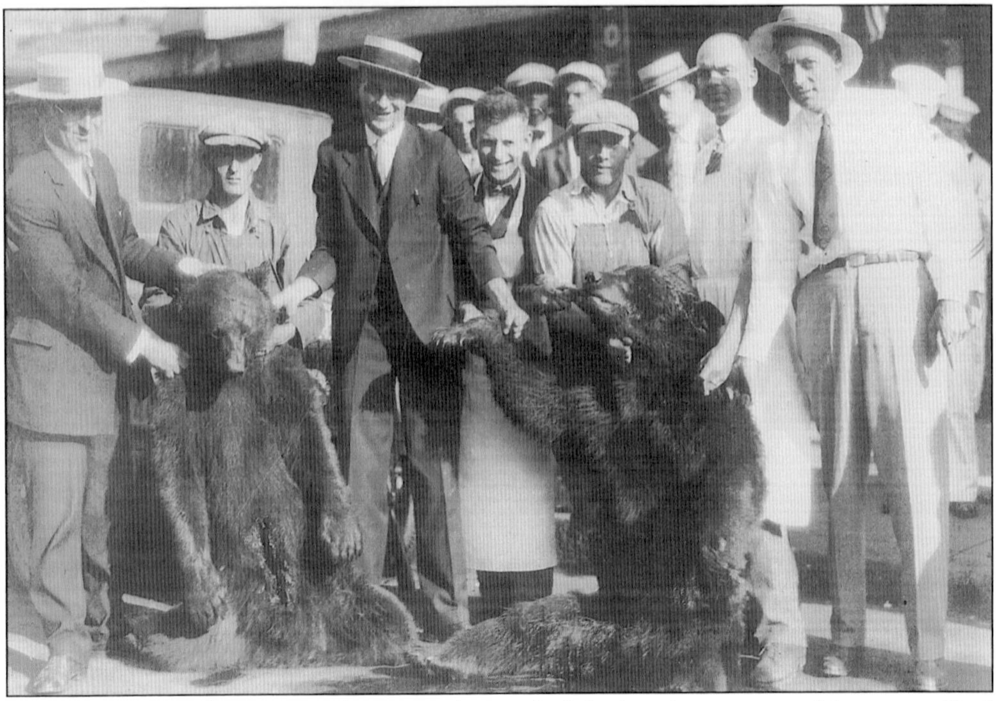

These locals wanted to get into the act, so they pushed the bear hunters out of the way and had their picture taken with the dead bears.

Here we see Doug Fuller, a 1947 Riverdale star, taking a practice swing at the ball. Doug was slated for a career in the majors but was called to active duty to serve our country in Korea.

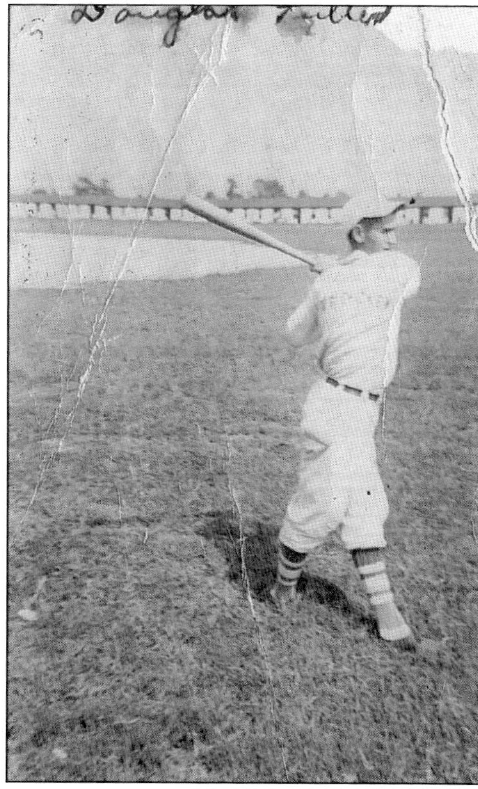

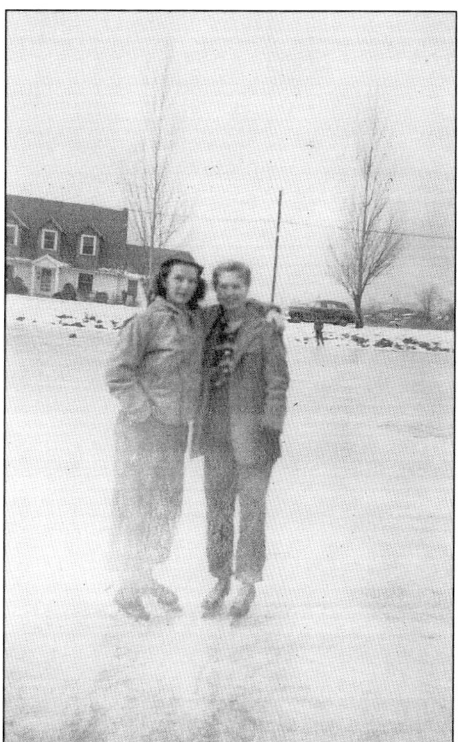

This c. 1947 picture was taken in the middle of the lake at Lakeside Park. The ladies are, from left to right, Alice Marie Meacom and Margie Townsend.

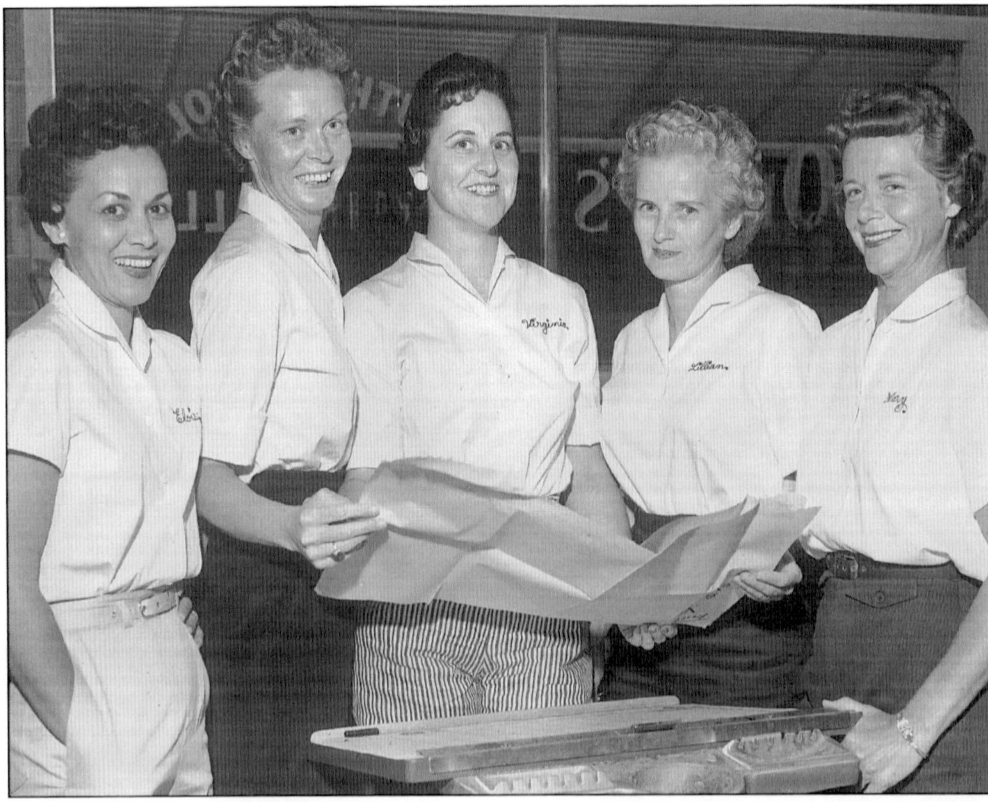

Mr. Robert Graham of Graham Funeral Home sponsored this bowling team, called Top Lady. These lovely ladies are, from left to right, as follows: Eloise Parker, Rivers Hall, Virginia Oglesby, Lillian Smith, and Mary Toler.

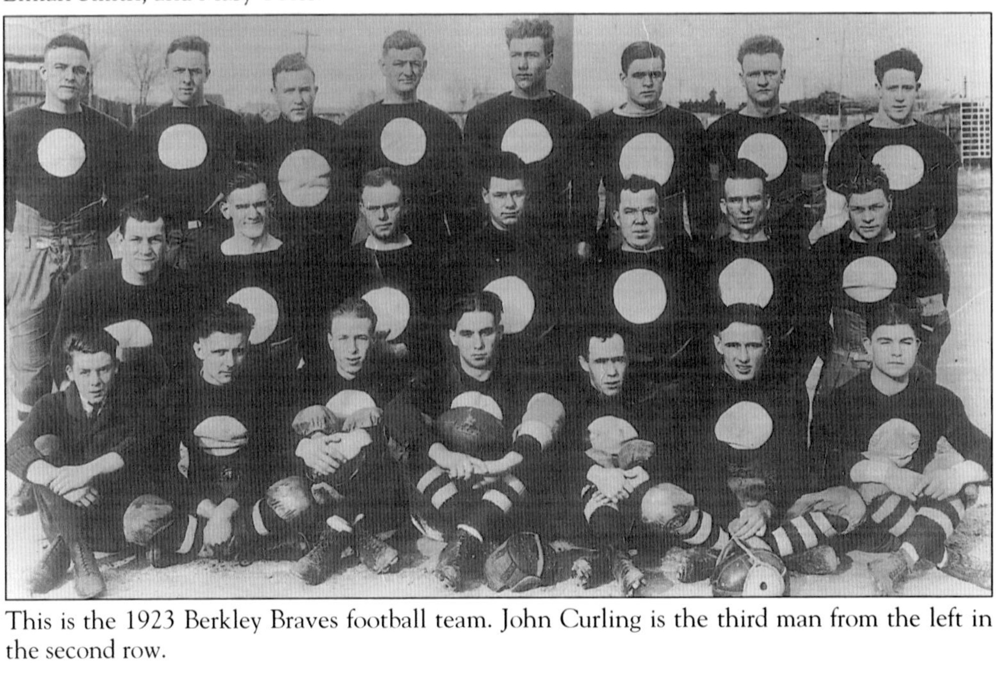

This is the 1923 Berkley Braves football team. John Curling is the third man from the left in the second row.

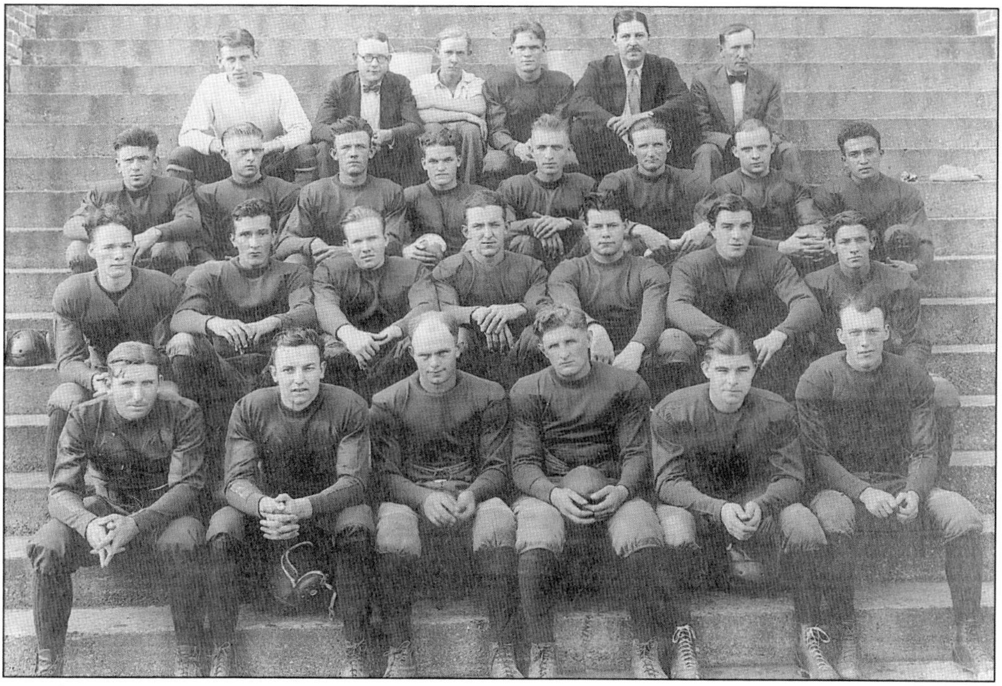

Merchants such as Dean Preston of Preston's Pharmacy and "Doc" Monroe of Monroe's Pharmacy sponsored the South Norfolk Aces football team. Only a few players are identified in this c. 1920 image by Acme Photo Co., and they are, from left to right, as follows: (first row) unidentified, unidentified, John Curling, "Bus" Howell, unidentified, and Charlie Pool; (second row) all unidentified ; (third row) unidentified, unidentified, unidentified, "Buddy" Morgan, unidentified, unidentified, unidentified, and Sid Harrell; (fourth row) coach Ted Myers, "Doc" Monroe, unidentified, unidentified, Dean Preston, and unidentified.

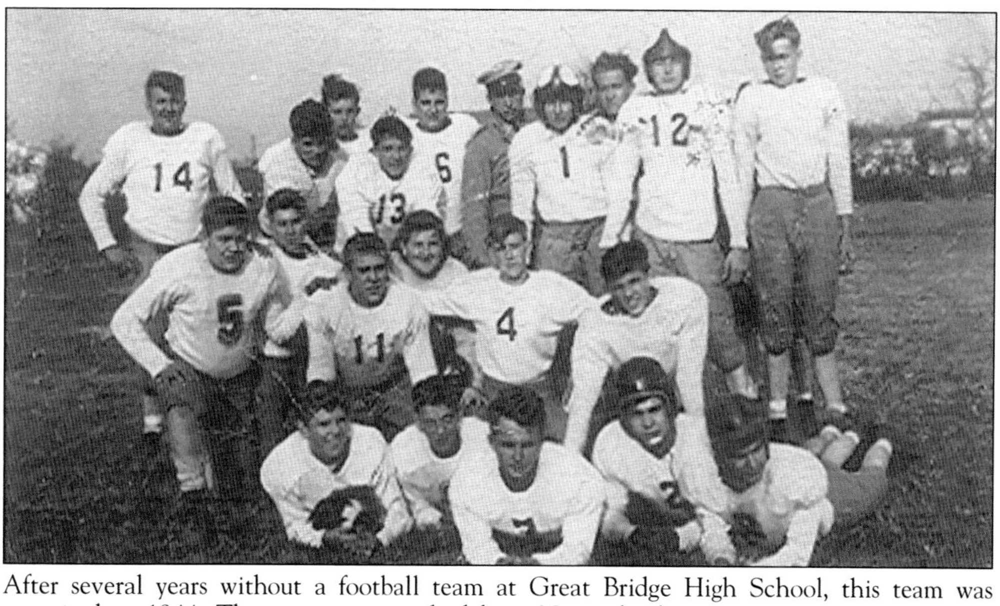

After several years without a football team at Great Bridge High School, this team was organized in 1944. The team was coached by a Navy chief petty officer who volunteered his time.

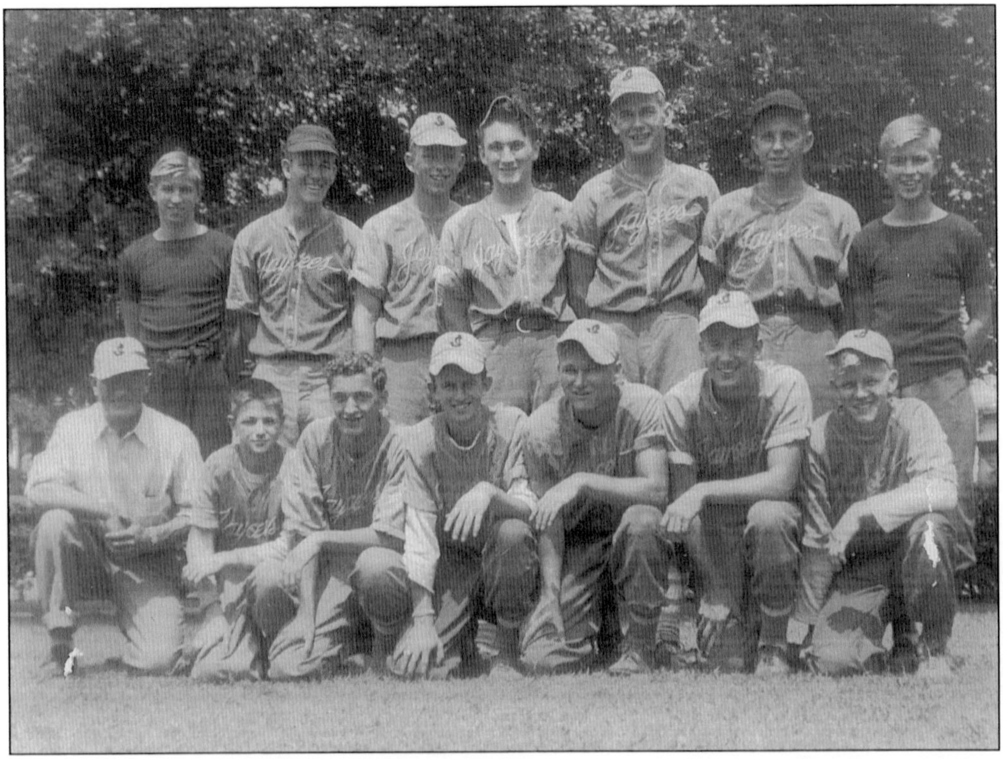

This team, sponsored by the Junior Chamber of Commerce, was known as the Jaycees. Mickey Harrell is the second man from the left in the front row. In the second row, from left to right, are Sidney Johnson and Donald Leet, and the man on the far right is Billy Johnson.

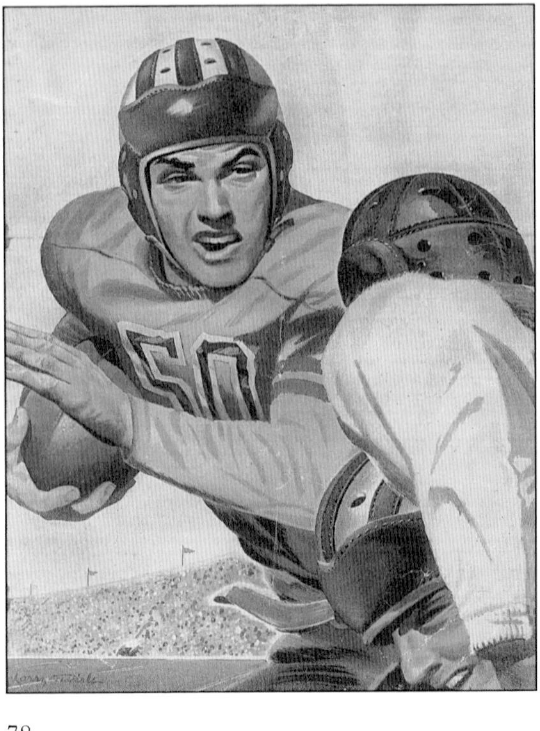

This is an old football program from the game between Holy Trinity and South Norfolk High Schools. The score, written on the third page, was South Norfolk, 18, and Holy Trinity, 6.

Seven

Early Industries

This is a difficult topic to cover, for there were many businesses and industries, both large and small, in the area. Along the Southern Branch of the Elizabeth River were lumber mills, creosote, fertilizer, guano, and chemical plants, just to name a few. Then the railroads came. But agriculture was the first business; people literally lived off the land. The Gosport Navy Yard started in 1801. Timber from the Dismal Swamp brought riches to the area, and let's not forget the local seafood industry. All of the above brought employment to the area's residents.

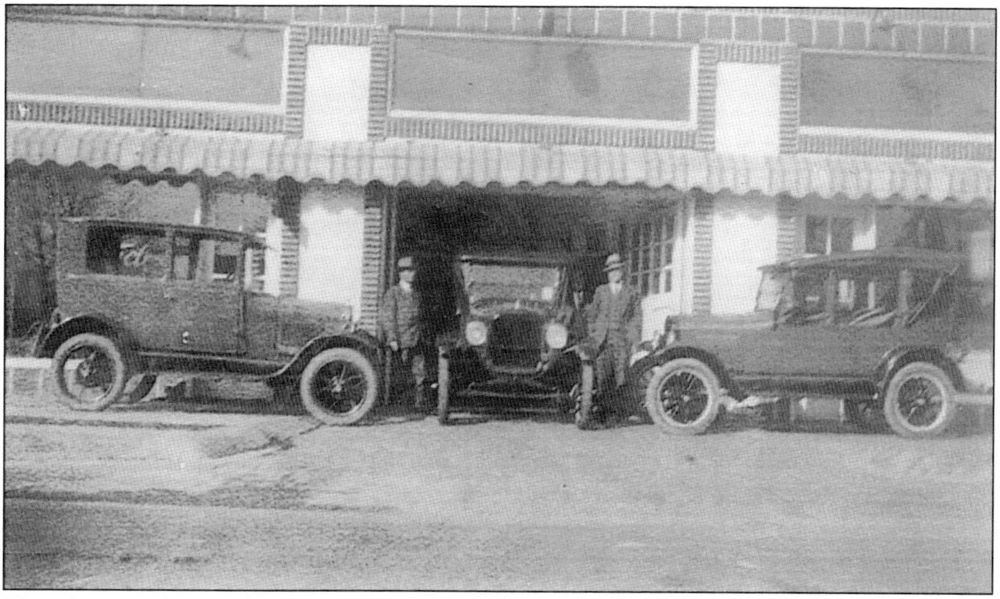

This photograph was taken in front of the Gibson Motor Corporation on Bainbridge Boulevard in Portlock, Virginia. Three models of Ford cars are shown here. The year was 1927 and to own one of these vehicles was pure luxury.

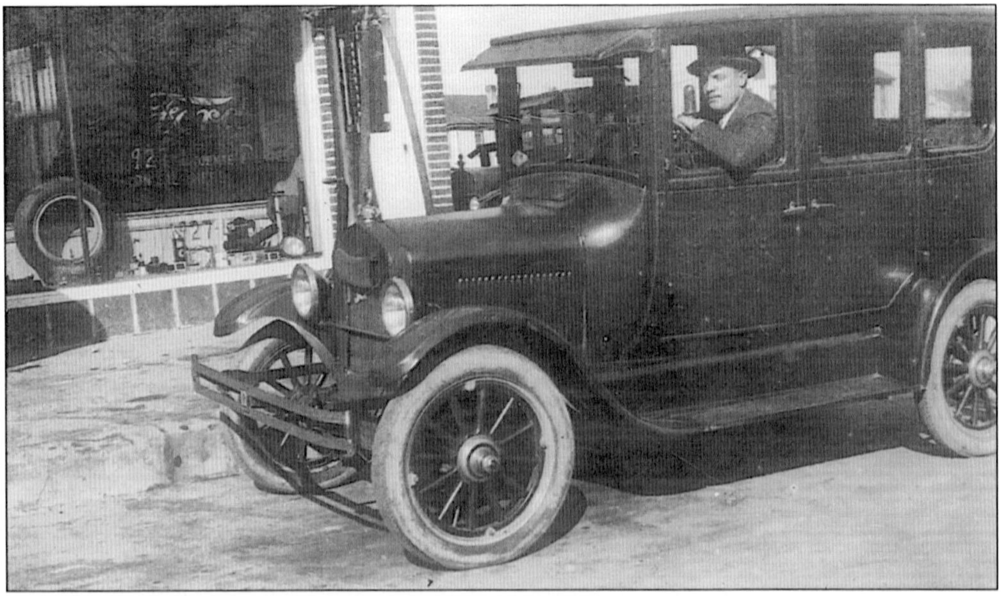

This is R.L. "Bob" Simpson, a salesman for Gibson Motor Corporation, as he prepares to test drive one of the new four-door automobiles with a sun visor over the windshield. A sign in the window of the showroom states that "1927 license plates are on sale here."

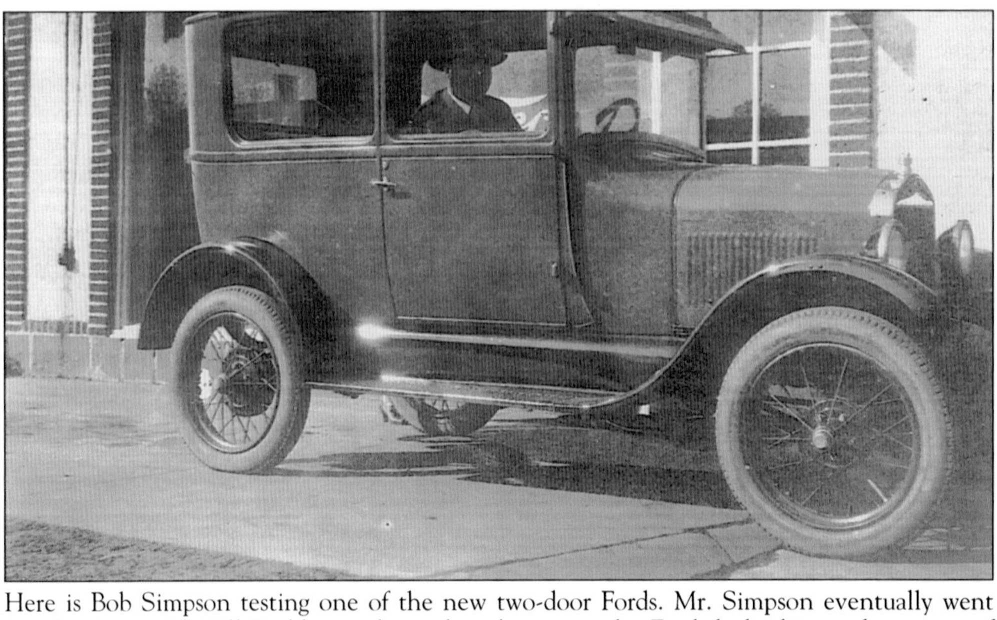

Here is Bob Simpson testing one of the new two-door Fords. Mr. Simpson eventually went into business with Bill Peebles, and together they opened a Ford dealership at the corner of Poindexter and Rodgers Streets in South Norfolk.

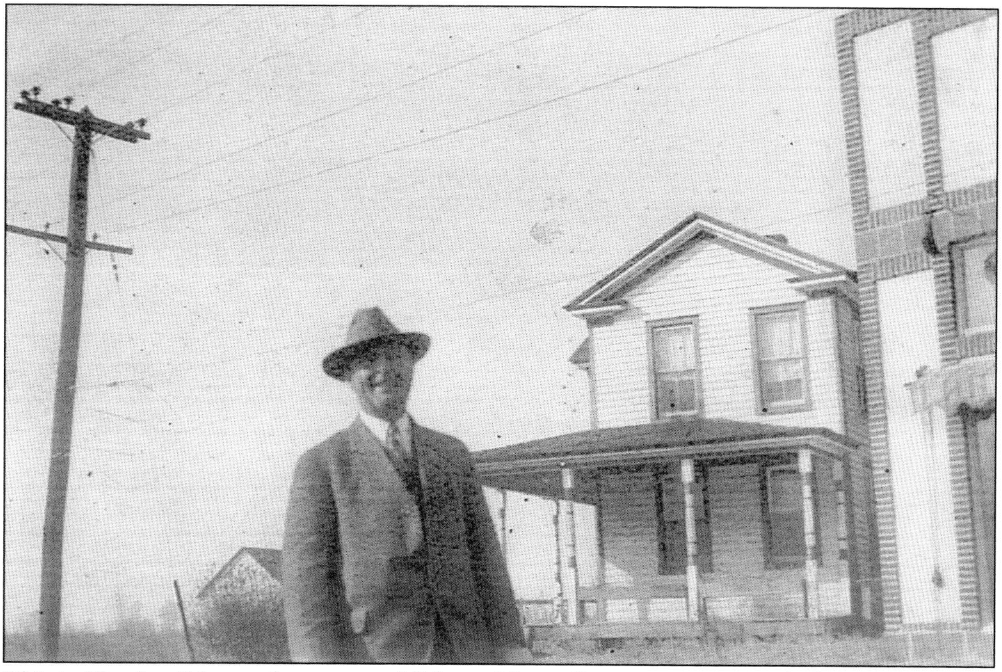

This is Charley Gibson, the owner of Gibson Motor Corporation in Portlock. His dealership and service department were located at the corner of Bainbridge Boulevard and Freeman Avenue. After Mr. Gibson moved his business, the building served many other purposes, including the site of the city garage. Eventually it was torn down, and now a Hardees Restaurant is on the site.

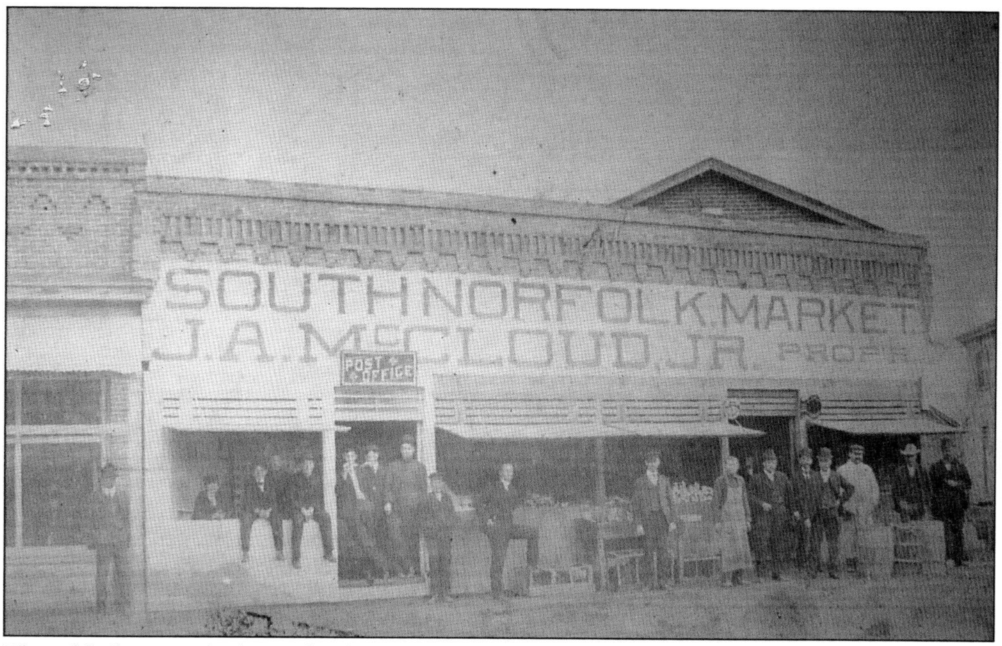

This old photograph shows the first store in the village of South Norfolk in Norfolk County, Virginia. The proprietor of the business was J.A. McCloud, and he opened the market in 1873. A close look reveals the entrance to the post office on the left side of the building.

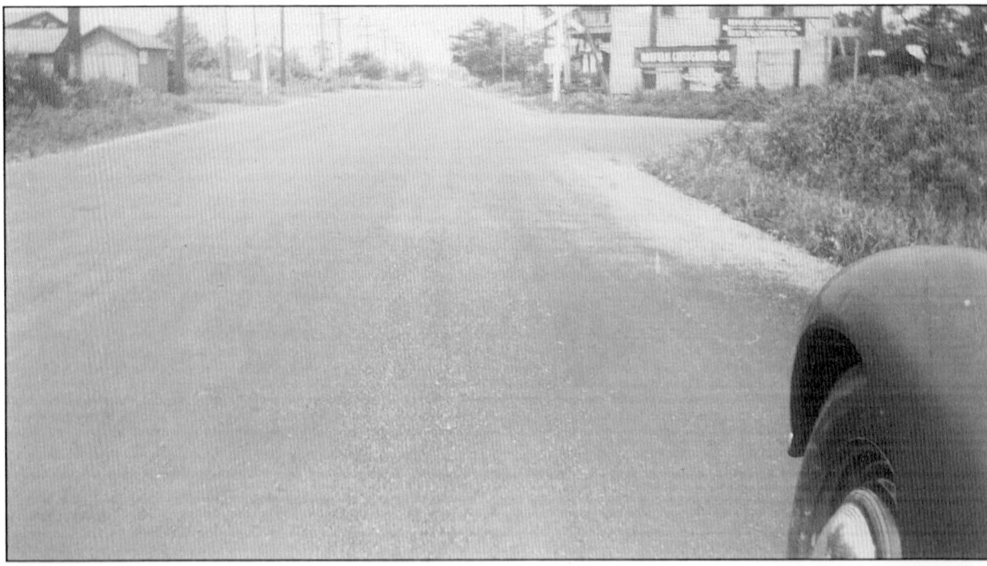

This picture of Buell, Virginia, was taken on Freeman Avenue in 1942. Nichols Fertilizer Corporation is on the left. The sign near the railroad crossing points to the Norfolk Creosoting Plant along the Southern Branch.

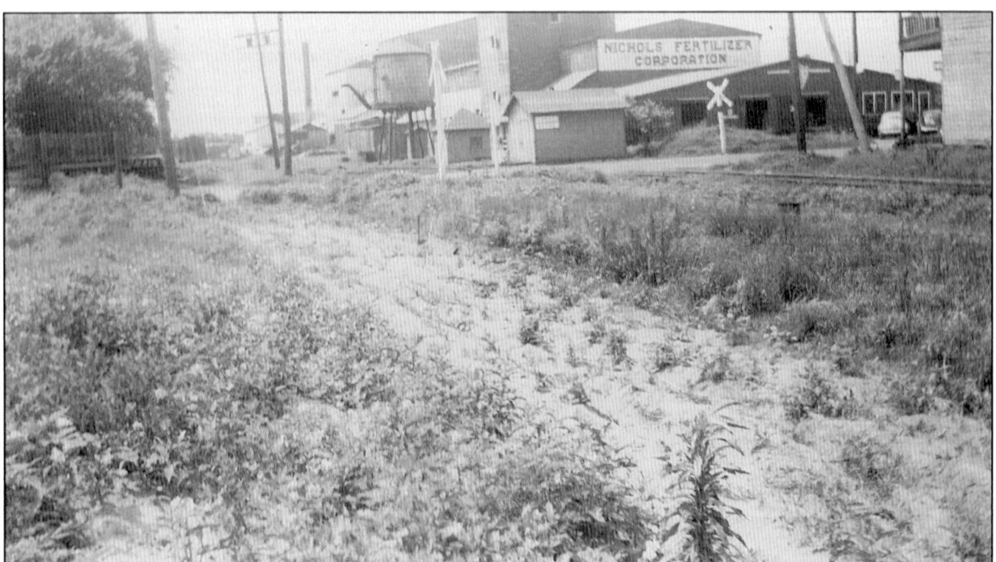

This photograph shows the complete plant of Nichols Fertilizer Corporation at Buell, Virginia. The large water tank, which was used by the railroad, can be seen beside the plant.

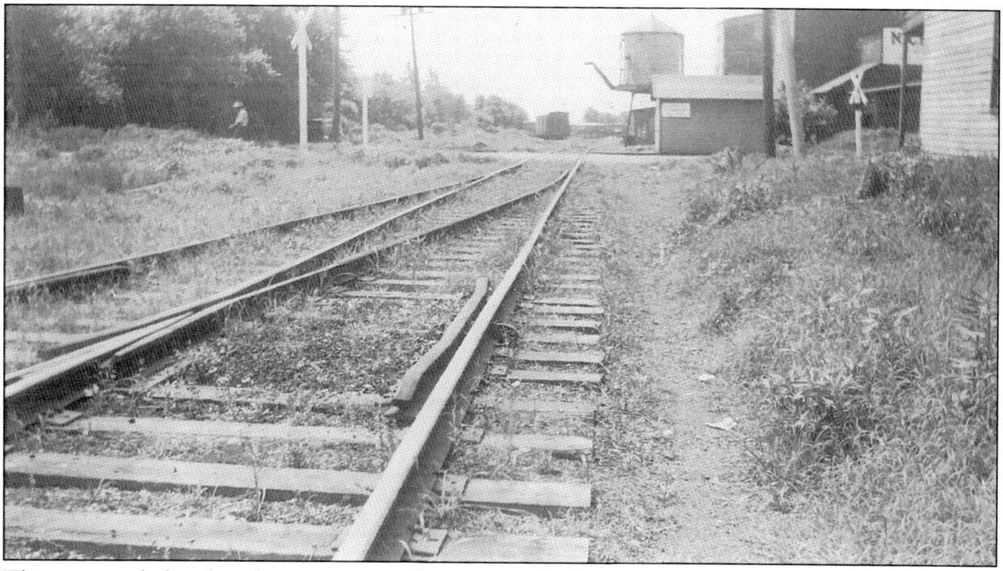

This unguarded railroad crossing was the scene of a bad accident in 1943, when a car hit a passing train. The car was totally destroyed, but no one was hurt. The crossing was near Nichols Fertilizer plant in Buell.

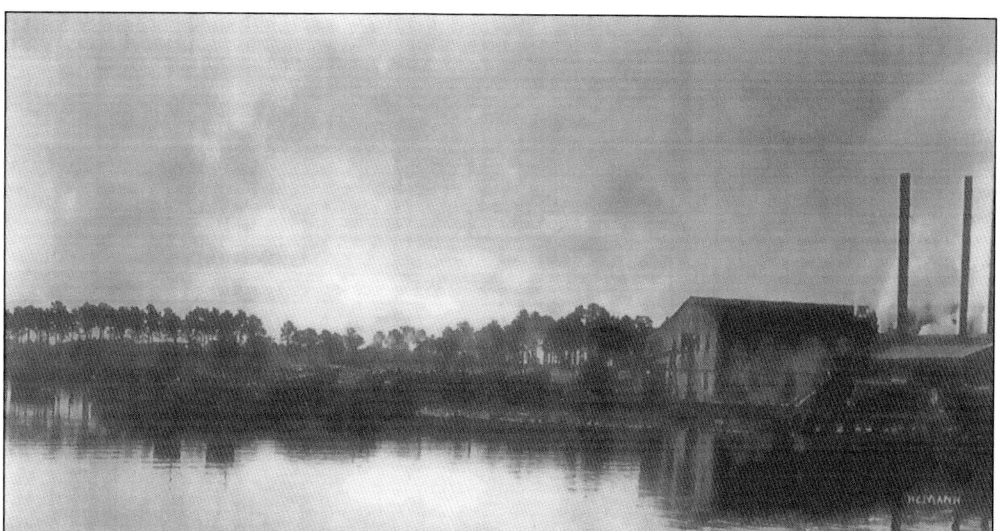

Harry C. Mann took this picture of one of the cedar mills in Gilmerton, Virginia, in 1910.

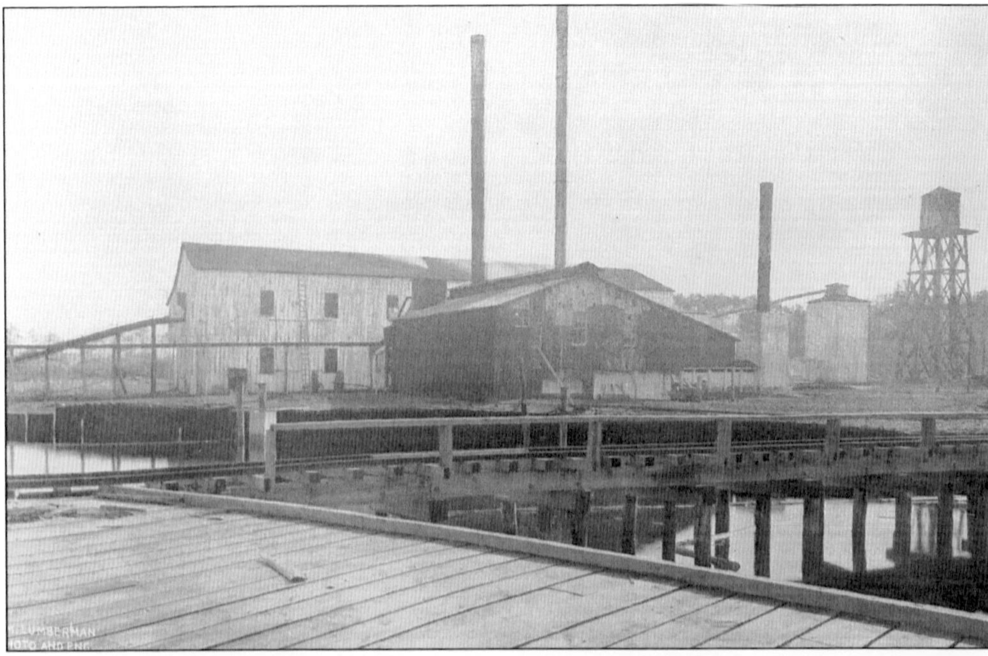

The next four photographs appeared in the *American Lumberman and Eng.* magazine on April 27, 1907, and show various mill operations at the John L. Roper Lumber Company Plant in Gilmerton, Virginia. The tall smokestacks, various buildings of the cedar band mill, railroad tracks, and part of the waterfront can be seen in this exterior view.

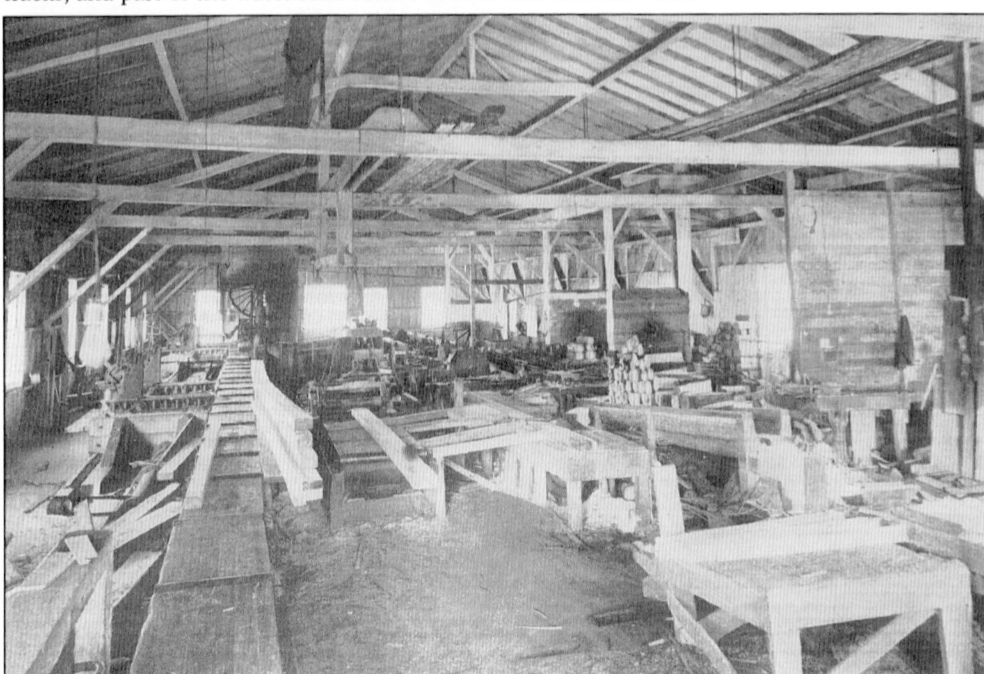

Here we see the interior of the cedar band mill. Taking a close look at the operation, cedar logs can be seen entering the plant, where they are stripped of bark, cut into various sizes, and dressed.

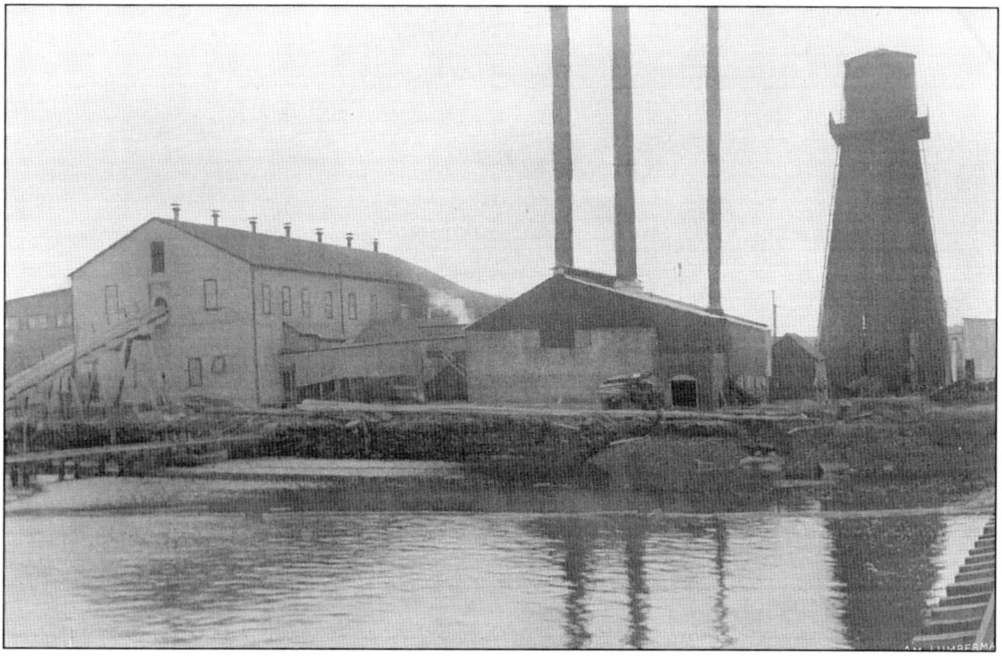

This is the exterior of Mr. Roper's "Elizabeth" band sawmill. Again, the tall stacks, various buildings, waterfront, and railroad tracks are visible.

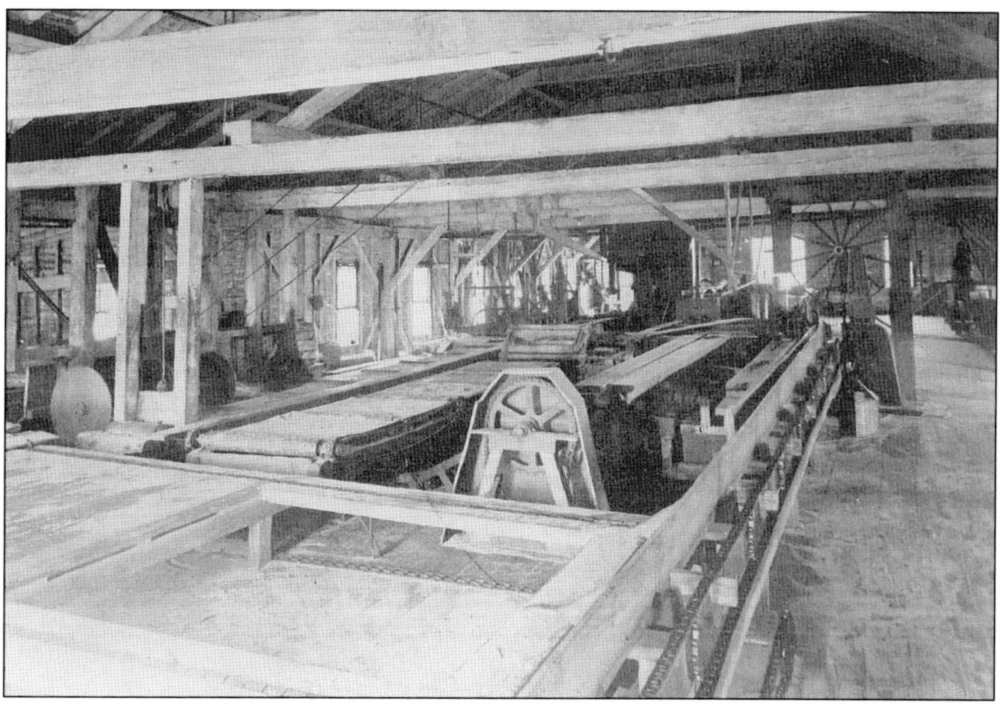

Here is an interior view of the "Elizabeth" band sawmill. Various saws, conveyor belts, and other pieces of equipment are used in operation of the mill.

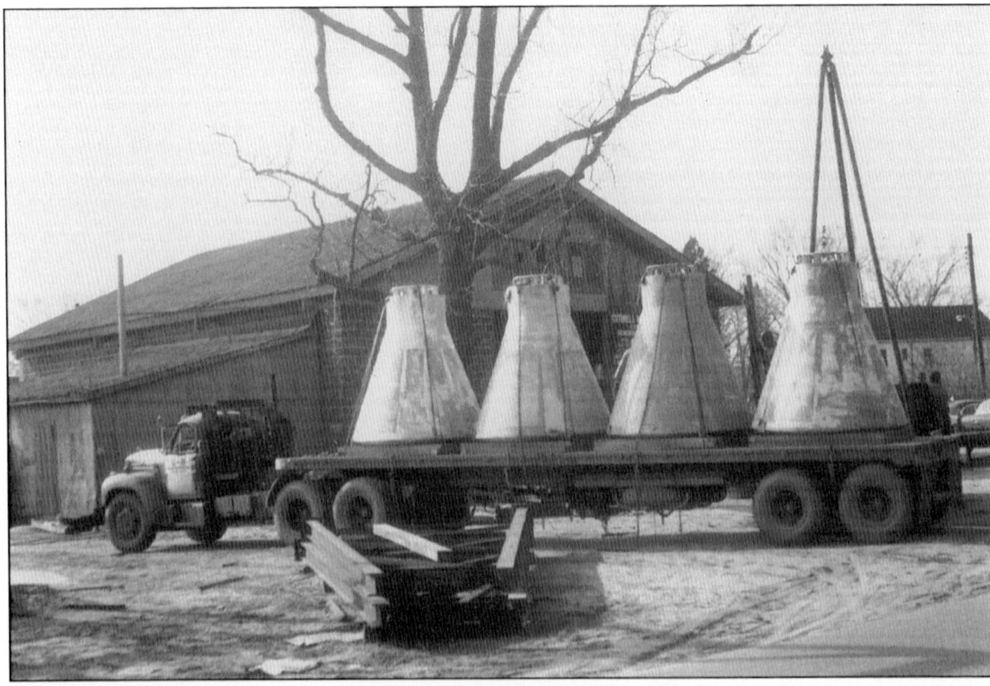

In 1930, Mr. E.H. Cuthrell established Cuthrell's Machine Works. His business grew from a one-man operation to more than 35 employees. Cuthrell built many things including a boat, but probably the most noted articles manufactured at the machine works were practice capsules for the National Aeronautics and Space Administration (NASA). He initially built 12 capsules for the Mercury program and then 18 for the Gemini program.

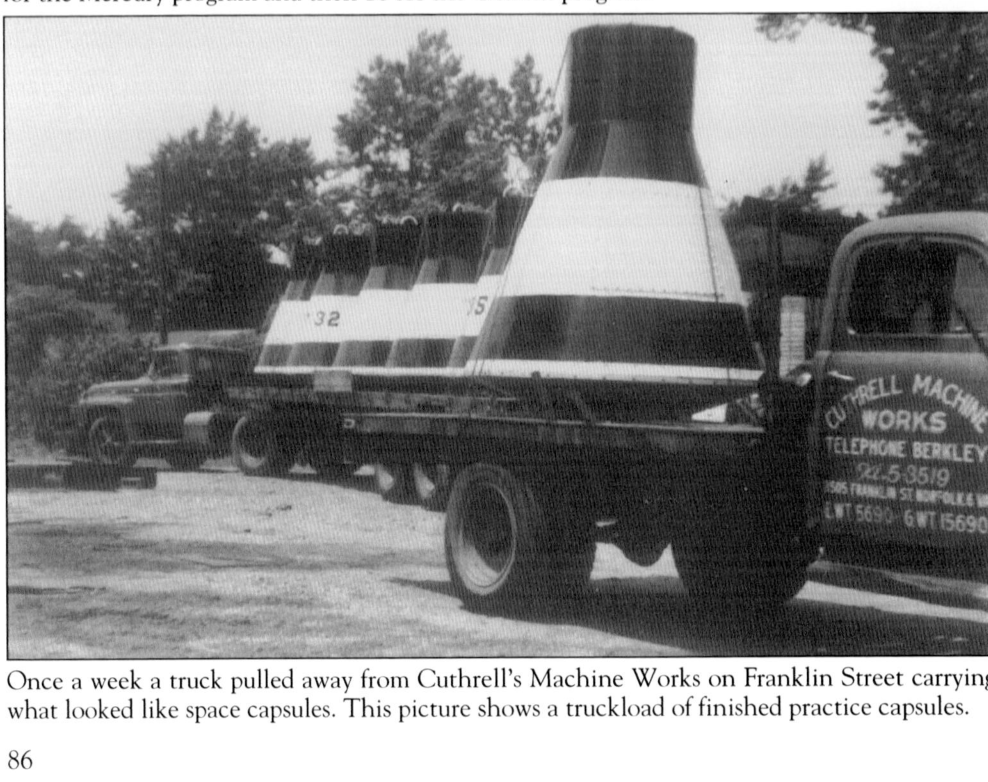

Once a week a truck pulled away from Cuthrell's Machine Works on Franklin Street carrying what looked like space capsules. This picture shows a truckload of finished practice capsules.

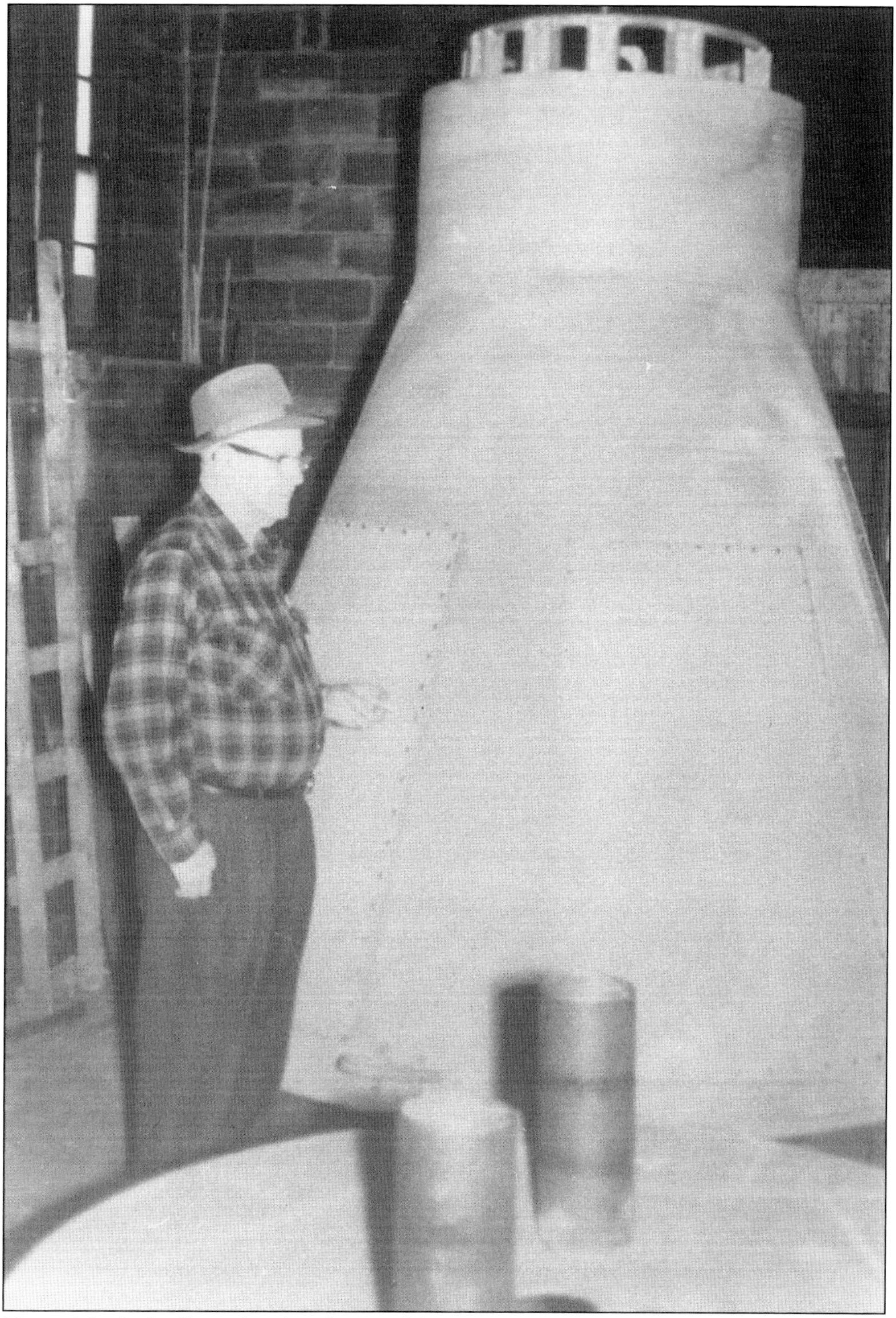

Here is Mr. Cuthrell standing beside one of the practice capsules.

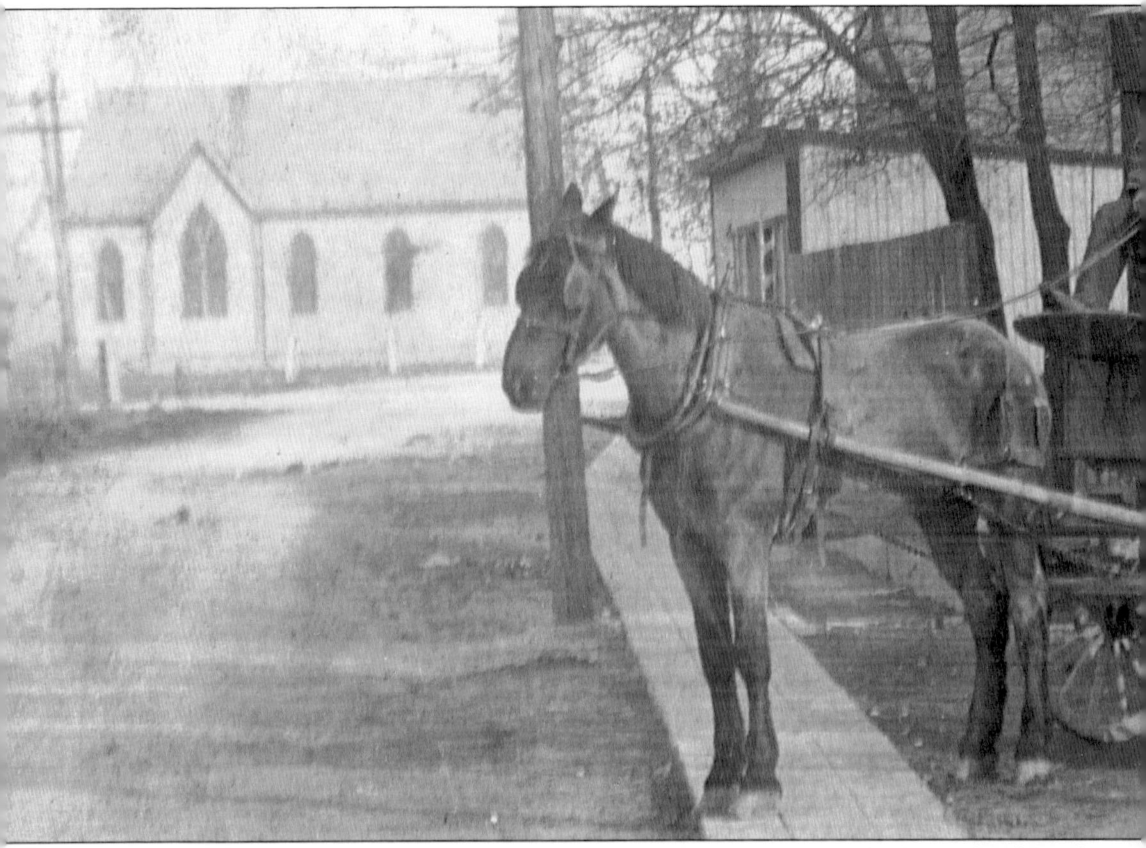

This c. 1892 photograph was taken on what is now Liberty Street in the borough of South Norfolk. The horse standing on the boardwalk pulled the Berkley express between the town of Berkley and the village of South Norfolk in Norfolk County, Virginia. The church in the left background is the new Liberty Street Methodist Episcopal Church, South. Where the church once stood is now the corner of Liberty and Twenty-second Streets.

Eight

County Courthouse and the Police

By an act of the legislature in 1789, Powder Point was chosen as the site for the Norfolk County courthouse. The land was purchased from Edmund Allmand for 25 English pounds in 1790, and the courthouse was built on the corner of what would become Walnut and Pine Streets. The court was moved to Portsmouth in 1801, and the building at Powder Point was afterwards used as a meeting place for church groups and lodge organizations. Later it became a gristmill and, even later, a knitting mill. The property was bought several years after this by Sam Fox and converted into an apartment house. A picture of the apartment can be seen in chapter two.

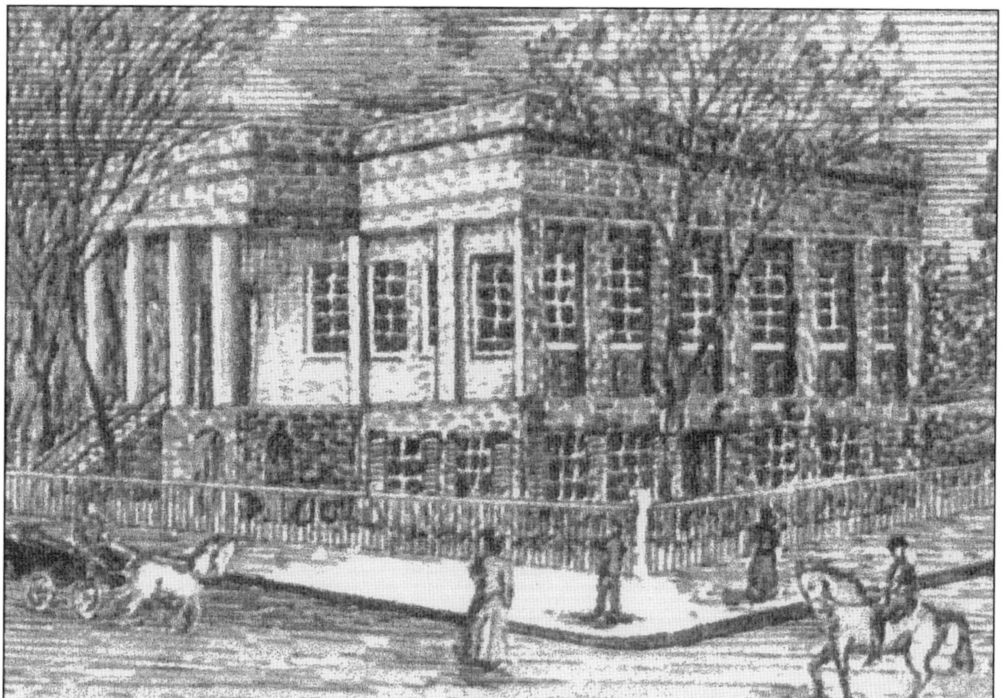

This image of the Norfolk County courthouse in Portsmouth was drawn in 1886.

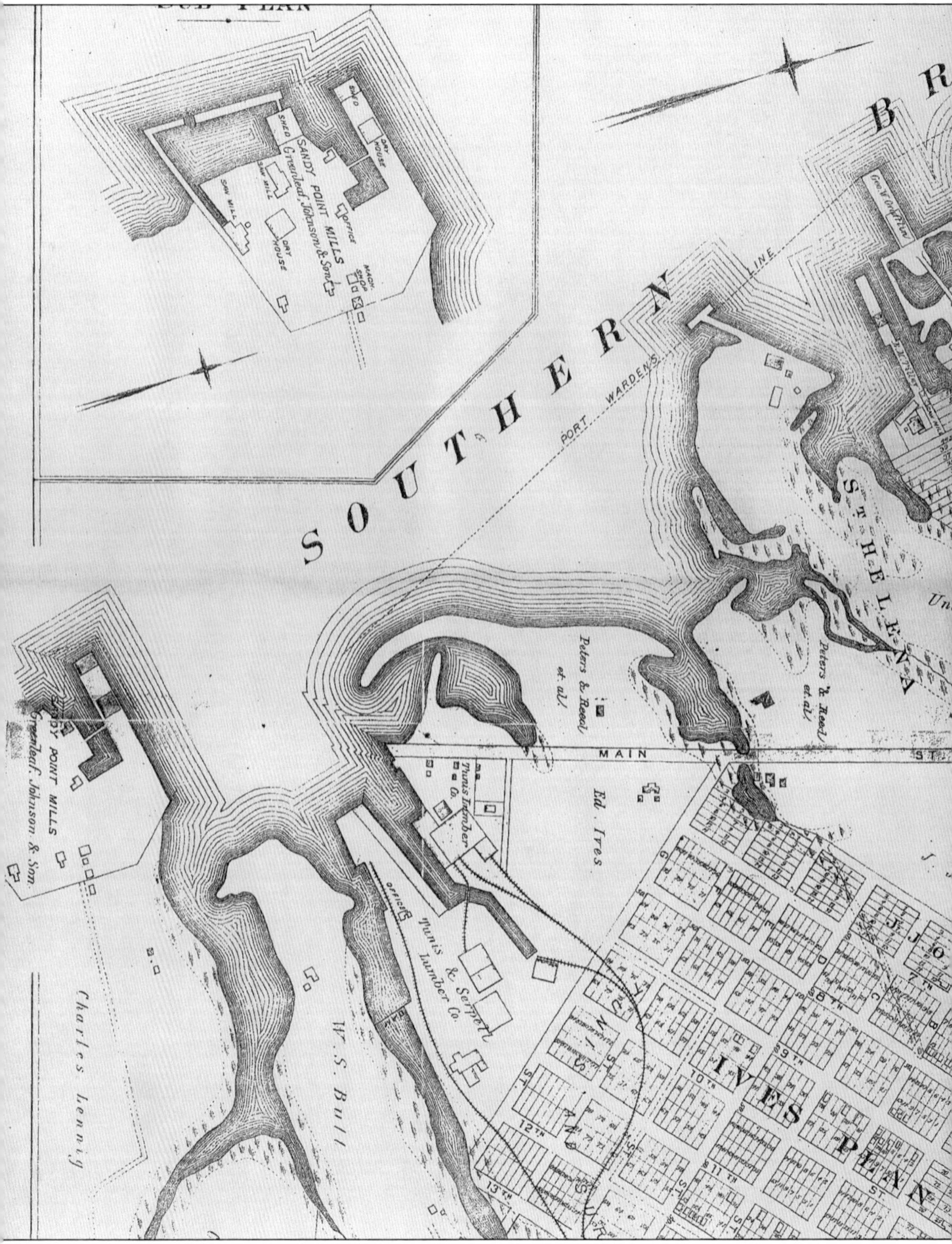

By the time this map was drawn in 1889, Powder Point had been renamed Berkley, and Liberty Street had been extended down to Washington Point where Baker Salvage Company was

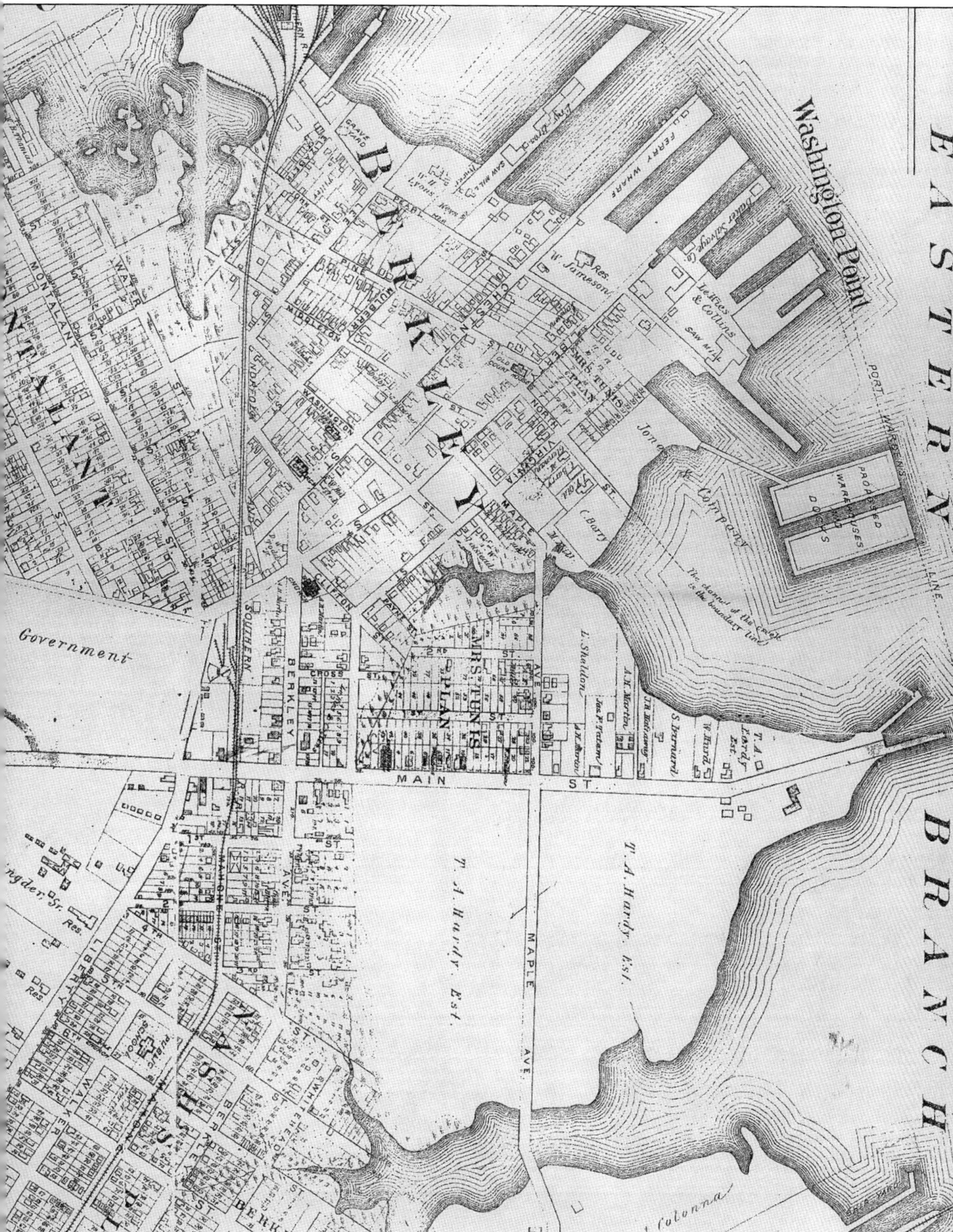

located. This extension took in Walnut Street, and therefore the old courthouse is at the corner of Pine and Liberty Streets.

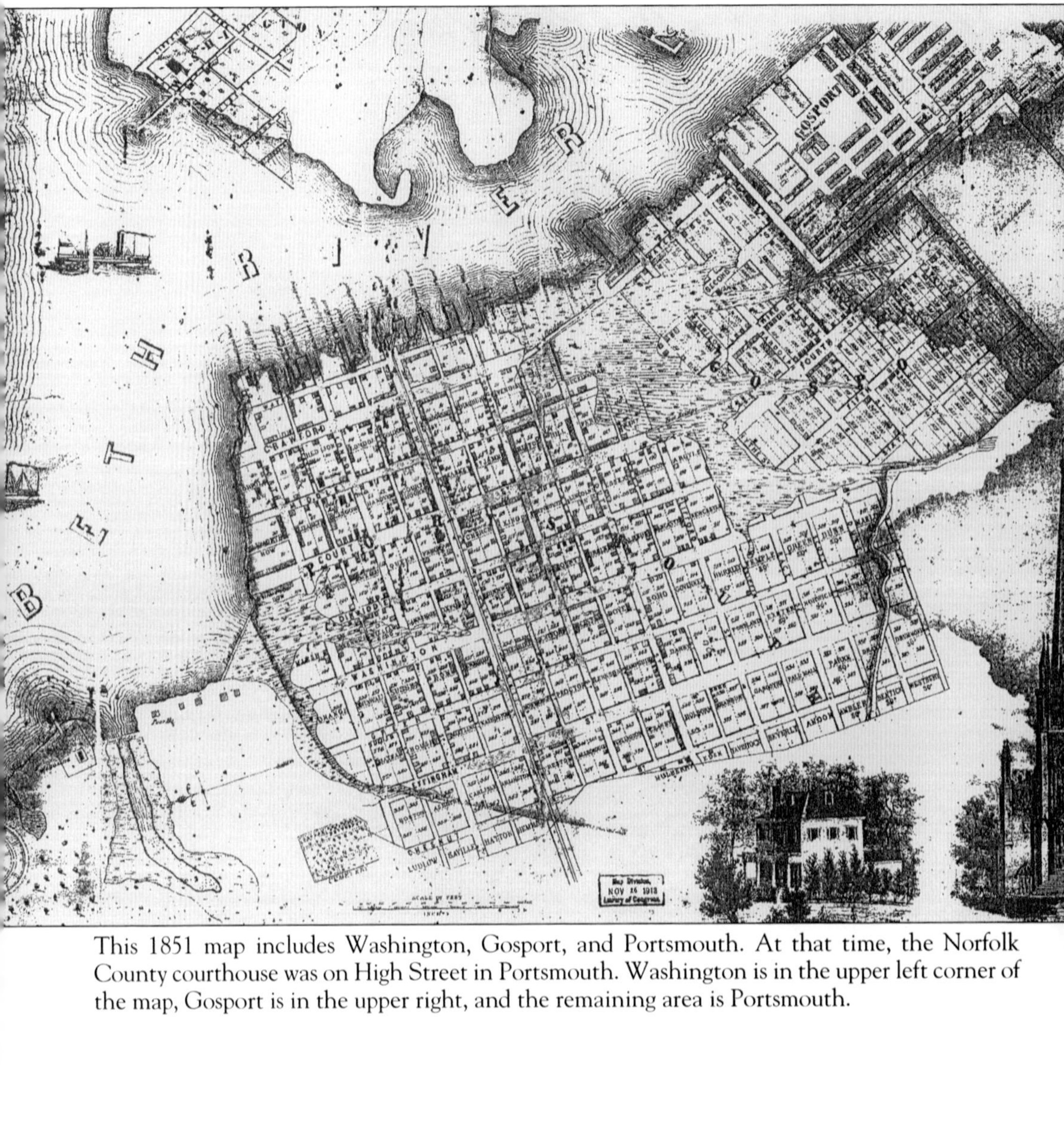

This 1851 map includes Washington, Gosport, and Portsmouth. At that time, the Norfolk County courthouse was on High Street in Portsmouth. Washington is in the upper left corner of the map, Gosport is in the upper right, and the remaining area is Portsmouth.

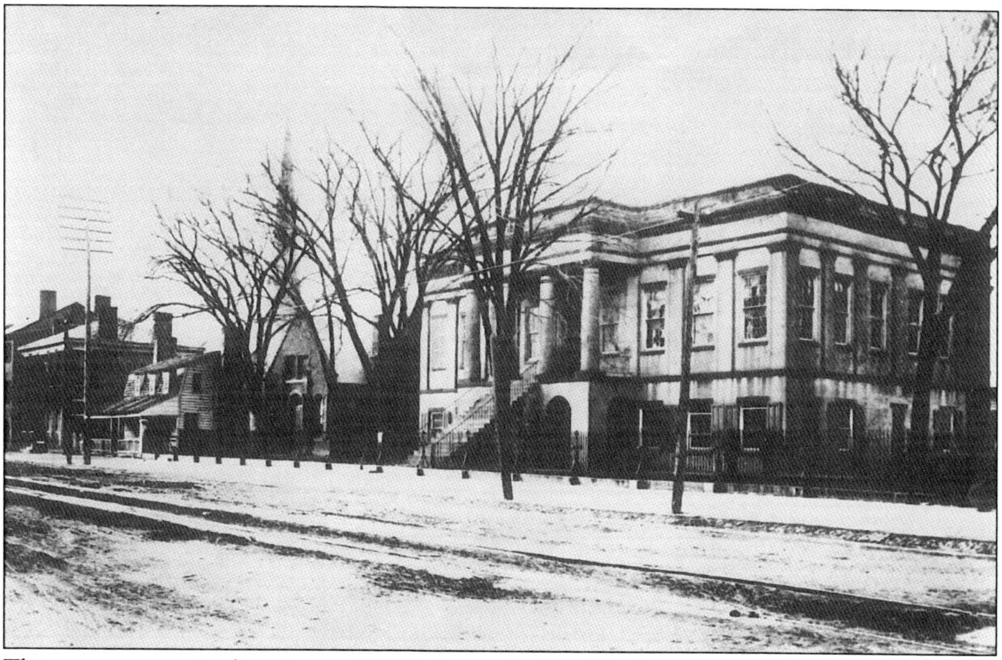

This snowy scene in the winter of 1895 shows the Norfolk County courthouse on High Street in Portsmouth. The clerk's office is to the left of the main building, and the house with the Dutch roof beside the clerk's office was the first home of the Bilisoly family. Colonel William H. Stewart, a lawyer, local historian, and officer of the Confederacy, had his law office on the first floor. The more modern brick house next to this structure became the next home of the Bilisoly family. The steeple of the Monumental Church can be seen in the background.

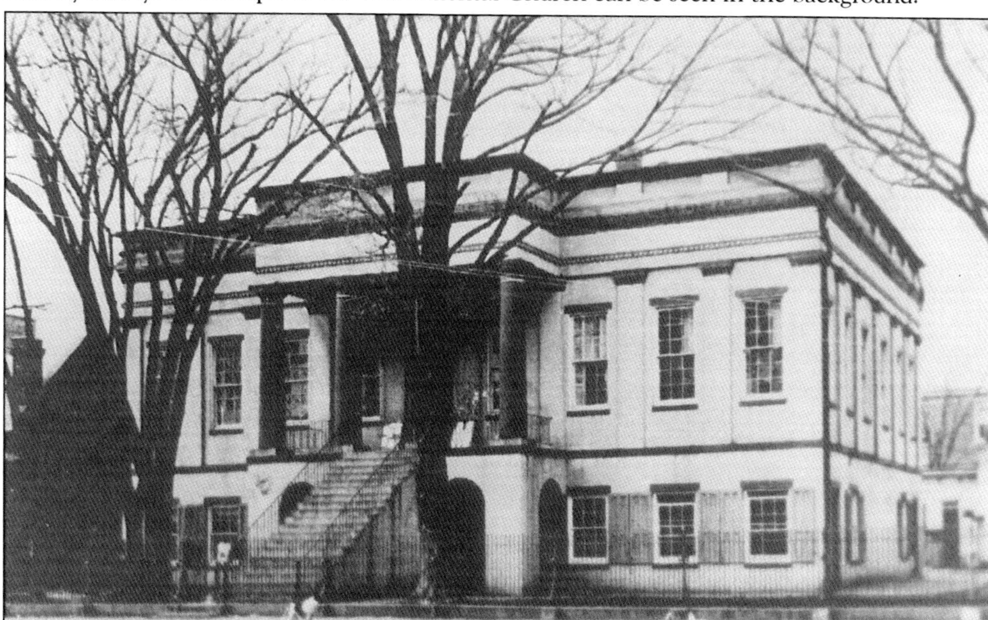

Here is the Norfolk County courthouse as it appeared in 1905. Its only visitor when this picture was taken was the dog standing out front. The building to the right and behind the courthouse is a tavern that served as the watering hole for the local male population.

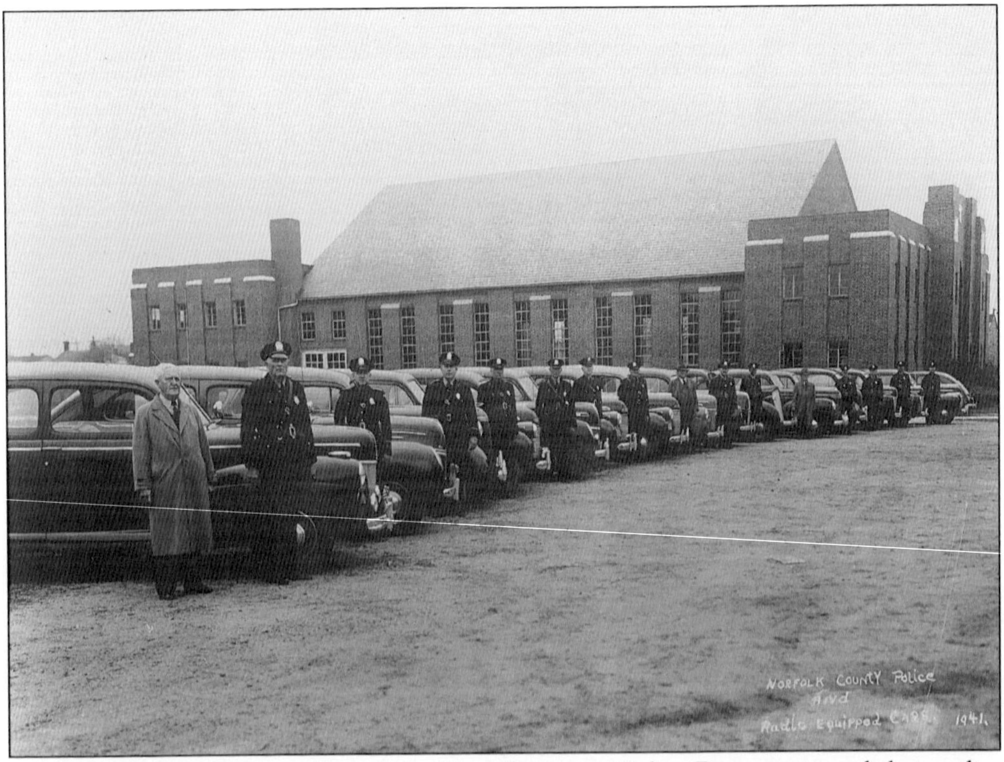

This photograph of the members of the Norfolk County Police Department and their radio-equipped cars was taken in 1941. The large building in the background is the armory on Elm Avenue in Portsmouth.

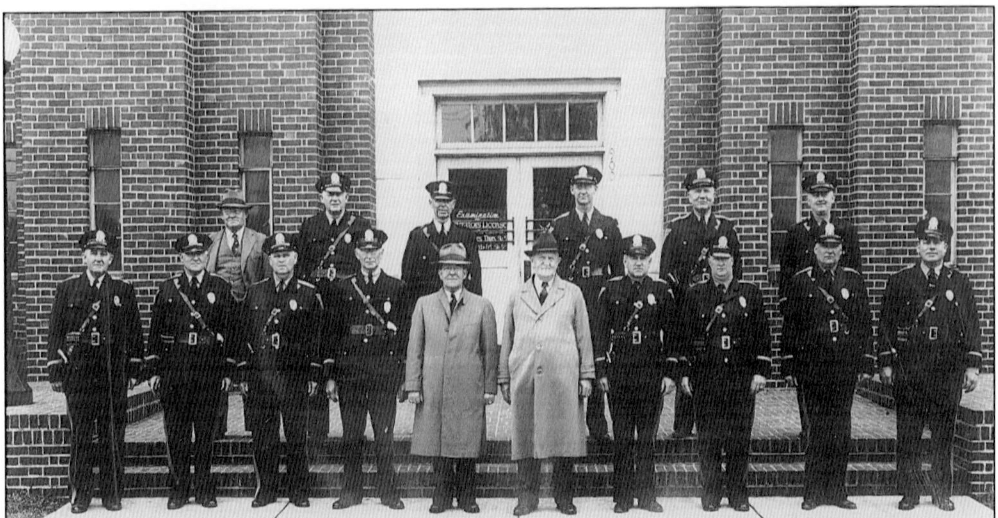

This picture of the 1941 Norfolk County Police Department was taken at the entrance to the armory on Elm Avenue. The members are, from left to right, as follows: (front row) unidentified, ? Parkerson, unidentified, Harry Jones, Frank Wilson, Sheriff A.A. Wendell, unidentified, Julian S. "Pop" Leonard, John Collins, and unidentified; (back row) unidentified, unidentified, ? Rowe, J. Arthur Hodges, John Peeples, and unidentified.

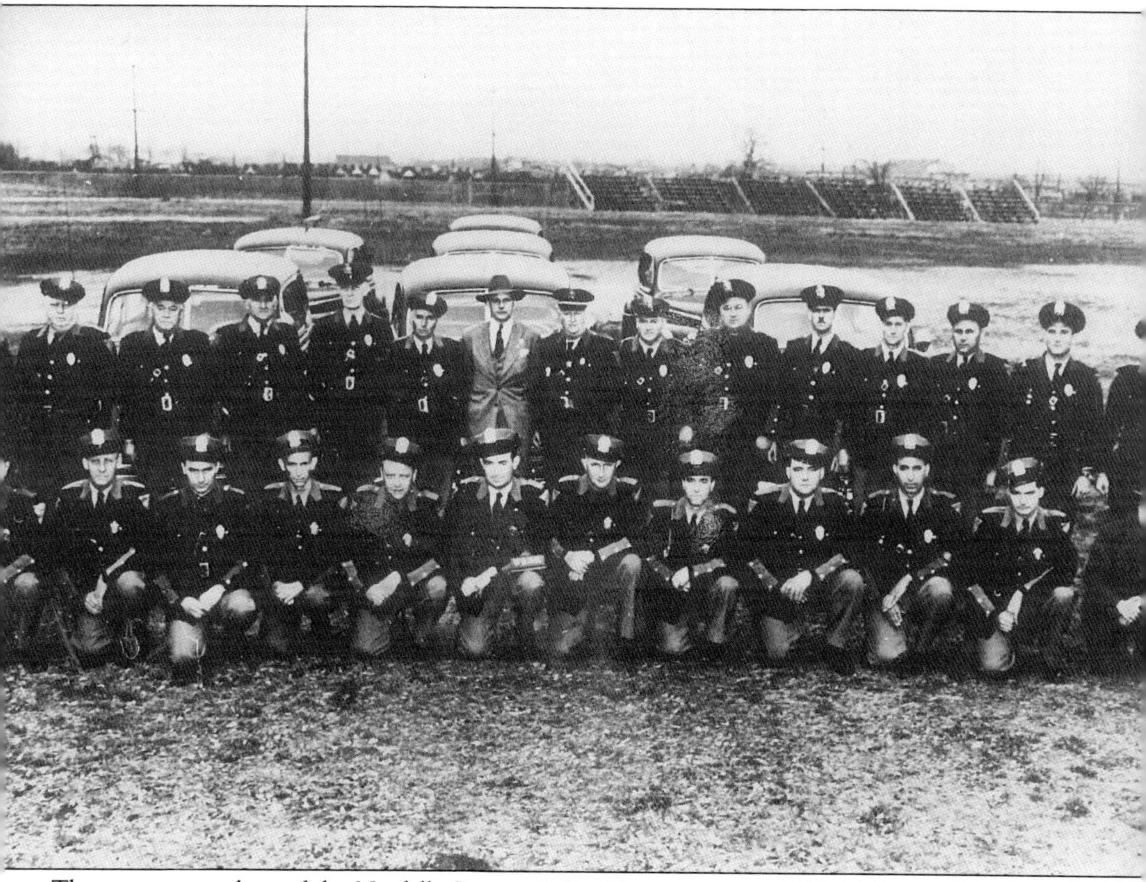

These men, members of the Norfolk County Police Department in 1948–1949, are, from left to right, as follows: (front row) ? Lyles, ? Brown, Wilmer "Snooky" Jones, ? Frost, ? Powell, ? Johnson, ? Schucker, ? Barrow, ? West, unidentified, George Murphy, and ? Wilson; (back row) Harry W. Jones, unidentified, unidentified, ? Parkerson, ? Powell, ? Brown, Perry Williams, Julian S. "Pop" Leonard, ? Kelly, ? English, ? Harkey, ? Twine, ? Williams, Denkly Barkley, and A.B. Roane.

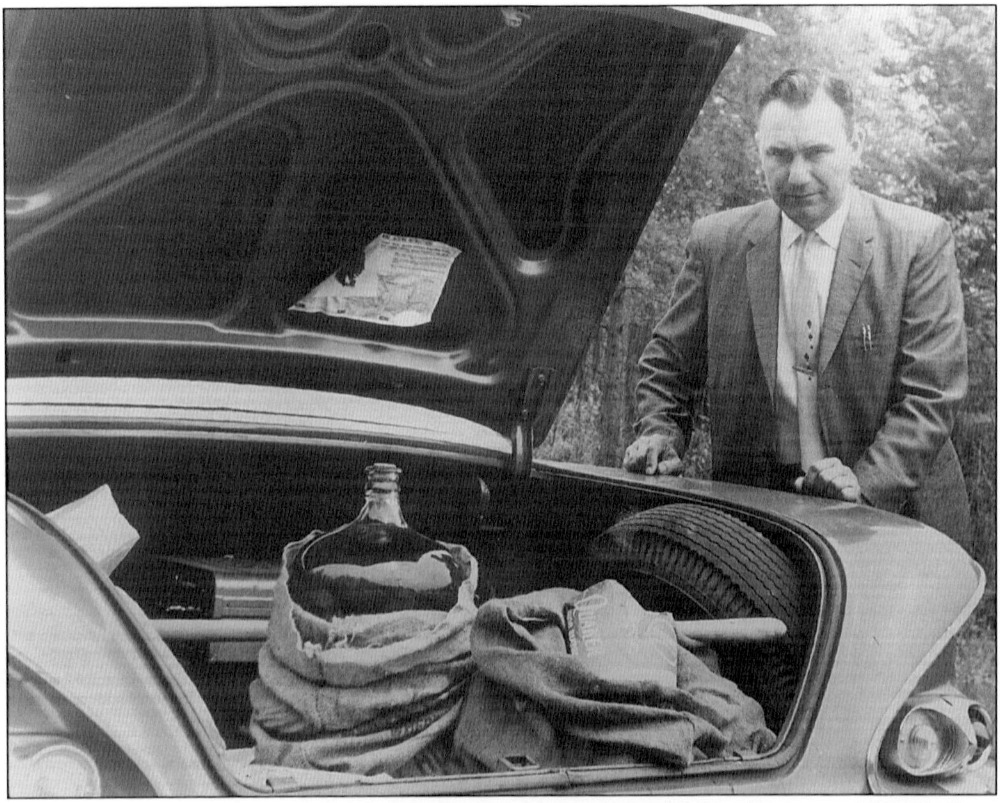

Wilmer "Snooky" Jones is shown here after having uncovered a 5-gallon jug of illegal white lightning, or moonshine. A partial bag of Quaker cane sugar, one of the necessary ingredients in the manufacture of the drink, was also found in the trunk of the car.

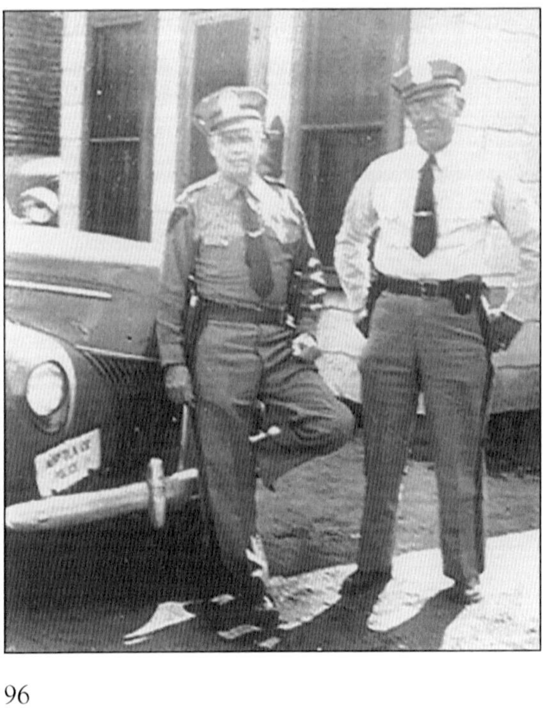

Here are two members of the Norfolk County Police Department standing in front of the small police station in the village of Portlock. They are, from left to right, Harry Gardner and Cecil Brown. When Portlock became a town in 1948, Harry Gardner served as the first city sergeant.

Nine

CHURCHES AND CEMETERIES

Many community activities revolved around the early churches. They served not only as places of worship, but also hosted such events as school graduations, picnics, and many other happenings of the day. In 1761, when the Elizabeth River Parish was divided, there were just a few churches, and as people began to move, those churches became too distant to travel to several times a week. As a result, religious groups formed and started their own. Many of the early meeting places were converted barns, log cabins, or any structure that was available. Some of the earlier churches had their own burying grounds or cemeteries. One of them is the Good Hope United Methodist Church on Benefit Road, which is now in the City of Chesapeake.

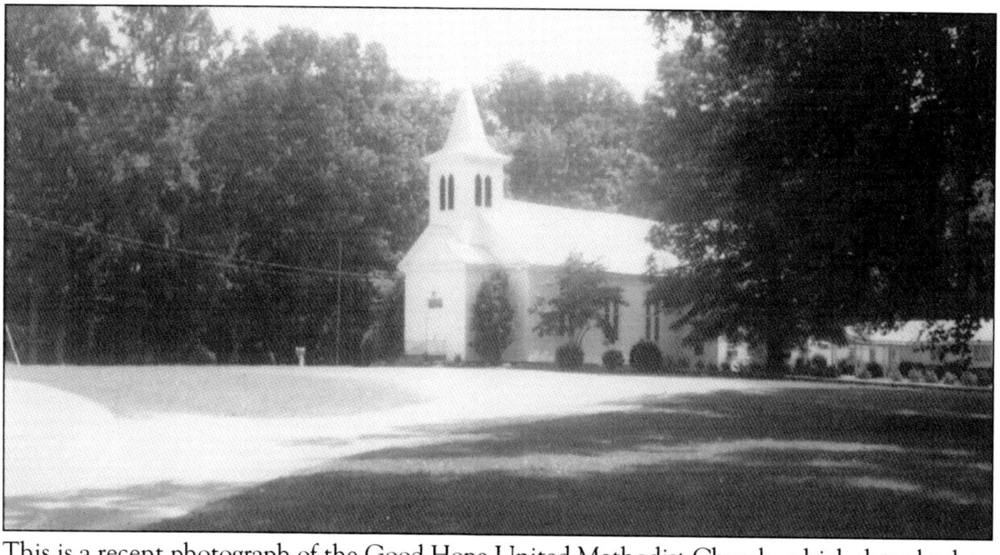

This is a recent photograph of the Good Hope United Methodist Church, which dates back to 1848. It was built on land donated by Laban N. Hall and Israel Foreman.

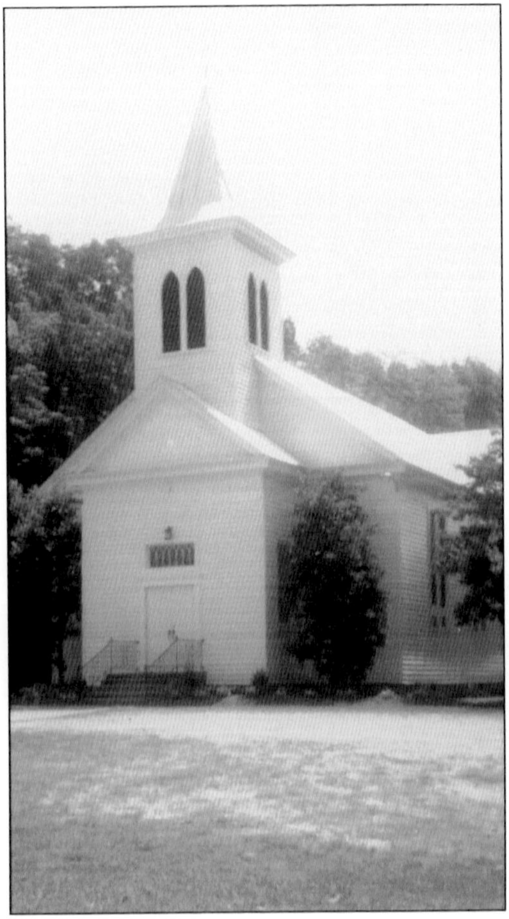

This is a front view that shows the main entrance to Good Hope United Methodist Church.

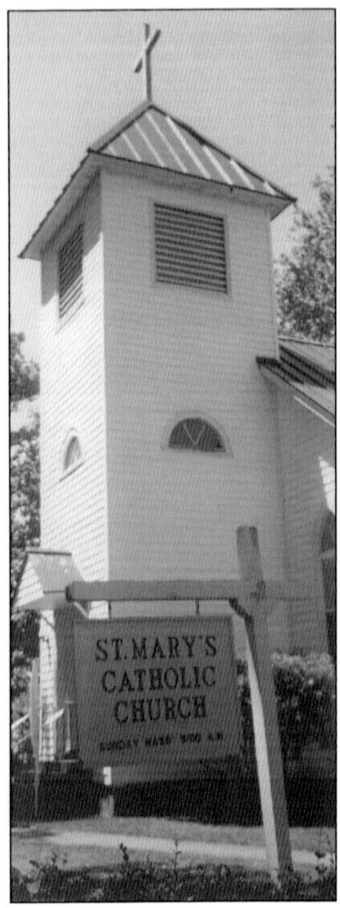

This picture shows the entrance and steeple to Saint Mary's Catholic Church on Homestead Road in Western Branch.

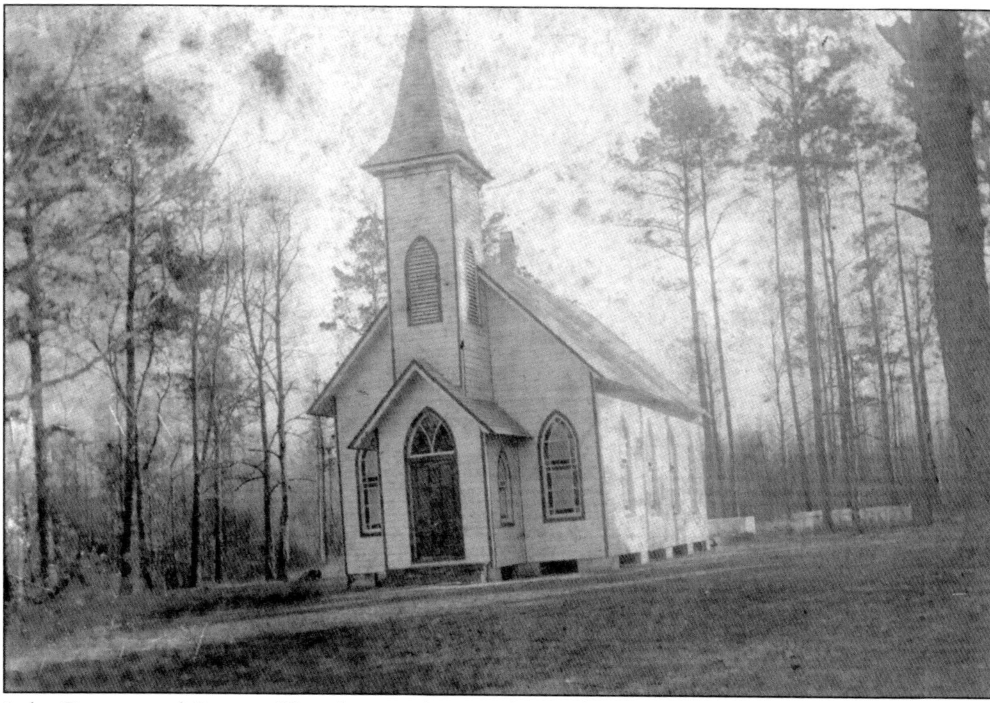

Lake Drummond Baptist Church, seen here, is located at 3873 Ballahack Road. The church, which was completed in 1851, was built on land donated by Michael Sykes. The church has its own cemetery, and Mr. Daniel Williams, the father of J.R. Williams, is buried there. Mr. J.R. Williams was the owner of a funeral home located in South Norfolk.

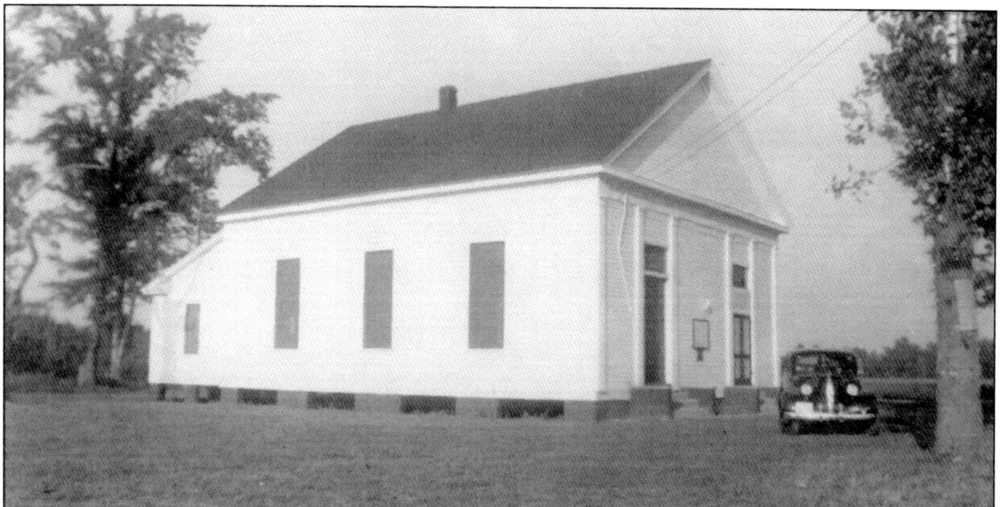

This small church is the Mount Pleasant Church as it appeared c. 1926. It is not known if this is the same Mount Pleasant Church that exists today. The history of Mount Pleasant indicates that it was one of 19 churches on the Princess Anne Circuit in 1846. There are several entries in the records of the Chesapeake Avenue Methodist Church that refer to activities involving Mount Pleasant. According to those records, on March 10, 1926, Mount Pleasant had a Sunday school but no other organizations. When new members were received at Mount Pleasant, their names were documented in the records of the Chesapeake Avenue Church.

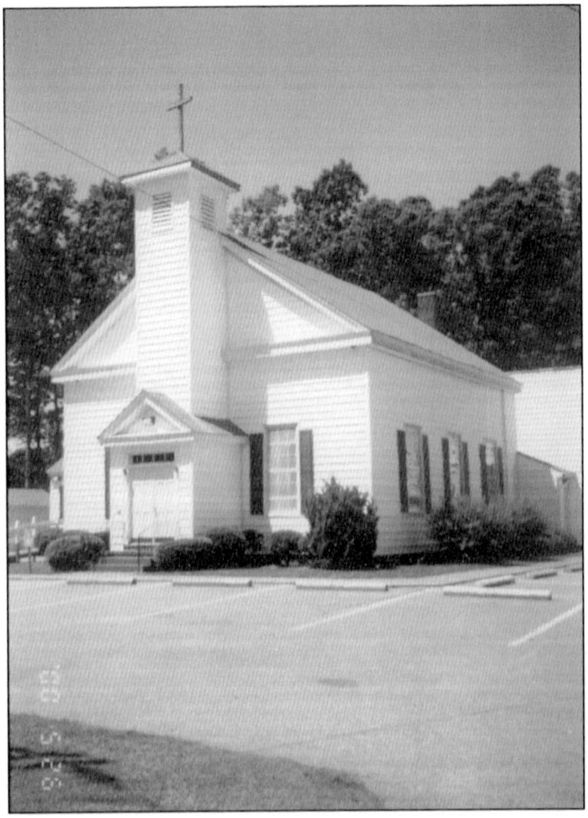

Jolliff United Methodist Church, which is located at 1836 Jolliff Road in Western Branch, has roots going back to c. 1798. At that time, the church was known as the Jolliff meeting house. The present church was erected c. 1850 and has been remodeled several times since.

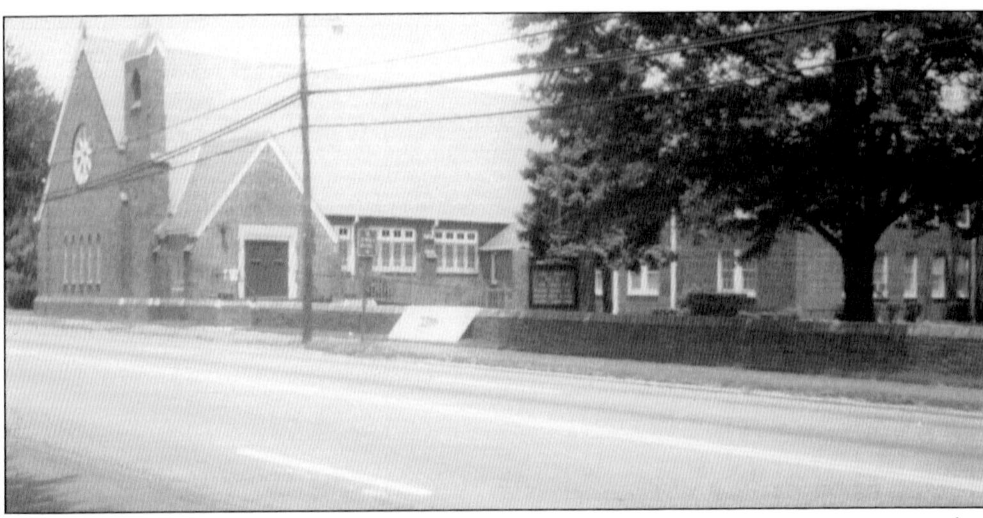

Around 1900, most of the people in Portlock, a part of Norfolk County, were attending the Providence Christian Church a few miles away, but leading citizens of the area were concerned about having a place of worship in their own community. When the Rosemont Christian Church was organized on August 14, 1902, many members of the Providence Church transferred their membership to Rosemont. Here is a recent photograph of Rosemont Christian Church.

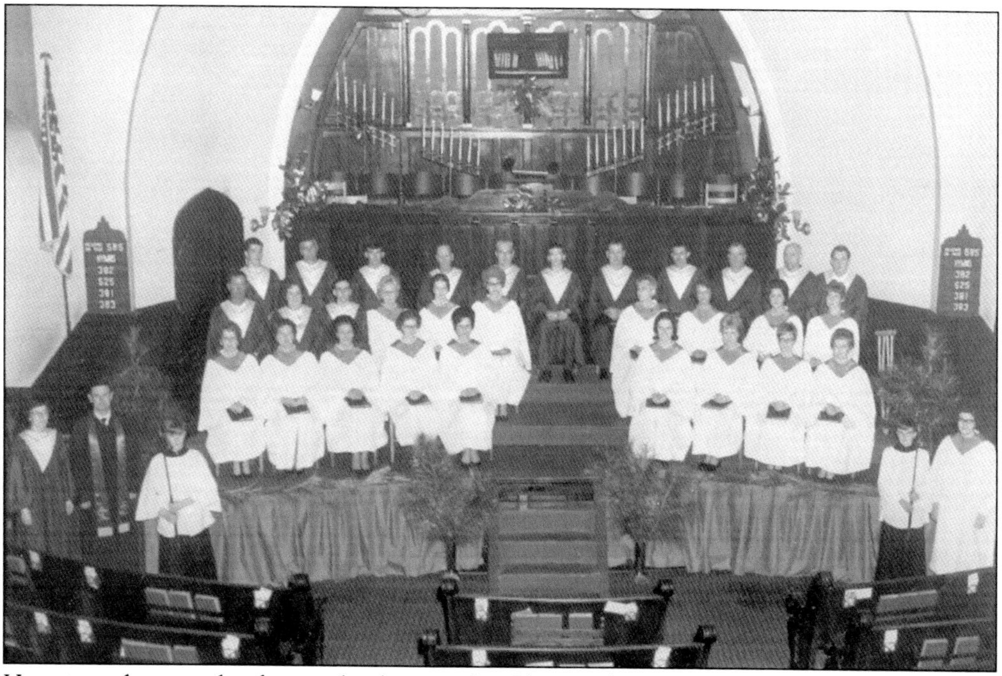

Here is a photograph of an early choir at the Chesapeake Avenue Methodist Church. Mrs. Elizabeth Lindsey, the choir's director, and Reverend C. Reginald Walton are on the left near the bottom of the picture.

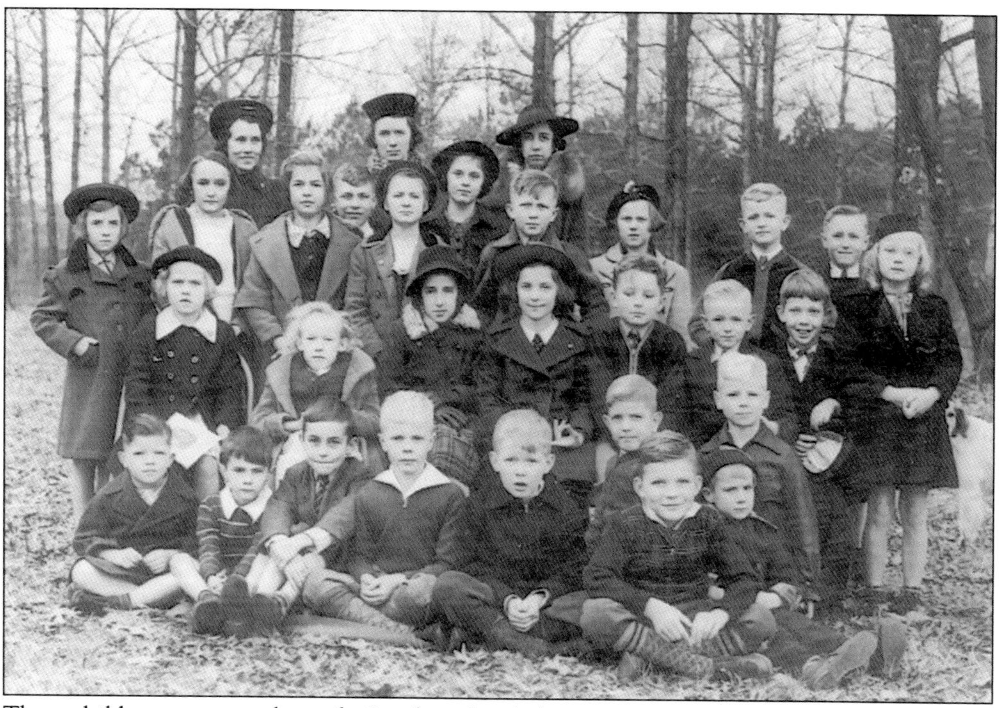

These children were members of a Sunday school class at Oak Grove Methodist Church.

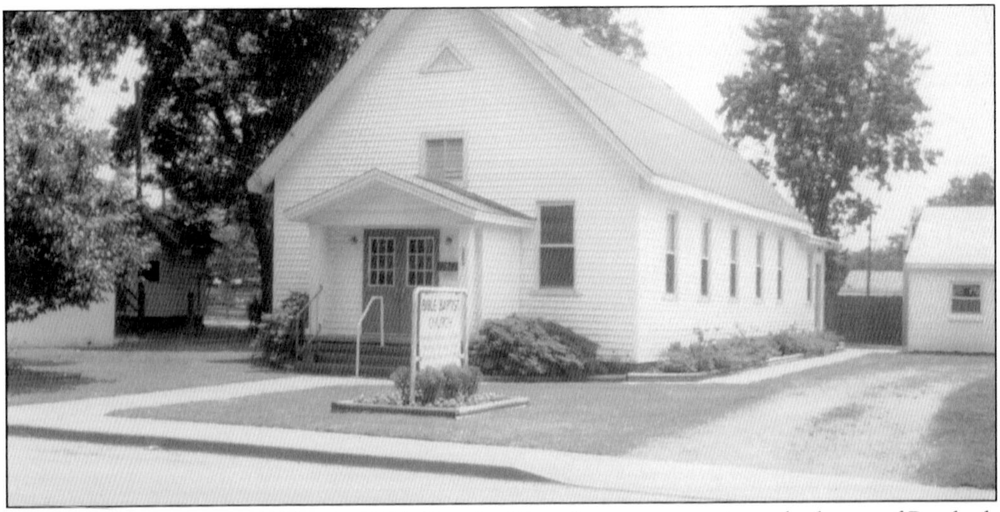

The building now occupied by the Bible Baptist Church was, at one time, the home of Portlock United Methodist Church. The Methodist church moved to a new sanctuary in 1969.

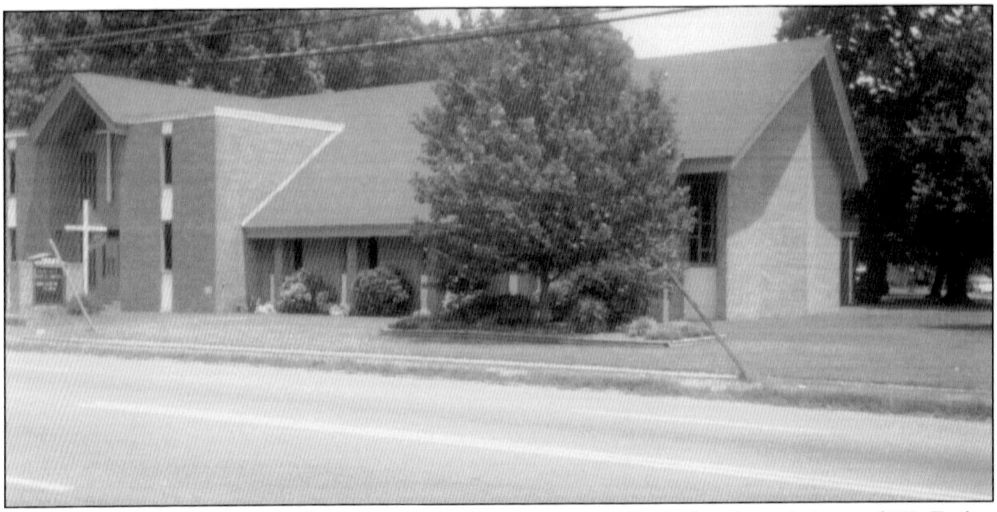

The Portlock United Methodist Church had its start in 1923 under the ministry of W. Farley Powers. The congregation met in a four-room schoolhouse on Bainbridge Boulevard, until eventually a church building was constructed on Edgewood Avenue. The first service in the new building was conducted on Sunday, May 3, 1925. In 1968, ground was broken for the building in this picture. A service of consecration was held on September 7, 1969.

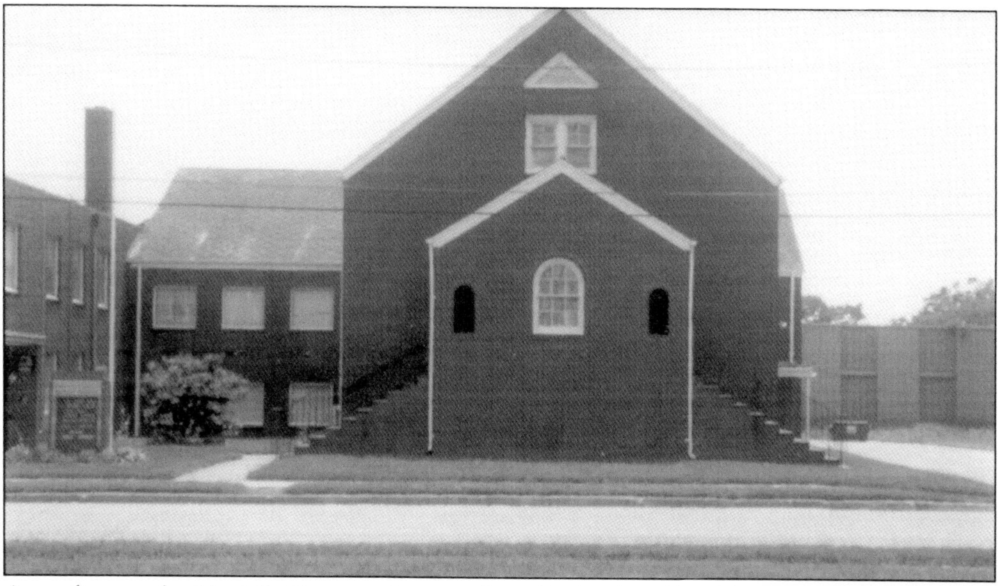

According to the Norfolk County Common Law Book, the official beginning of the Raleigh Heights Baptist Church was on November 10, 1897. Its first meeting place was an old log barn, and this photograph shows that portion of the building as it was in 1951.

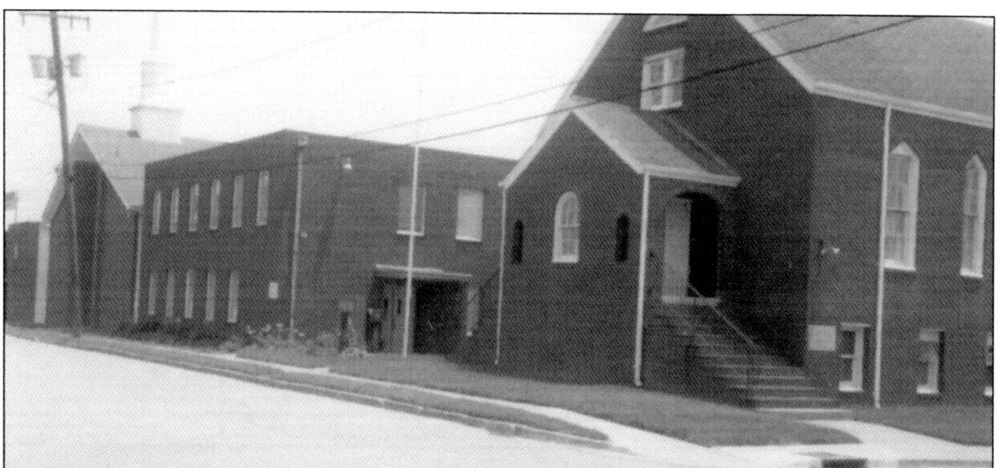

This picture of Raleigh Heights Baptist Church shows the major buildings that make up the present-day church. As can be seen, the church membership and physical plant have grown considerably throughout the years.

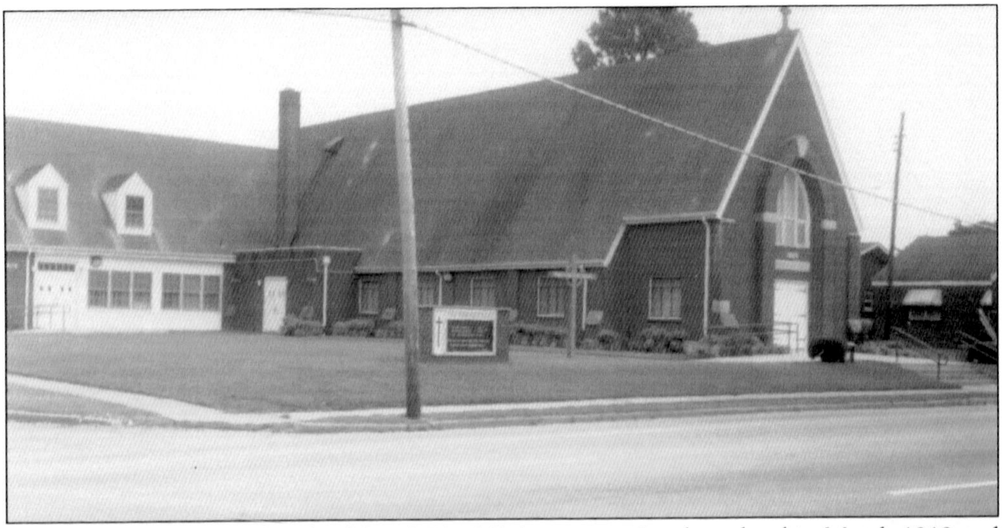

The First Presbyterian Church of South Norfolk began as a Sunday school in March 1919 and was first called the Geneva Presbyterian Mission. The Geneva Presbyterian Church was formed on November 1, 1920, and its first pastor was the Reverend Hugh Fitzpatrick.

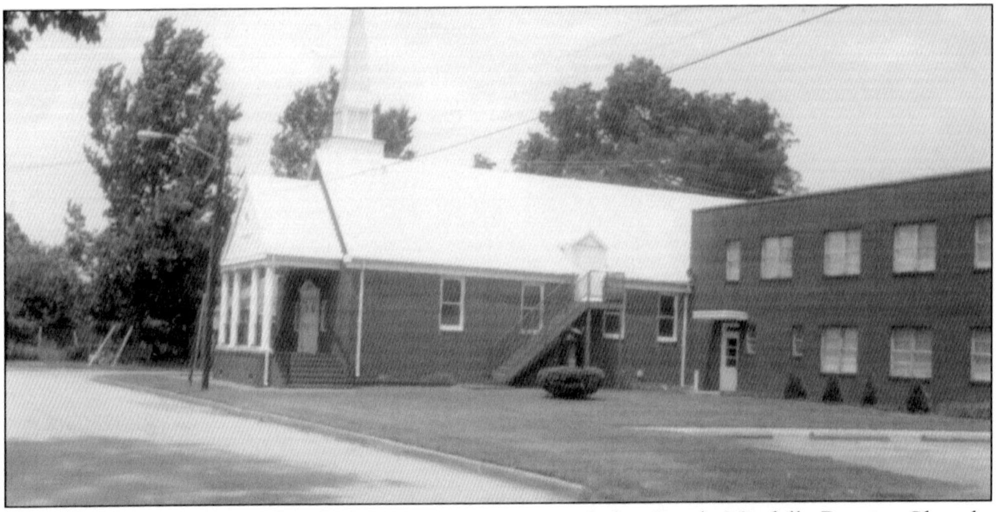

The Southside Baptist Church began as a mission of the South Norfolk Baptist Church. Southside was officially organized in March 1952, and its first pastor was a lay minister by the name of Mr. W.L. Bristow. This photograph shows the church as it is today.

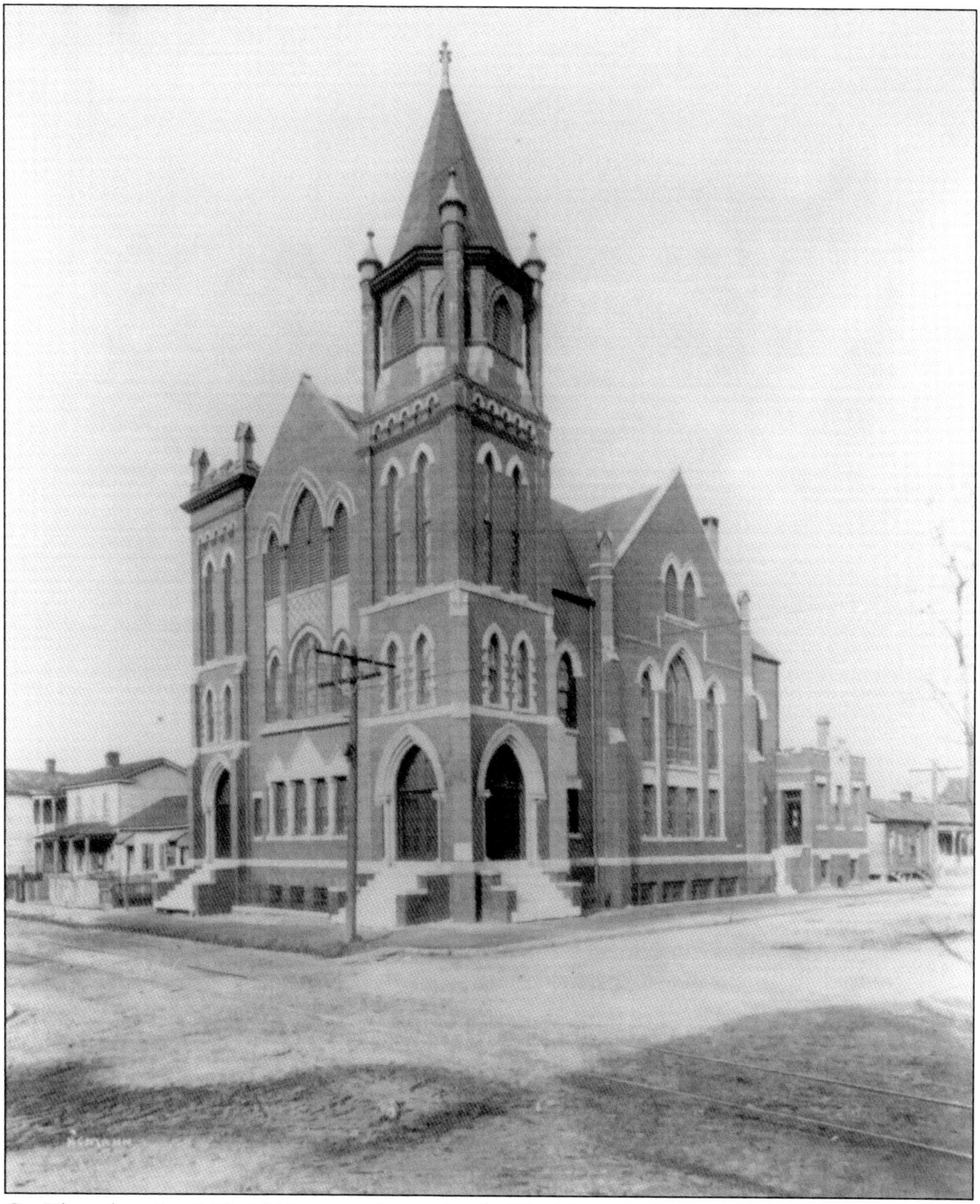

On Thursday, April 13, 1922, more than a third of Berkley was destroyed by fire, and along with it, the Central Baptist Church. This photograph by Harry C. Mann shows the New Central Baptist Church at 712 Walker Avenue.

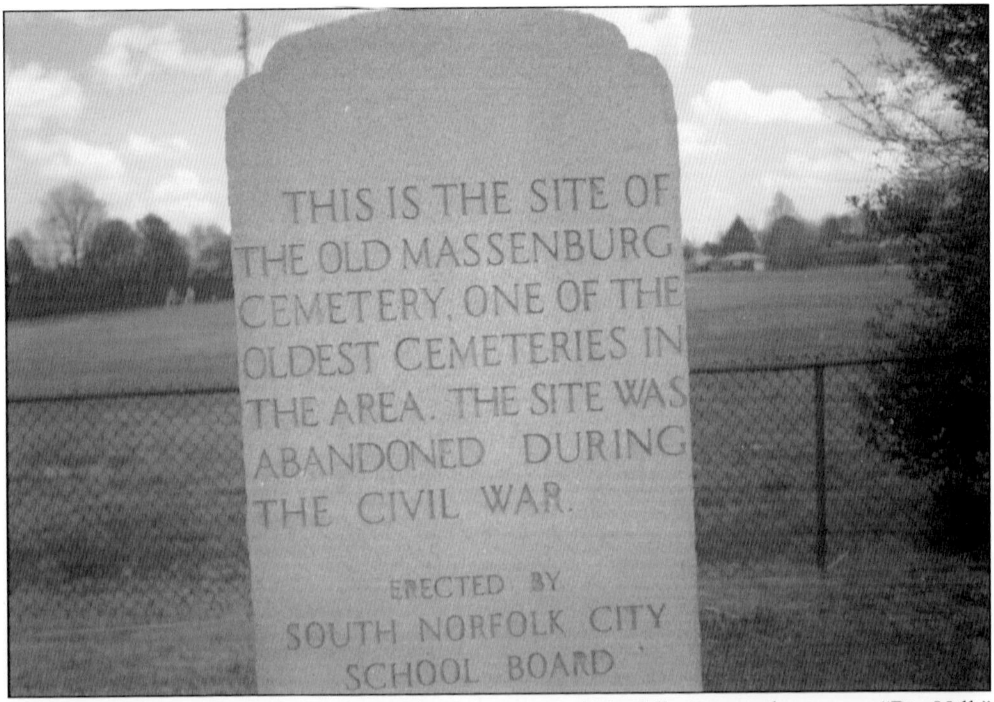

The Massenburg Cemetery was located in a section of Norfolk County known as "Big Hill." During this author's youth, it was the final resting place of approximately three dozen early citizens. The information on one side of the marker states that the cemetery was abandoned during the Civil War, but this is not accurate. Anne Frances Tatem's last will and testament was signed by William H. Etheridge, Elton Williamson, and Thomas Williamson on July 18, 1867. Anne lived another nine years, died on August 16, 1876, and was buried in the Massenburg Cemetery. The Civil War ended 11 years before her death, so apparently the cemetery was abandoned sometime after 1876. It was probably in use from 1731 until that time.

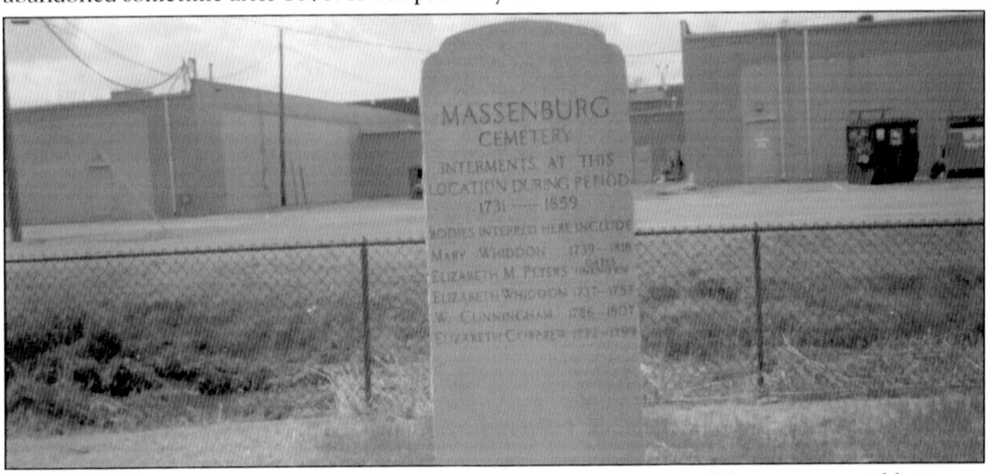

This is the reverse side of the marker. When the cemetery was moved from its original location, there were only five tombstones remaining, and those names were engraved on this marker. The information included the following names and dates: Mary Whiddon (1739–1818), Elizabeth M. Peters (dates unknown), Elizabeth Whiddon (1737–1757), W. Cunningham (1786–1807), and Elizabeth Corprew (1722–1799).

This picture was taken in the Good Hope Cemetery. The marker is on the grave of John West, a veteran of the Confederacy and a longtime superintendent of Norfolk County schools.

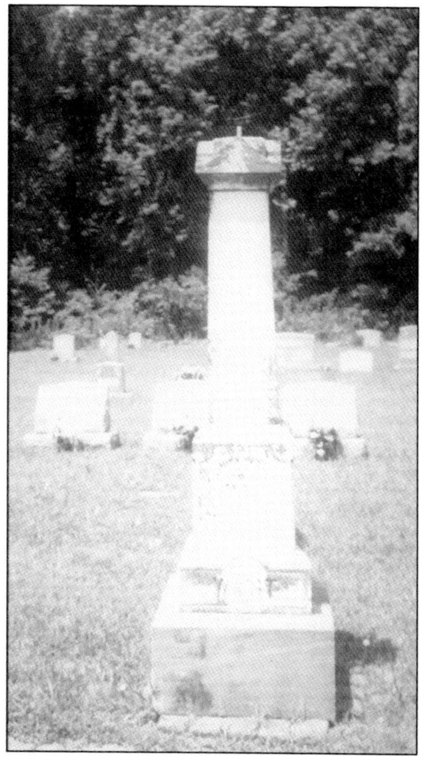

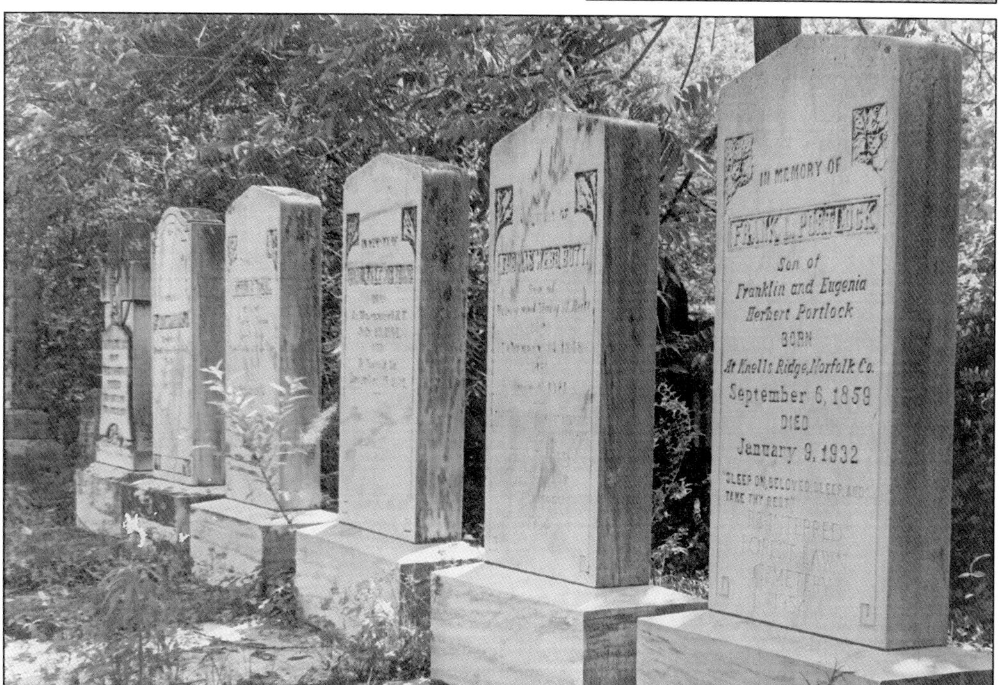

Here are 6 of about 50 tombstones in the Portlock Cemetery. The remains of approximately 18 people were removed to Forest Lawn Cemetery in 1954; however, the stones were left in place.

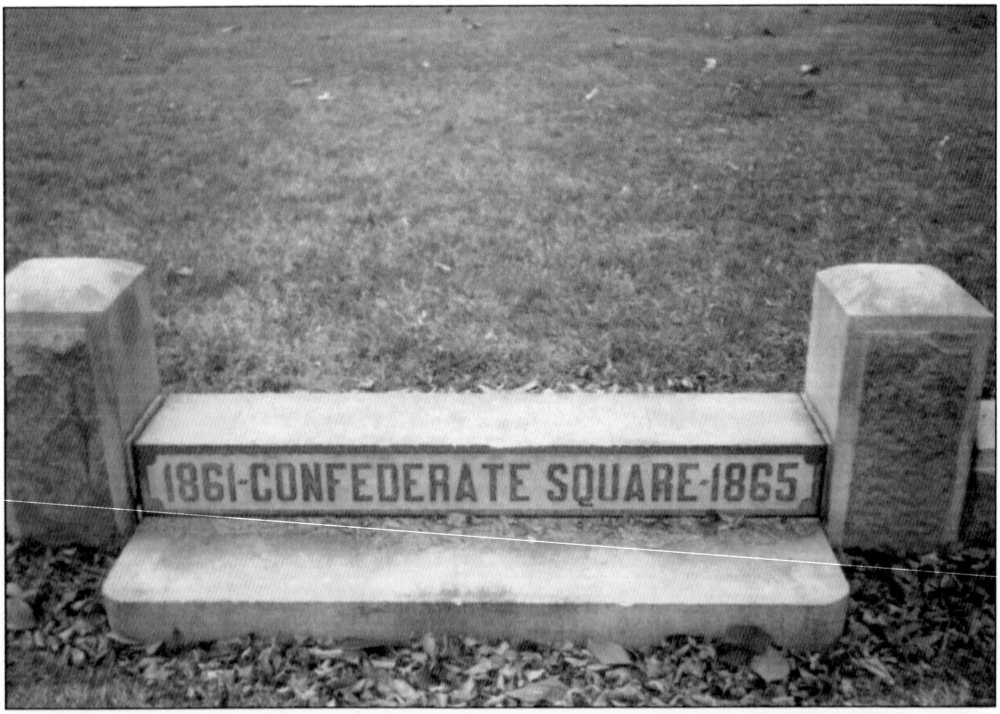

Magnolia Cemetery in Berkley was a part of Norfolk County until 1906, and pictured above is that section known as Confederate Square. As the story goes, four Confederate soldiers killed in the Civil War were buried in an open field, and this field became Magnolia Cemetery.

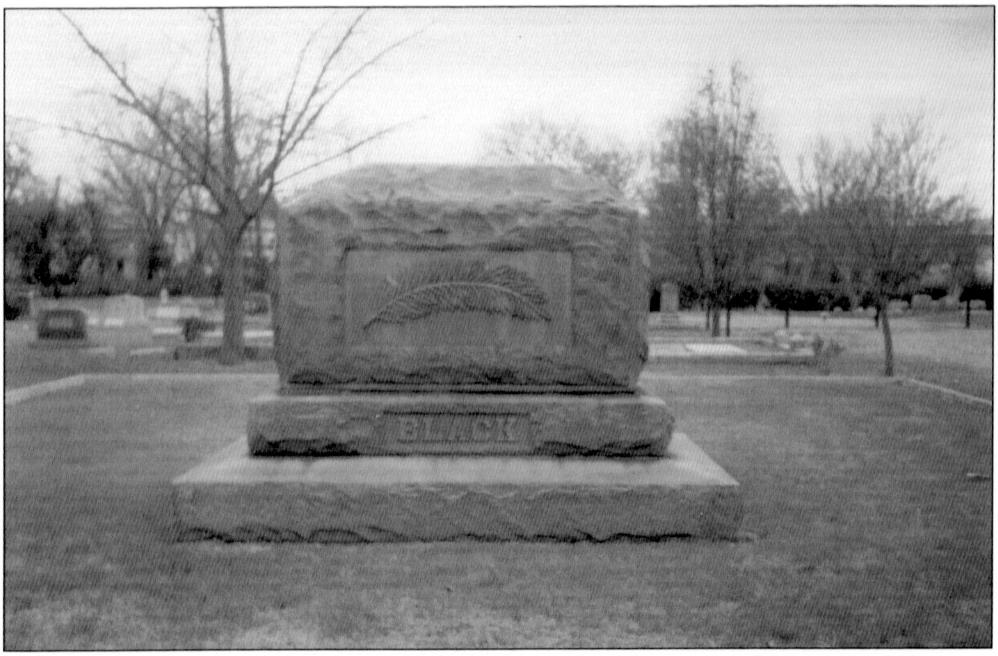

There are many large stones and monuments in Magnolia. This one marked the area belonging to the Black family. Foster Black, who was buried here in 1903, came from Scotland and made a fair amount of money in the knitting mills.

Needless to say, Magnolia Cemetery is filled with large magnolia trees such as this one. This tree has horizontal limbs that extend 20 to 30 feet in length. A close look reveals several small stones that have been almost devoured by the tree. Also, one side of the metal fence has been demolished by the growth of the tree.

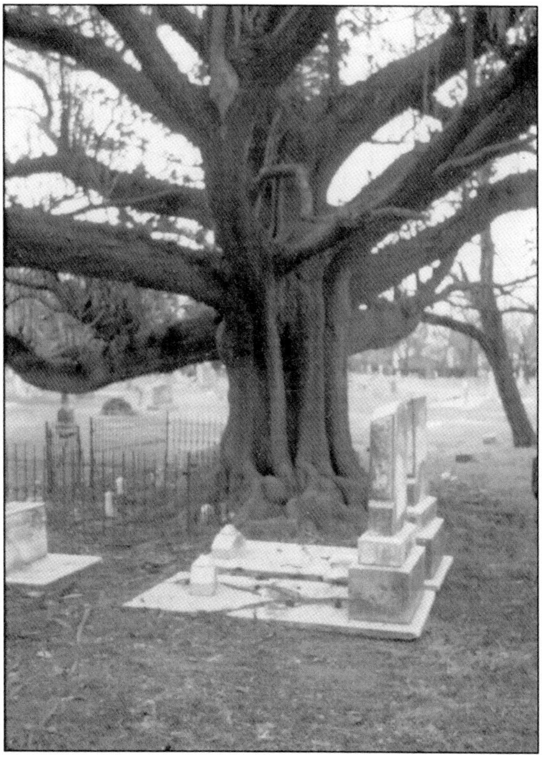

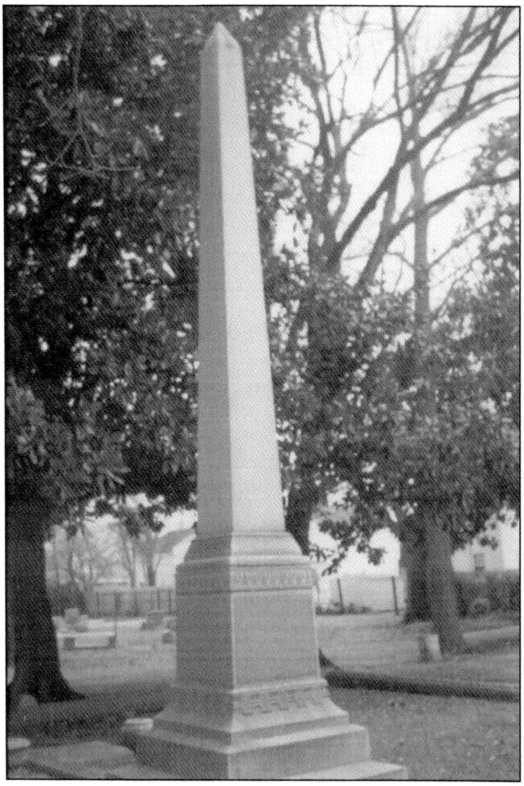

The large monument seen here is typical of the expensive markers of some family plots in Magnolia Cemetery.

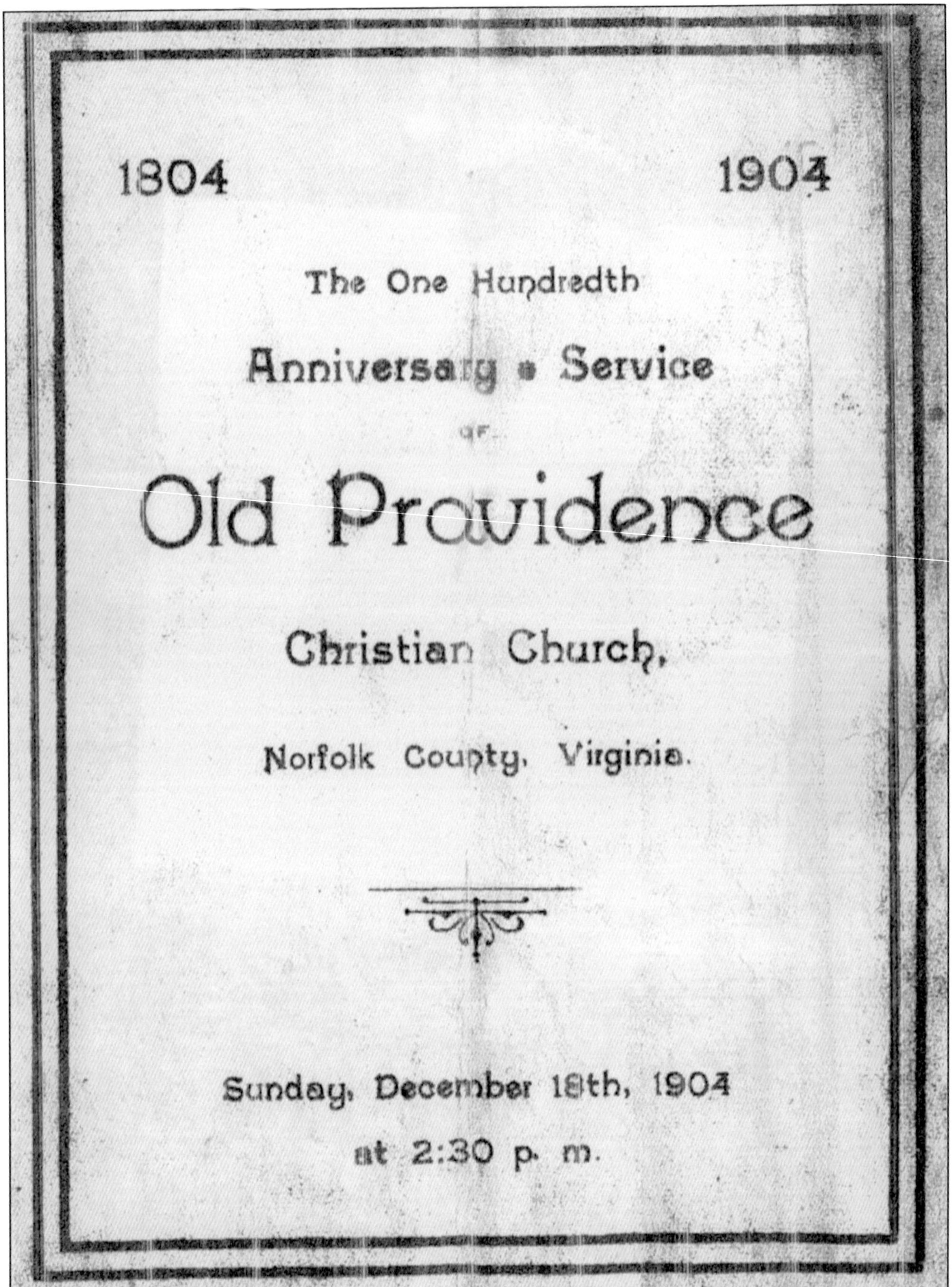
1804 1904

The One Hundredth

Anniversary Service

of

Old Providence

Christian Church,

Norfolk County, Virginia.

Sunday, December 18th, 1904

at 2:30 p. m.

Providence Christian Church was one of the earliest churches in Norfolk County. Elder N.P. Tatem organized it in 1804 with the assistance of a group of ministers. The church was 4 miles from Norfolk on the highway to Great Bridge, and the land on which it was built was purchased with English pounds. The information available places the sanctuary at the corner of Campostella and Providence Roads. Pictured here is a copy of the bulletin used at the 100th anniversary service held on Sunday, December 18, 1904.

Ten

LASTING MEMORIES

Someone once said, "that it's nice to remember, but nicer to be remembered." In this author's youth, there were many street vendors with horse-driven wagons. The owners of wooden ice boxes were dependent upon the daily delivery of ice. A sign was placed in one of the front windows of each home, and this let the ice man know how many pounds of ice to deliver. There were no refrigerators for home use, so grocery shopping was a chore that had to be accomplished every day except Sunday. Due to the "Blue Law," all stores were closed on Sunday. Kids sold newspapers or Cloverine Salve to earn money. In the spring of each year, children had marble and yo-yo contests in the school yard. These are just a few of many "lasting memories."

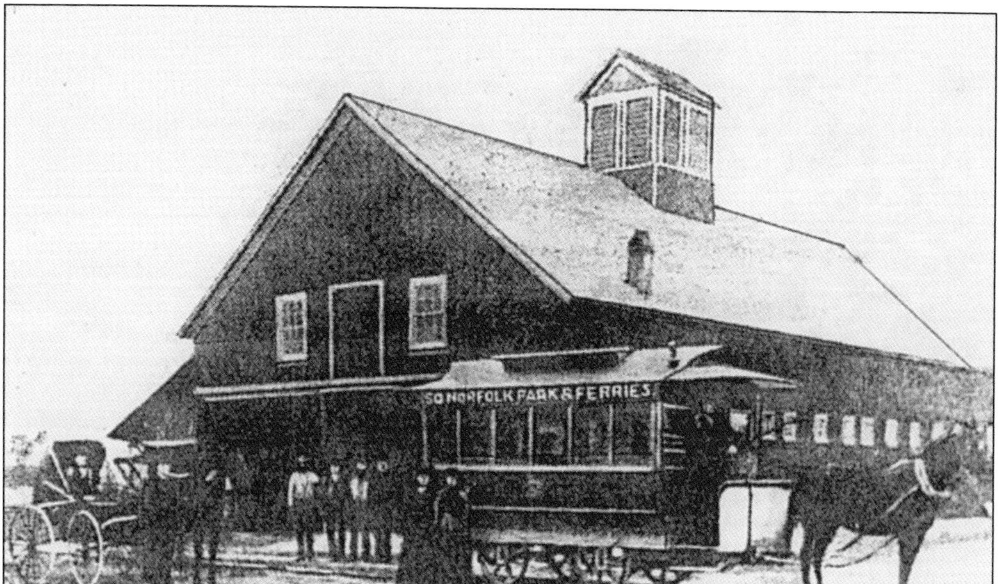

Horse-driven streetcars were used to carry passengers from one part of the area to another. In 1893, this one carried passengers from the Berkley Ferry Wharf to South Norfolk. The streetcar company was required to keep the tracks clean as well as those spaces immediately to the sides of the track.

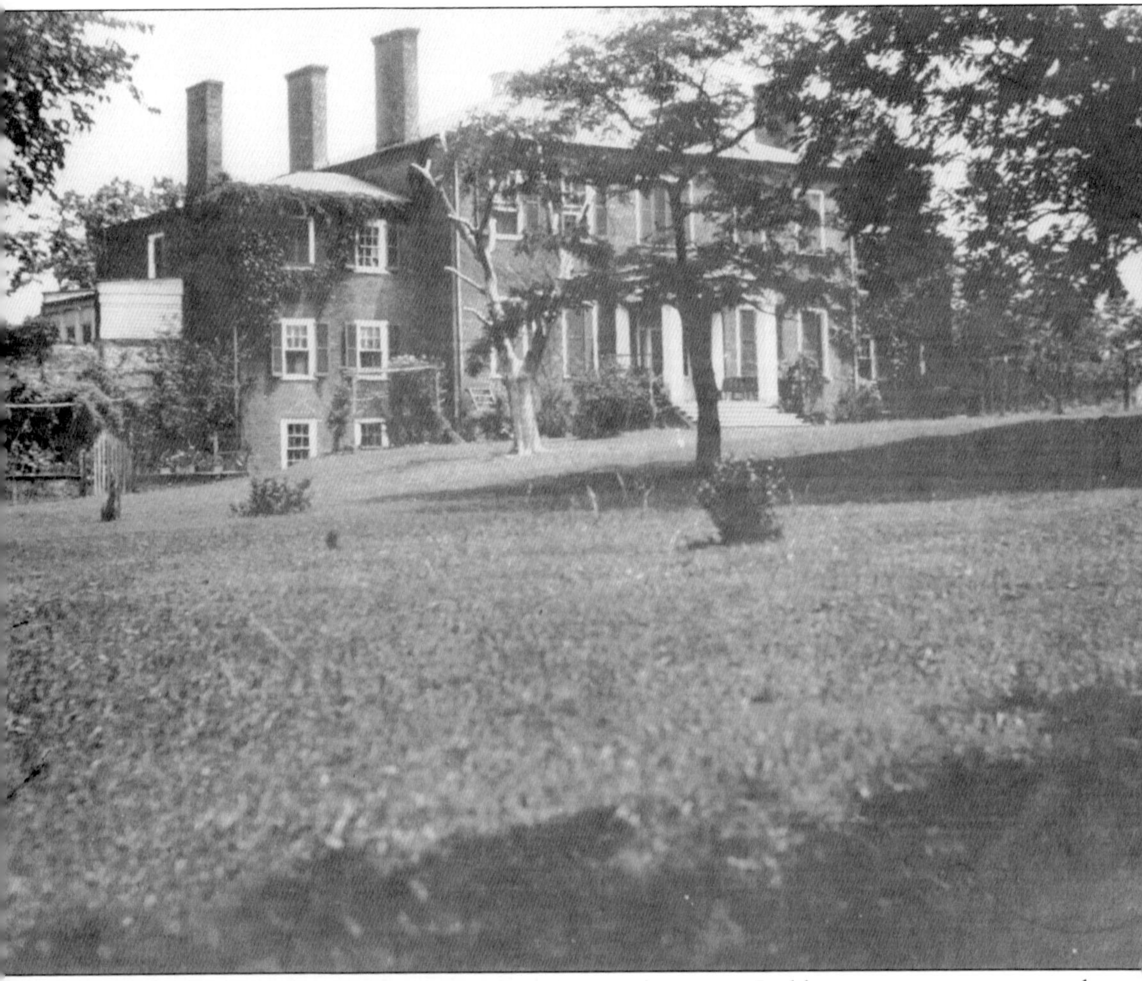

Practically the entire section of what later became known as Berkley was at one time owned by the Herbert family, and the area was originally given the name Herbertsville. The family acquired the land by virtue of land grants from King Charles II in 1664 and 1667. This lovely home, which became known as Riveredge, was built along the Southern Branch of the Elizabeth River near where the Berkley bridge was built in 1916. It has been said that the home had more than 20 rooms. About 1840, Mr. Herbert sold his home and the section east of Main Street and north of Poplar Avenue to Thomas Hardy. It was at Riveredge that Mary Pinckney "Pinky" Hardy was born on March 22, 1852. Pinky married Arthur MacArthur and became the mother of General Douglas MacArthur.

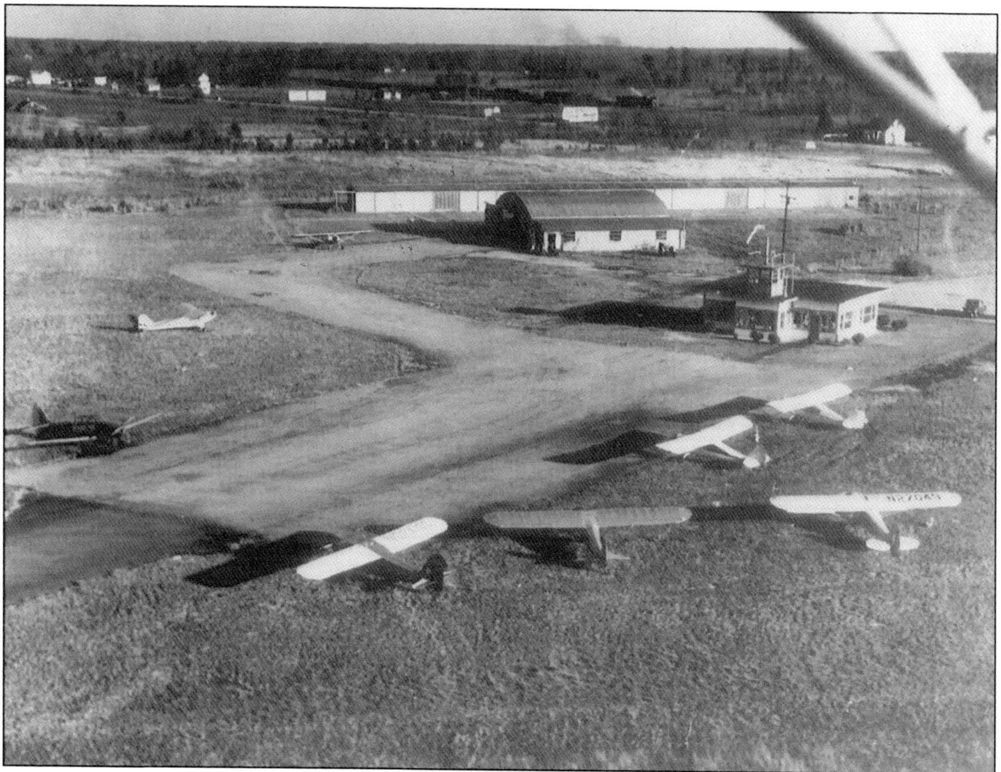

Pictured here in 1958 is the airport located in the Bowers Hill area of Norfolk County. Throughout the years, the airport's name has changed several times; it is now known as the Hampton Roads Airport.

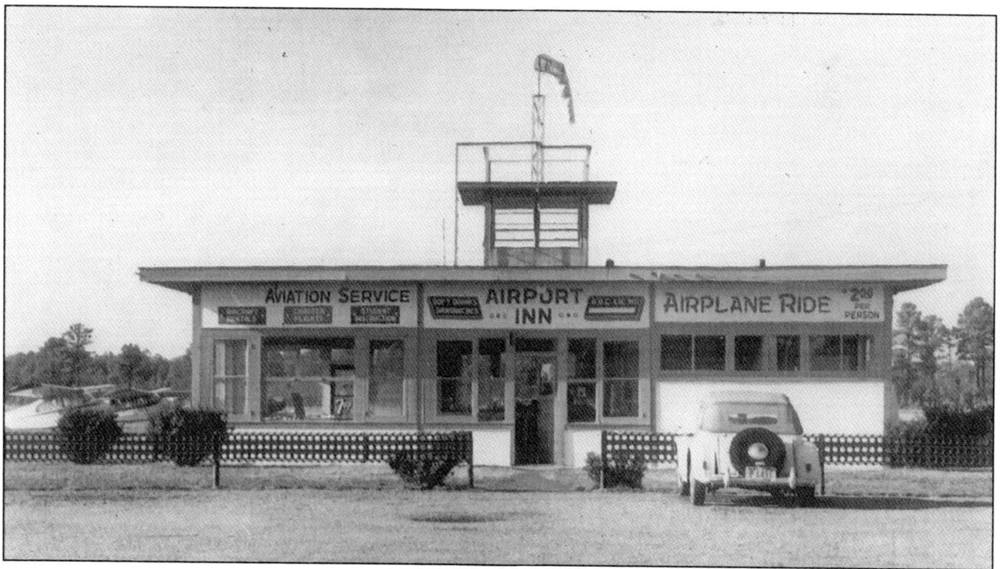

This is the restaurant located at the airport in Bowers Hill. When this photograph was taken in 1958, the establishment was known as the Airport Inn; at another time it was Clayton's Restaurant. As can be seen, the aviation services available included aircraft rentals, chartered flights, student instruction, and one could purchase an airplane ride for only $2.

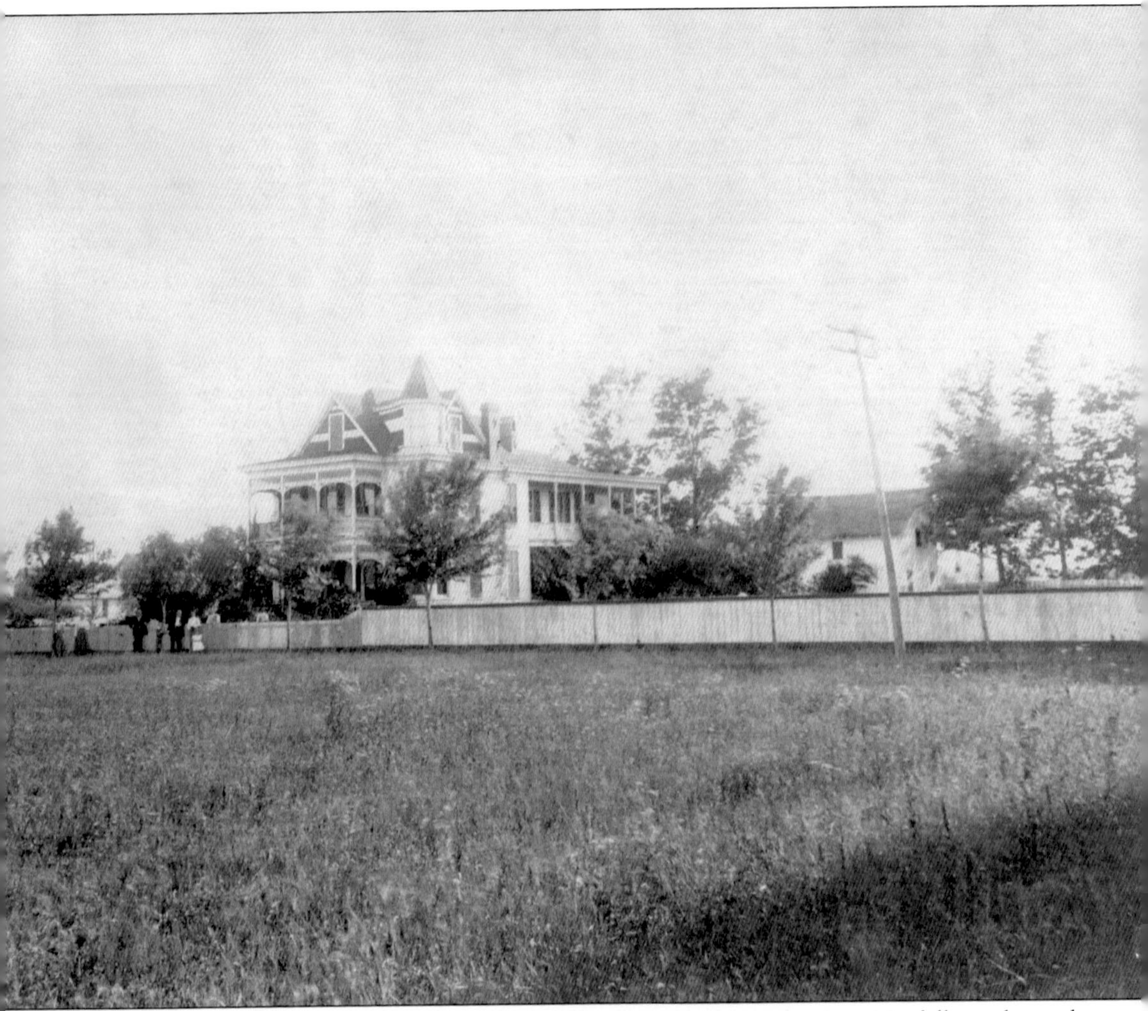

This is the Smith family home located on Chautauqua Avenue in Port Norfolk in the early 1900s. Because of its massive size and lavish ornamentation, including the gingerbread trim, this house might be considered of the Victorian style. The home had at least four porches, several fireplaces, and a huge barn behind the main dwelling.

These two drum majorettes, Virginia Oglesby (left) and Weeda Simpson, are members of the American Legionnaires. The lovely ladies are pictured here in the 1930s.

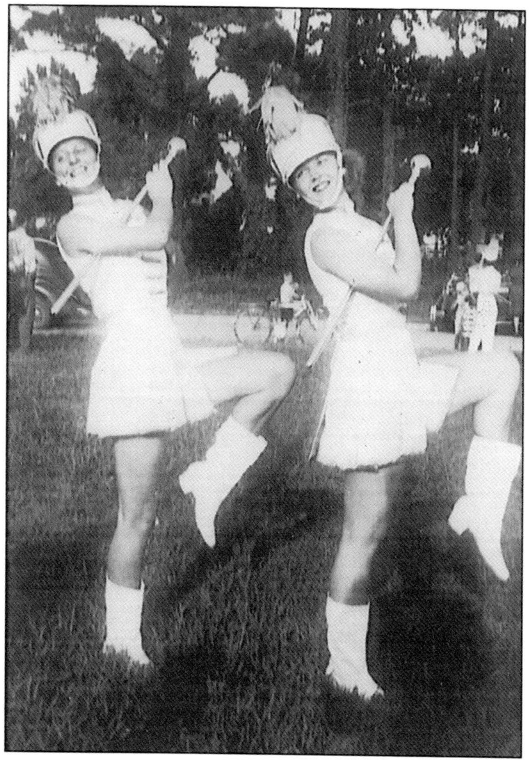

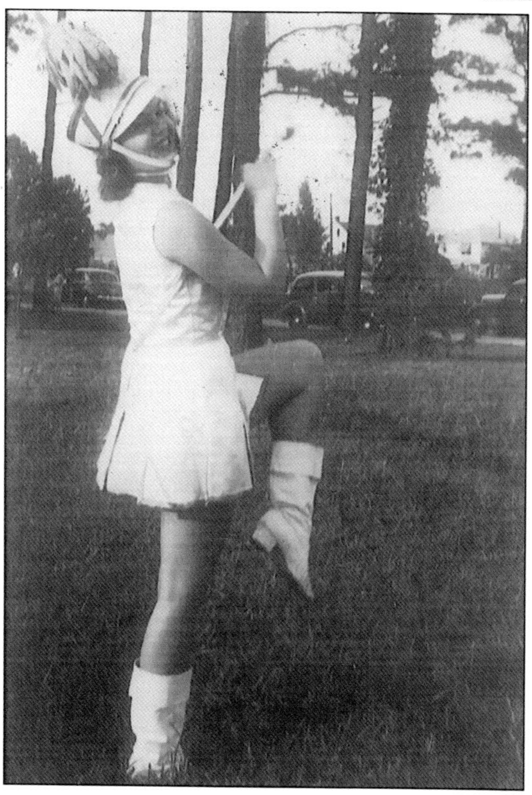

This is a 1930s photograph of Weeda Simpson, a drum majorette with the American Legionnaires.

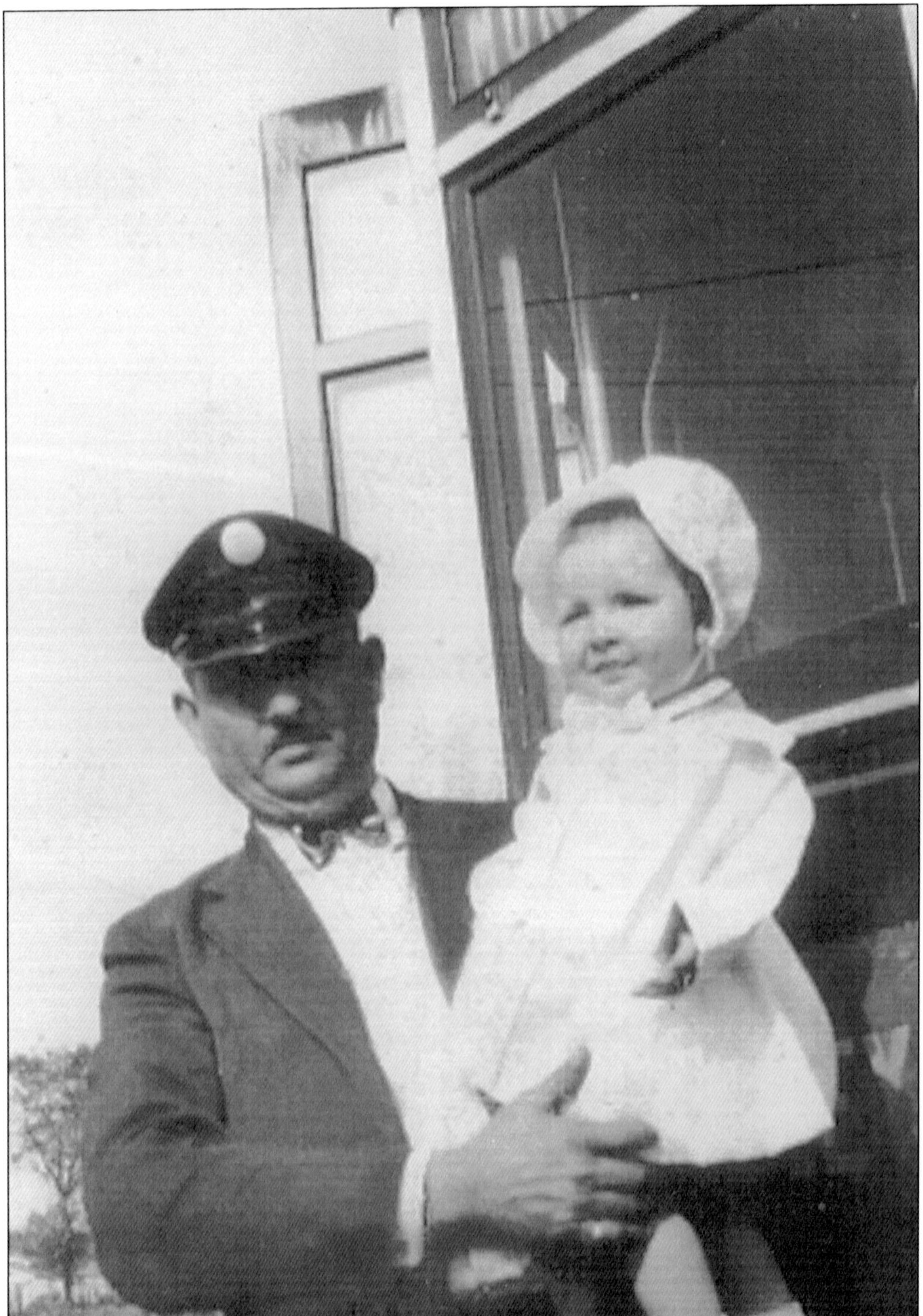

This early picture shows Will Phelps with his granddaughter Sherry standing in front of the Money Point streetcar. Mr. Phelps served many years as a streetcar motorman for the Virginia Electric & Power Company (VEPCO).

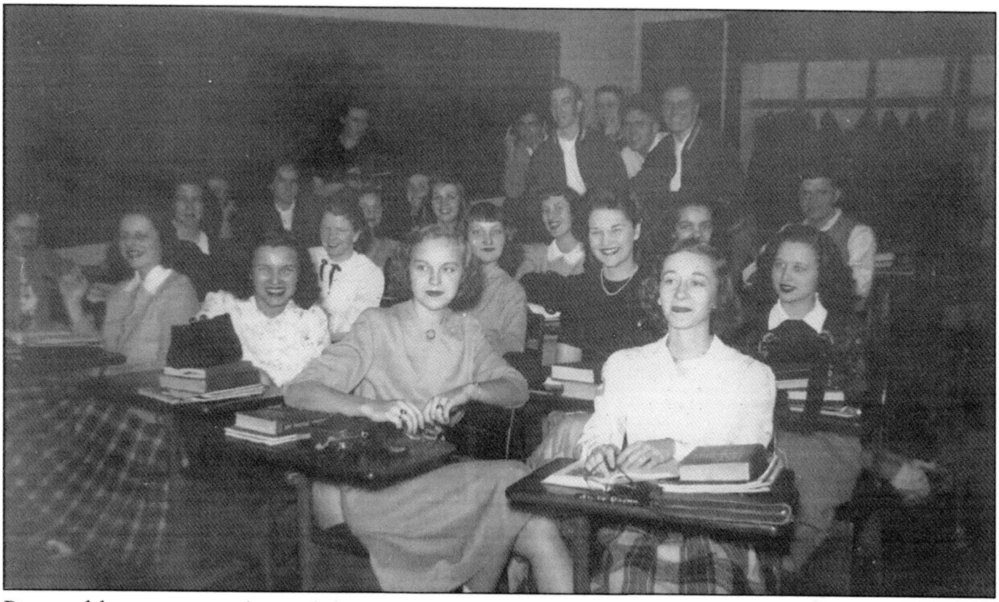

Pictured here are members of the 1948 South Norfolk High School senior English class. It is not possible to name them all, but those that are recognizable are, from left to right, as follows: (front row) Barbara Alvis, Elizabeth Williams, Jackie Creef, Francene King, Betty Joe Sykes, Janet Carter, Annis Pegram, Ruby Mcpherson, Barbara Harrell, Ginger Harrell, Florence Bryant, Anne Forbes, and Becky Hardison.

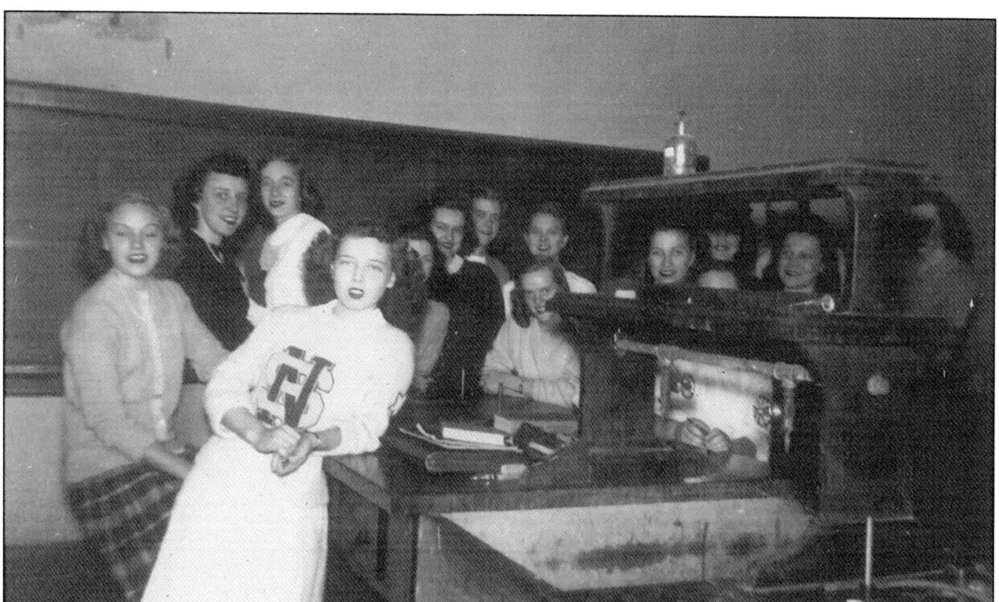

Some of the members of the 1948 South Norfolk High School senior chemistry class are Jackie Allen, Jackie Creef , Francene King, Marilyn Burgess, and Ann Page.

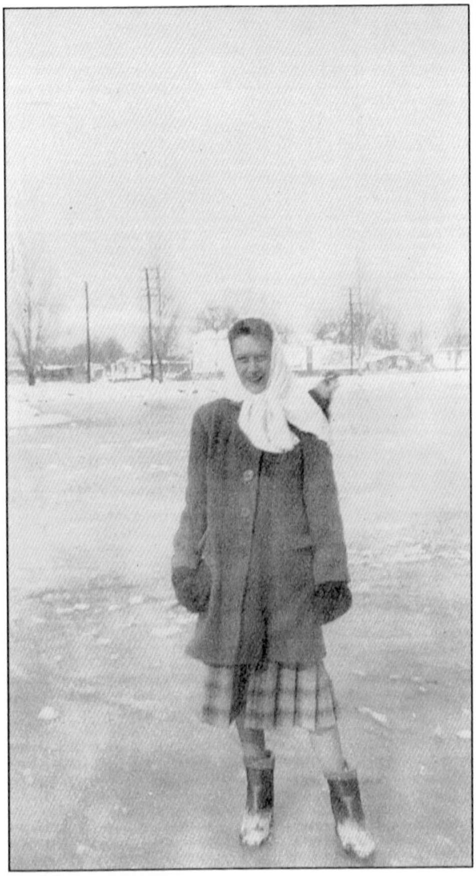

Jackie Jones stands on the frozen lake in Lakeside Park, *c.* 1948.

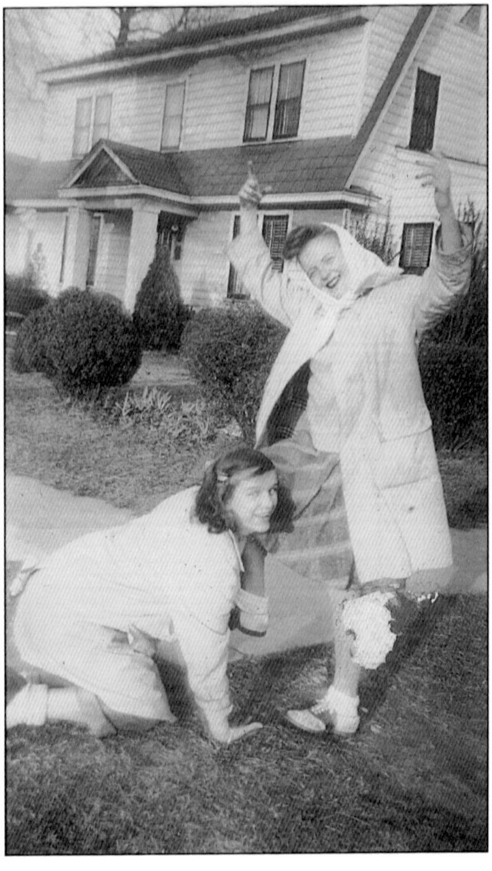

These two high school students are just clowning around at the corner of Rodgers and Jefferson Streets. The house in the background was the home of the Bray family.

A favorite hangout for many high school students was Preston's corner, and this day was no exception. Here are, from left to right, Johnny Landers and Tommy Henderson.

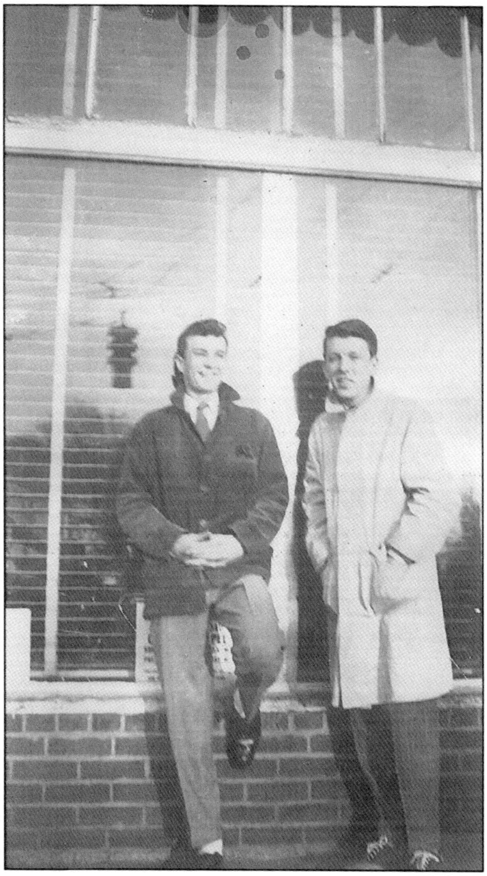

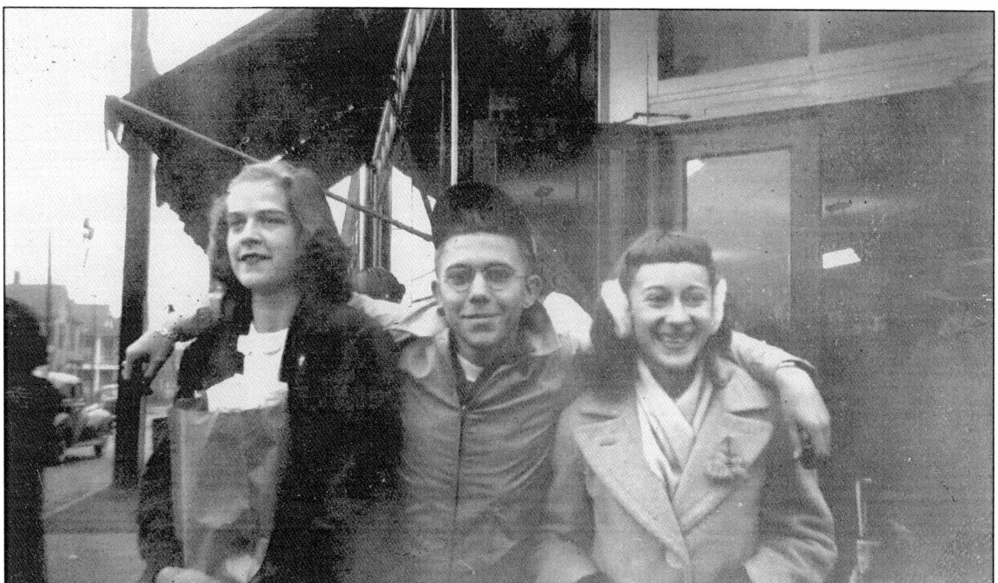

Another group of students at Preston's corner includes, from left to right, Marilyn Burgess, William Horton, and Francene King.

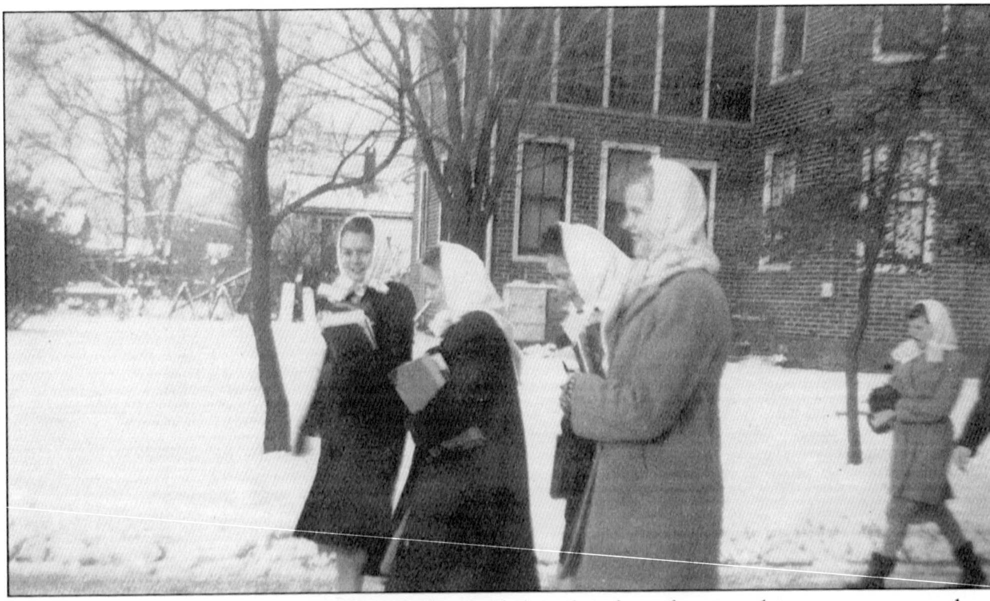

It was a snowy day in 1948, and these ladies had their heads tied up in white scarves, wore long coats, and fur-lined boots in order to keep warm.

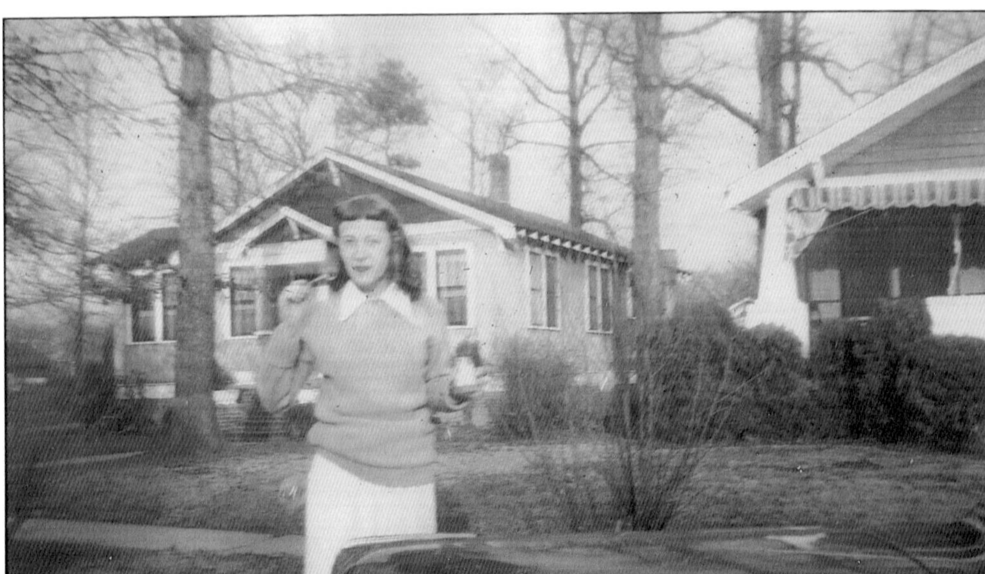

This picture, taken on Rodgers Street in South Norfolk, caught Francene King blowing soap bubbles.

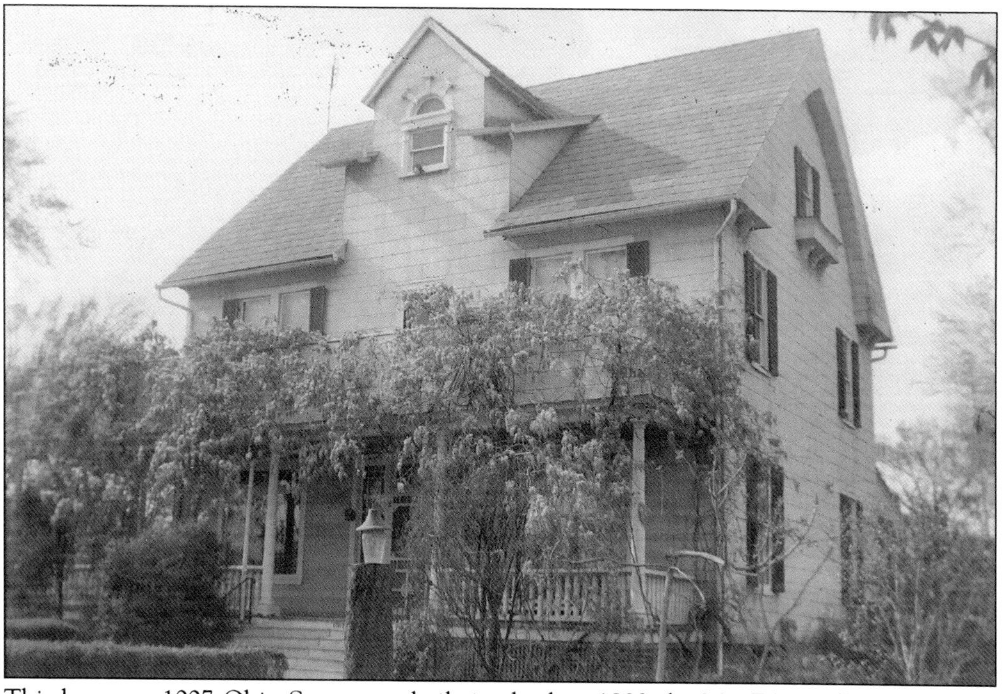

This house at 1007 Ohio Street was built in the late 1800s by Mr. E.M. Tilley for his son William. The Portlock family acquired the house in September 1910. A large amount of wisteria is growing around the porch in this view.

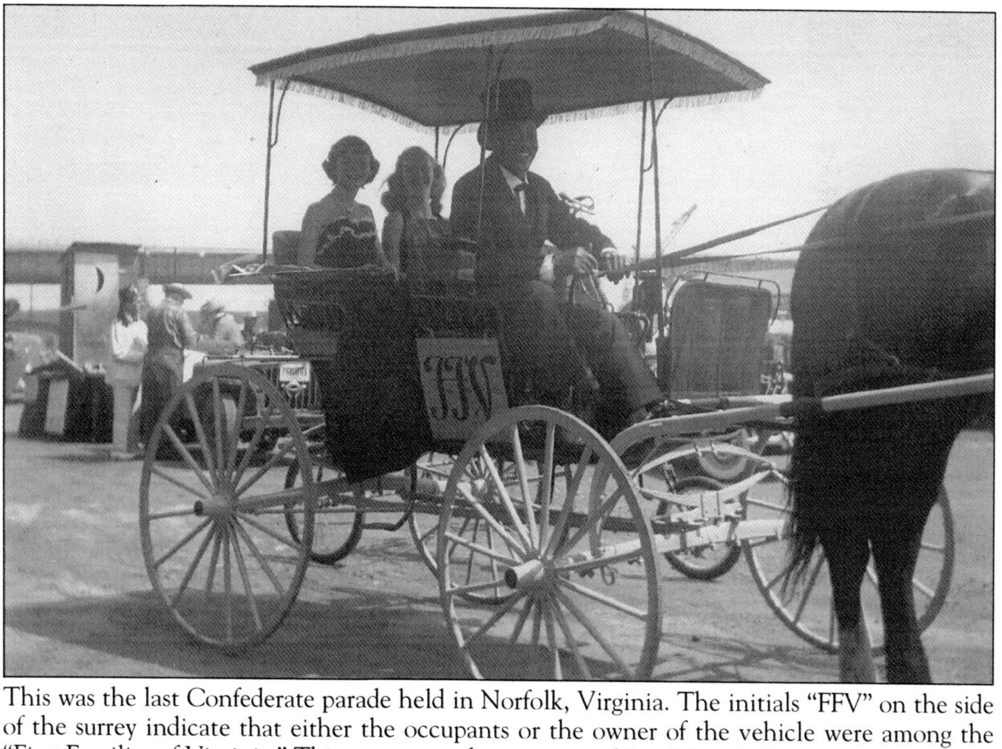

This was the last Confederate parade held in Norfolk, Virginia. The initials "FFV" on the side of the surrey indicate that either the occupants or the owner of the vehicle were among the "First Families of Virginia." This surrey was the property of Frank Portlock Jr.

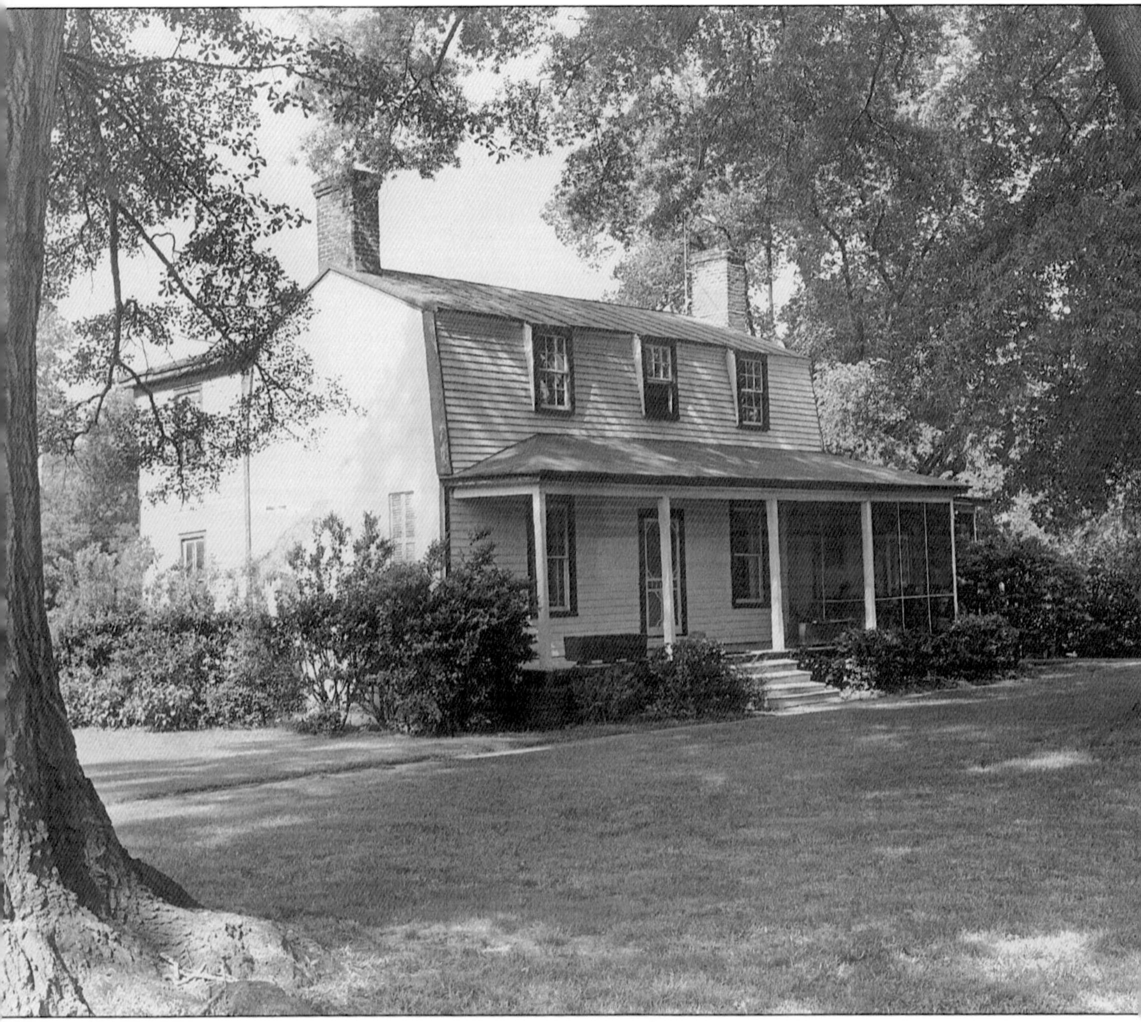

Pictured here is the Tapley Portlock homestead, which was built in Norfolk County in 1789. It became the property of Benjamin F. Gibson in 1884 and is now owned by Mr. Roy Spencer.

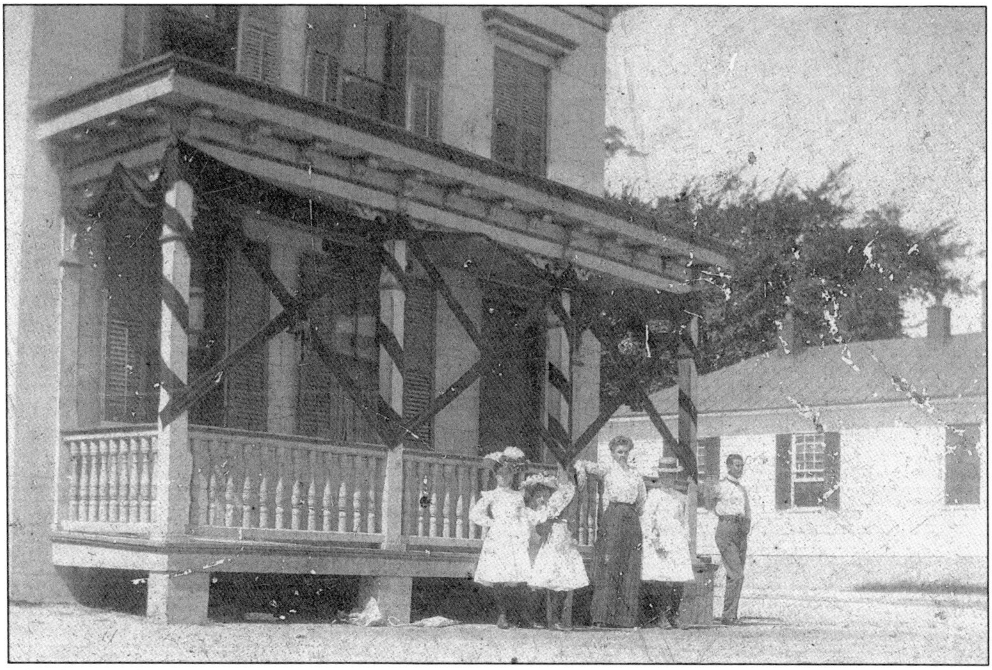

This house, located on "B" Street in South Norfolk, is decorated for the July 4th holiday. The children are too well dressed to watch a parade, so it is possible that they are participants. Around 1900, this was the home of Samuel F. and Susan Sanderlin Toxey.

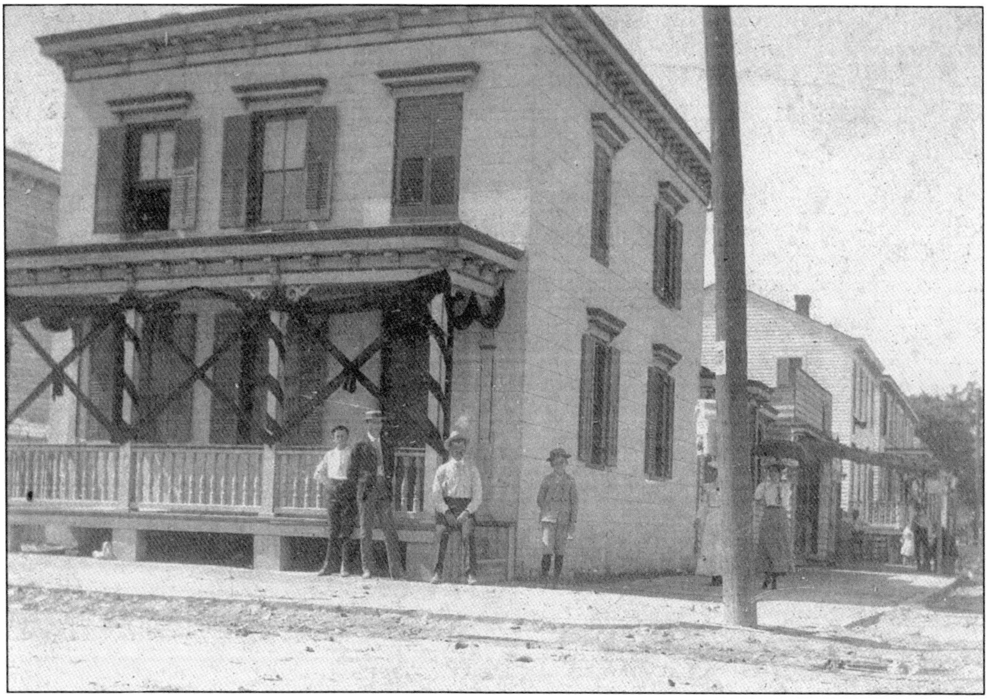

This *c.* 1900 view of the Toxey home on "B" Street shows that it is on a corner. The people on the side street are returning home, possibly from the July 4th parade. There is a store and several two-story homes on the side street.

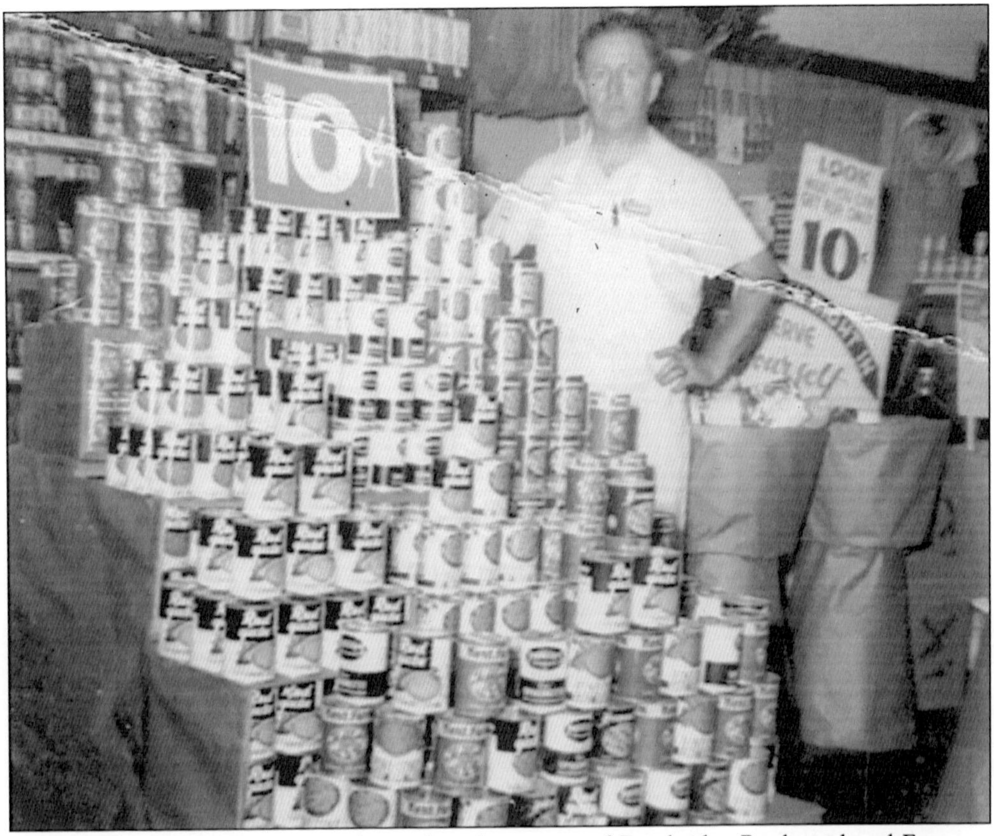

A David Pender (DP) store was located at the corner of Bainbridge Boulevard and Freeman Avenue in Portlock in Norfolk County, Virginia. Mr. Archie Pritchard was the manager. A large display of canned goods, which sold for 10¢ per can, is seen here.

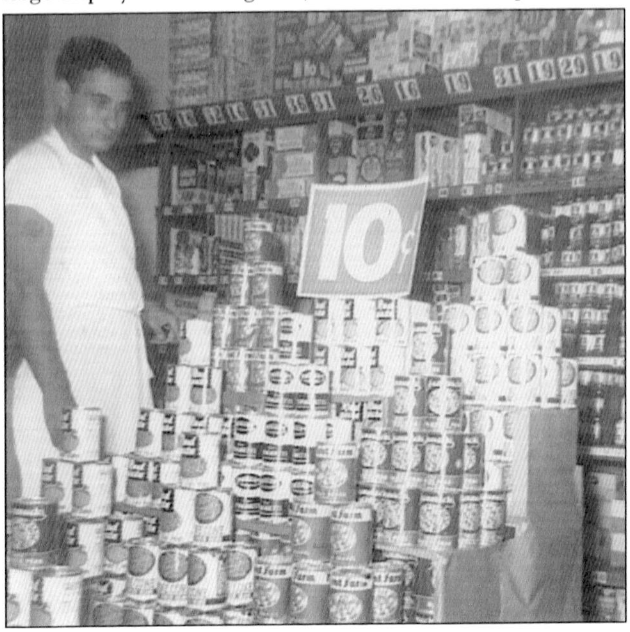

Here is another view of the canned goods on sale for 10¢ per can. Among this large display were products such as Red Gate corn, Phillip beans, and Great Farm vegetables.

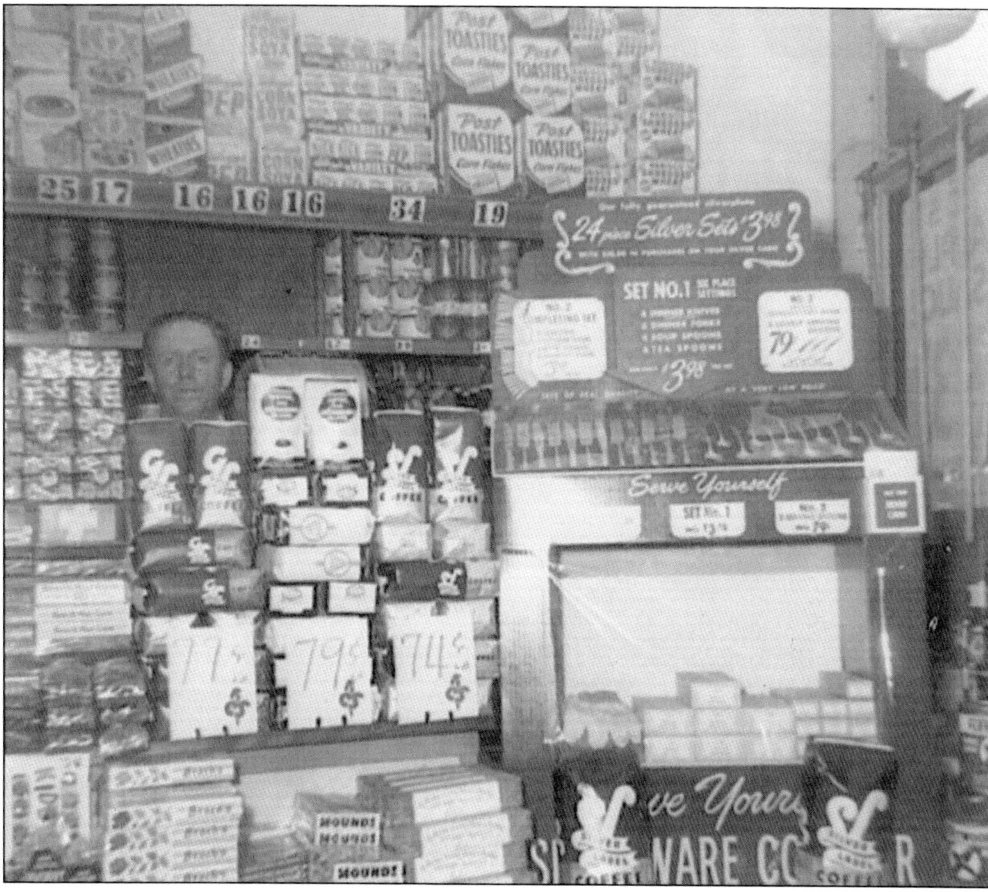

In this photograph of the interior of the DP store, there is a display of silverware. A 24-piece setting could be purchased for $3.98. There were several brands of coffee, the most expensive of which was 79¢ per pound. Taking a look at the top shelf, one can see the price of breakfast cereals—a large box of Post Toasties was 19¢.

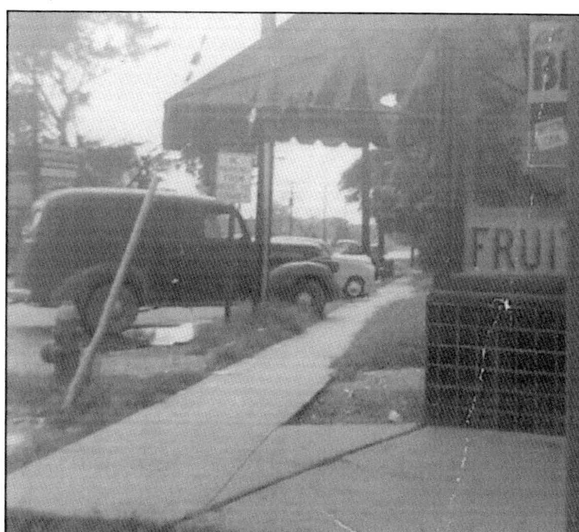

Parallel parking was available beside the DP store. The truck seen here was used to deliver groceries to the homes of local customers.

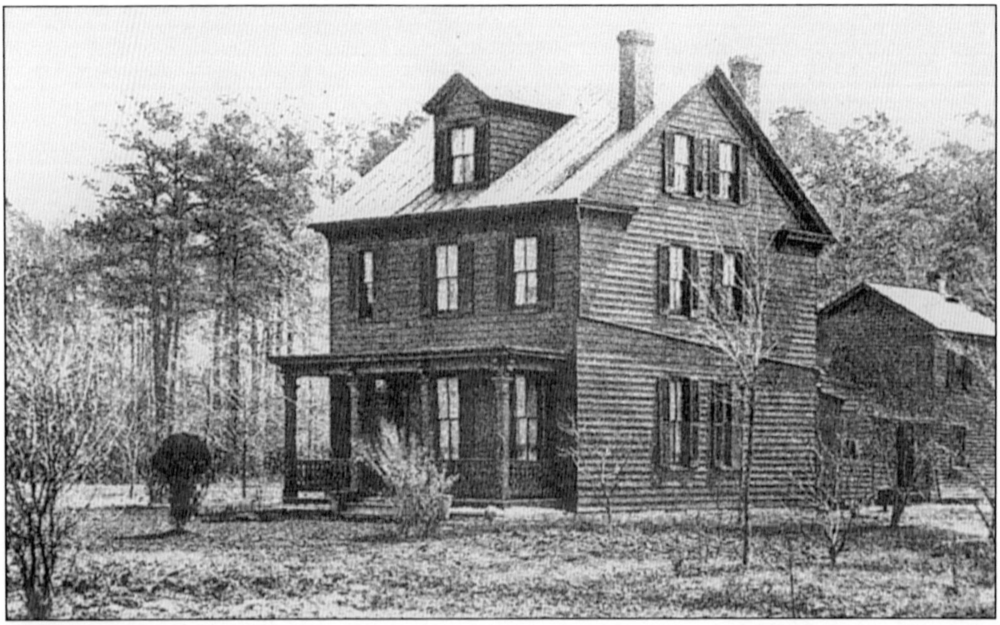

C.W. Poindexter built his first home, the "Anchorage," on the waterfront across from the Gosport Navy Yard. Poindexter later built this home on Ohio Street. This drawing depicts the house as it looked in 1894; the kitchen and dining areas were on the back. Eventually the house was removed to Stewart Street, where in 1918, one of the boys in the neighborhood set fire to it, completely destroying the kitchen and dining areas. It was rebuilt, but those areas were not replaced.

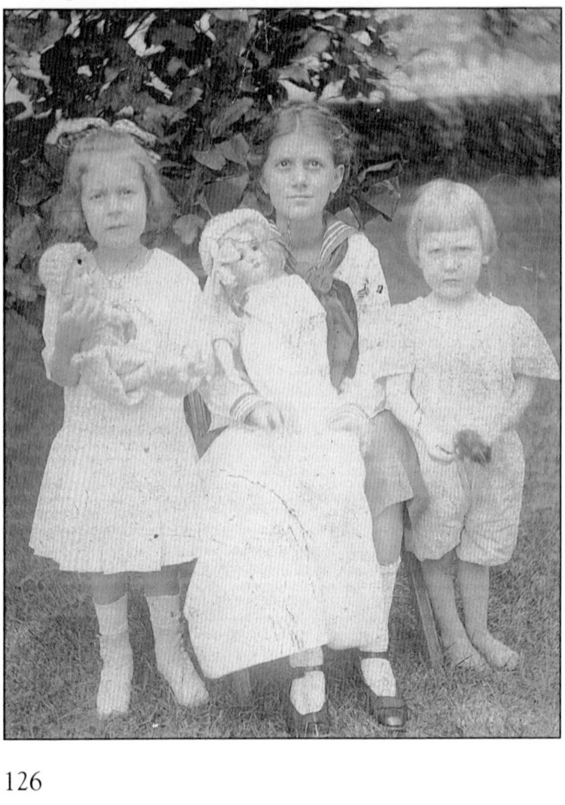

One fine day, the Portlock children posed for this picture. They are, from left to right, Eugenia, Marion, and Frank Jr.

Frank L. Portlock Sr. was born at Knells Ridge in Norfolk County on September 6, 1859. His first job was that of a schoolteacher at Oak Grove, just 1 mile north of Great Bridge. In 1890, he was elected road commissioner of Norfolk County. In addition to this job, Portlock carried on general farming and stock raising. This picture of Mr. Portlock was taken in 1924.

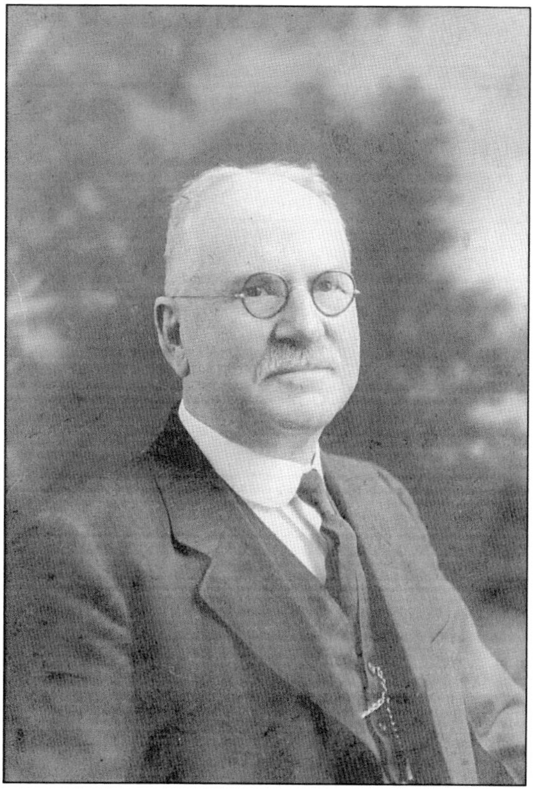

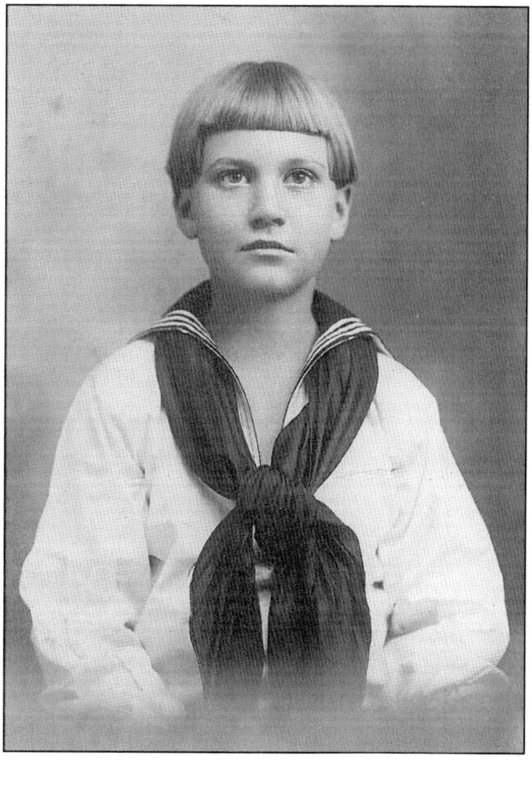

This photograph shows a young Frank L. Portlock Jr., who was born on July 18, 1908, in Norfolk County. He maintains an interest in local history and is very knowledgeable about the area. The Portlock section of Norfolk County was named for his family.

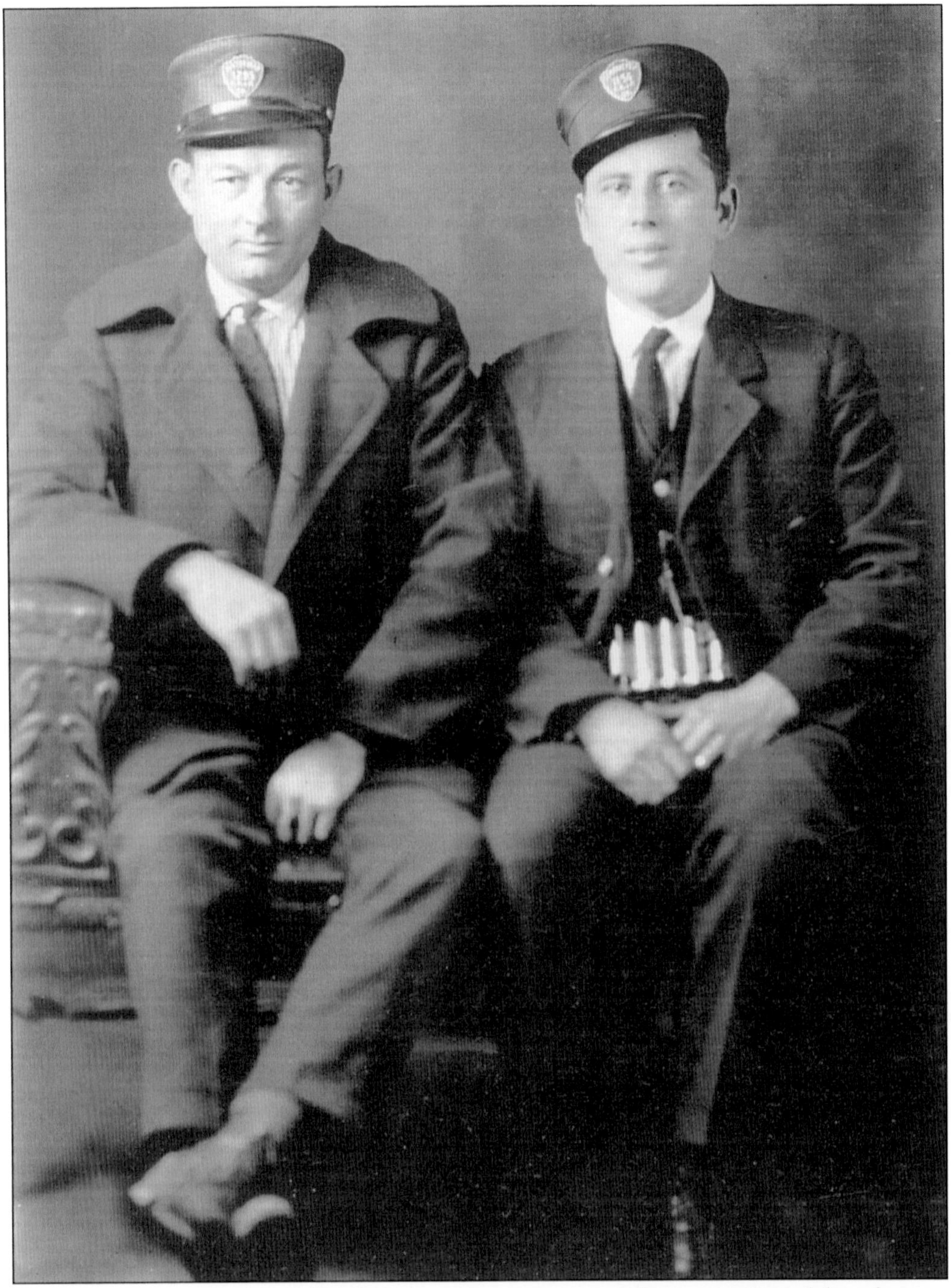

The streetcars at one time employed two men per car—one was the motorman and the other was the conductor. The motorman drove the streetcar while the conductor collected the fares, but each had to know the other's job. The two gentlemen seated here are Will Phelps, motorman (left), and Joe Forbes, conductor.